Customer Service In Insurance:
Principles and Practices

To learn more about customer service, look at this book's companion volume:

Customer Service in Insurance: Improving Your Skills

LOMA (Life Office Management Association, Inc.) is an international association founded in 1924. LOMA is committed to being the pre-eminent provider of education, research, information sharing, and the resources needed to facilitate effective management and operations for members of the insurance and financial services industry.

The **Associate, Customer Service (ACS) Program** consists of five courses. The first four courses are taken from the FLMI Insurance Education Program. They are FLMI Course 1, "Principles of Life and Health Insurance," FLMI Course 2, "Life and Health Insurance Company Operations," FLMI Course 3, "Legal Aspects of Life and Health Insurance," and FLMI Course 4, "Marketing Life and Health Insurance." The fifth course in the ACS Program is CS1 "Foundations of Customer Service," a comprehensive introduction to customer service in insurance companies. Students may not enroll for CS1 without first completing or being concurrently enrolled for FLMI Courses 1 through 4. Upon completion of all required ACS courses, the student is designated an Associate, Customer Service, receives an ACS diploma awarded by LOMA, and is entitled to use the letters ACS after his or her name.

Customer Service
In Insurance:
Principles and Practices

KENNETH HUGGINS, FLMI/M

LOMA Series in Customer Service

Associate, Customer Service Program • LOMA
Atlanta, Georgia

Textbook Project Team:

Author	Kenneth Huggins, FLMI/M
Project Editor, Curriculum	Dani L. Long, FLMI, ALHC
Production Editor, Text Design	Richard Bailey, FLMI
Project Manager	Dennis W. Goodwin, FLMI, HIA
Cover Design	Zoila Harmouche
Typography	Fishergate, Inc.

ISBN 0–939921–02–2

Library of Congress Catalog Card Number: 91–061151

Printed in the United States of America

Contents

Chapter 2: Building a Customer Service Culture 34

Chapter 3: Developing a Customer Service Strategy 60

Preface

Too often in the past, customer service has been treated like the poor stepchild of business: "Sure, we provide customer service . . . when we can . . . if it's profitable." In today's business environment, this stepchild appraisal no longer works.

Customer service is not just a smile and a nod and a "Have a nice day." Customer service is an essential, demanding, and rewarding part of doing business in the insurance industry. Customer service is part marketing, part strategic planning, and part research and systems. It requires thorough training and a heavy doese of interpersonal skills. And it combines all these into a single area of expertise. Customer service is about getting to know the customer and learning how to think like a customer. It's about creating systems and providing training that allow employees to provide the best service possible. It's a value-added benefit that can help a company put itself one notch above its competition.

Customer Service in Insurance: Principles and Practices is designed to help you understand not only how customer service is planned and implemented but how important it is to you, your company, and the entire insurance industry.

In this book, we describe the customer service challenges facing the insurance industry and the steps that insurers are taking to develop their strategic plans for customer service. We also describe ways to

- develop a customer service culture in your company,
- conduct customer service research,
- develop systems that support customer service, and
- train employees to provide quality customer service.

All in all, this book will help you understand the necessary steps for establishing and managing excellent customer service practices in your company.

Throughout the book we also include a number of short articles about current developments in customer service. In the articles called "Customer Service in Action," we give you first hand accounts of what insurance companies are doing to provide excellent customer service. And in "Issues in Customer Service," we feature articles written by some of the leading authorities in customer service, discussing some of the most important questions facing customer service today.

In the companion volume to this book, *Customer Service in Insurance: Improving Your Skills*, we show you ways to improve the interpersonal skills that are essential when working with customers. *Improving Your Skills* helps you learn how to identify customers' wants and understand how they perceive the service you provide. It helps you communicate with customers more effectively and recommends ways to improve your listening skills, organize your time, and manage stress. Both books are assigned reading for LOMA's Foundations of Customer Service course, which is the capstone course in LOMA's Associate, Customer Service Program.

Welcome to the world of customer service. It's a challenging and rewarding field, one that's essential to your company's success — and to yours. Good luck!

Acknowledgments

This book could never have come about without the help of a large number of people. First and foremost of these, I must thank the industry experts who volunteered their time, energy, and critical attention to make sure we produced an accurate book that met the needs of the insurance industry. The role of these experts was to read the manuscript of this book and let me know where I was missing the boat and what I needed to do to get things right. I am pleased and honored to have had the opportunity to work with this group of talented and dedicated people:

Joan Ehman, CLU, ChFC
Second Vice President, Financial Services Department
The Travelers Companies

Ann J. Goergen
Corporate Vice President, Customer Service Department
New York Life Insurance Company

Richard L. Low, FLMI (retired)
formerly Director, GSD Customer Service
London Life Insurance Company

Pattie McWilliams, FLMI
Assistant Vice President, Life and Health Policyowners
USAA Life Insurance Company

Joan Prevalnig, FLMI
Vice President, Agency Operations
Great-West Life Assurance

Sandra Reynolds
Vice President, Policy Administration
Fidelity Union Life Insurance Company

Louise B. Romano, FLMI
Assistant Vice President, Marketing Communications
Pacific Mutual Life Insurance Company

Harry L. Ruppenthal
Director, Policyowner Service
Northwestern Mutual Life Insurance Company

Leonard F. Stecklein, FLMI, ASA, MBA
Vice President, Policyowner Services
Northwestern Mutual Life Insurance Company

Linda L. Swanson
Vice President, Administration
First Capital Life Insurance Company

Ursula Wanko, FLMI, CLU, FALU, ALHC
Assistant Vice President, Administrative Services
Westfield Life Insurance Company

At the Prudential Insurance Company, Walter Graczyk, CLU, CHFC, Director of Market Analysis, provided me with great assistance by sending the manuscript to almost two dozen of Prudential's quality service experts. While I don't have room to name them all here, I would like to offer my special thanks to the many employees of Prudential's offices in Jacksonville, Minneapolis, and Newark who read the manuscript and improved it with their thoughtful comments.

In addition to the industry experts who provided me with invaluable assistance, many other people also helped me throughout the project.

I would like to thank Stephanie C. Consie, who helped me recruit this fine panel of experts and did extensive research for me during the early stages of the project; Richard Bailey, FLMI, who oversaw the design, typesetting, and printing of the book, and thereby took a great load off my shoulders; Sharon L. Bibee, who, besides handling a variety of other tasks, patiently contacted dozens of publishers and authors to get permission to reprint the various articles that appear in "Customer Service in Action" and "Issues in Customer Service"; and Alexa Selph, who copyedited the final manuscript and developed, with the help of Sharon Bibee and Richard Bailey, both the glossary and the index.

Finally, my special thanks go to Dani L. Long, FLMI, ALHC and Dennis W. Goodwin, FLMI, HIA, who read the manuscript through every draft and provided me with thoughtful editing, encouragement, and guidance throughout the project.

Kenneth Huggins, FLMI/M
Atlanta, Georgia
April 1991

Customer Service In Insurance:
Principles and Practices

CHAPTER 1

What Is Customer Service?

After studying this chapter, you should be able to

- Define customer service and describe some of the activities involved in providing customer service
- Explain the difference between customer service and policyowner service
- Identify who an insurance company's customers are and who provides customer service in insurance
- Describe why customer service is increasing in importance
- Understand the rewards that insurance companies can reap by providing high-quality customer service
- Understand the importance of the consumerist movement as it affects the insurance industry
- Explain some of the customer service issues that face the insurance industry

Introduction

Customer service is one of the most important functions performed in business. Customer service interactions — whether good or bad — are experiences that both an insurance company and its customers long remember. As a result, a company's ability to provide excellent customer service is essential for that company to develop and maintain a positive, lasting, and profitable relationship with its customers.

Regardless of our job responsibilities, most of us engage in some sort of customer service activities in our work. For example, as a representative of an insurance organization, you might be called on to provide a variety of services, such as recommending a particular type of coverage to meet a customer's changing needs, helping a customer understand the policy provisions in a new variable universal life policy, evaluating a policyowner's supplementary benefit rider request, or answering an insured's questions about reasons why a medical expense claim was denied. You might be asked to explain to an agent why an applicant's policy has been rated or declined or why it has taken you so long to approve an application for coverage. You might have just received an angry customer's misrouted phone call.

If you work in your company's accounting, information systems, or human resources areas, your customers are your fellow employees. The service you provide them is crucial in helping them meet the needs of your company's external customers. In fact, no matter what your job is, the better you are at providing quality customer service, the better prepared you will be to meet new challenges in business.

Customer service — and how we can make it better in the insurance industry — is the subject of this book. In this chapter, we begin our discussion by presenting some of the basic concepts of customer service: what customer service is, who the customer is, and who provides customer service. Next, we discuss the importance of customer service and the rewards that insurance companies can reap by providing high-quality customer service. Finally, we introduce some of the customer service challenges that the insurance industry faces.

What Is Customer Service?

Customer service refers to the broad range of activities that a company and its employees undertake in order to keep customers satisfied so they will continue doing business with the company and speak positively about the company to other potential customers. Providing customer service involves learning what customers want and taking whatever reasonable steps are required to make sure they get it. All companies — whether they manufacture physical goods, such as cars or radios, or provide intangible products, such as insurance and other financial services — offer some type of customer service.

Customer service activities can range all the way from providing customers with free parking to letting them transfer funds from their money market accounts to their IRAs or RRSPs without being charged handling fees. Businesses that sell physical goods, for example, often provide their customers with repair and warranty services, the option to return unsatisfactory goods, home delivery, telephone ordering, and lines of credit.

In the insurance business, customer service consists of a variety of activities aimed at both external and internal customers. For example, some insurers offer agents an 800-number hotline they can call for information about applications they have submitted. Other insurers guarantee that they will process any policy loan request within two working days of its receipt. By giving added value, each of these services provides an extra incentive for customers to do business with the company that provides the service. Thus, these value-added customer service activities help a company (1) become more appealing to customers, (2) attract new customers, (3) keep its customers once it has attracted them, (4) create additional sales opportunities with existing customers, and (5) differentiate itself from its competitors.

The importance of providing quality customer service cannot be overestimated. The more valuable a company is to its customers, the more likely it is that those customers will continue doing business with the company. By providing its customers with the kinds of service and the quality of service that they need and expect, a company improves its chances of meeting or exceeding its bottom-line business goals.

In an insurance company, the most visible customer service activities are generally policy administration functions, such as changing policyowners' addresses and processing policy loan requests. However, a wide variety of insurance company activities fall under the customer service heading. Each of the activities listed below is an example of a customer service function in an insurance company:

- Having agents provide service to customers in their homes.
- Maintaining company listings in local telephone books even though the company no longer markets insurance in that location; the company maintains the listings for the benefit of consumers who bought its products in the past and still own them.
- Letting customers conduct all their business with the company using a toll-free number.
- Giving each customer the name of a service representative who the customer can contact for any type of insurance service that the company offers.
- Setting up a telephone network that allows customers to get information and conduct transactions on a 24-hour basis.
- Training agents in the use of personal computers to maintain policyowner data.
- Providing fast turnaround on new business applications, enrollments, and fund reallocations.
- Establishing computerized systems that are oriented toward the needs of the customer; for example, using a system that files records by customer rather than by policy, so that all information on a single customer can be accessed at one time.
- Establishing a complaint-handling mechanism, such as a department of consumer affairs, through which customers can present their concerns and have them resolved.

Each time a company establishes a service like one of those listed above, the company is creating a special incentive for doing business with the company. For a closer look at a value-added customer service provided by an insurance company, look at Customer Service in Action 1–1.

A Money-Back Guarantee

In 1989 State Mutual Life Assurance Company offered what is believed to be the first money-back guarantee of its kind in the financial services industry. The warranty applies to full-service 401(k) retirement savings and other defined contribution plans.

According to the terms of the warranty, if State Mutual performs a service incorrectly and fails to correct it by the promised date, or performs contracted service after a specified date, the company will refund a client's fee for that service without question. Albert W. Buckbee II, Vice President of Group Pensions, personally handles client calls and, when appropriate, arranges for refunds.

"This warranty is intended to demonstrate the confidence we have in our ability to provide a high level service of unparalleled quality," said Buckbee.

Source: Adapted with permission of the publisher from Jill Conversano, "State Mutual Offers 401(k) Money-Back Guarantee," *Resource*, January/February 1989, pp. 56–57.

One of the goals of this book is to present customer service from a broad perspective — showing that customer service includes a wide variety of activities provided by every company representative for the benefit of many different kinds of customers. Although we will emphasize the work of employees who are specifically assigned to work with external customers, we will also make it clear that any insurance company employee may be called on at any time to provide customer service.

Who Is the Customer?

Typically when we speak of a customer, we are referring to the person who buys a product. However, the people who buy insurance products are not the only customers an insurance company has. Many other types of customers are associated with insurance companies. For example, the agents and brokers who sell insurance products are customers of the home office, and the home office must ensure that these agents and brokers get the support they need to do their jobs. Policyowners, of course, are customers, but so are beneficiaries and insureds. Claimants and group policyholders, company stockholders, investors who own shares in insurance company mutual funds, annuity contract holders, third-party administrators, employee-benefit consultants, and financial planners are also insurance company customers. In addition, insurance company employees are themselves frequently the customers of other employees at the same insurance company.

External Customers and Internal Customers

An insurance company's customers can be divided into two general categories: external customers and internal customers. An ***external customer*** is any person or business who is not on the insurance company's employee payroll *and* who is in a position either to (1) buy or use the insurance company's products or (2) advise others to buy or use its products. The best known among these customers are, of course, the people who actually use insurance products, for example, individual policyowners, annuity contract owners, insureds, beneficiaries, and group policyholders (such as corporations, proprietorships, and unions that buy insurance coverage for their group members). Throughout this book, we will refer to anyone who is a current or potential buyer or user of insurance products as a ***consumer***. In this sense, a consumer is a type of external customer. Consumers are an insurance company's most important customers. After all, they are the ones who buy the company's products.

Besides consumers, however, insurance companies have other external customers. Some of these other customers are third-party administrators, who work with insurance companies to administer insurance contracts for group policyholders; others are brokers, employee-benefits advisors, and other insurance consultants who help group insurance purchasers choose the insurance products they need.

Internal customers are the employees of an insurance company who receive service from other employees of the company. At any given time any employee may be the customer of any other employee in the same company. For example, when a company's middle managers ask the accounting department to develop a new financial report, the middle managers become the customers of the accounting department. When the accounting department asks the information systems department to program the company's computer system to produce the new report, the accounting department becomes a customer of the information systems department. Similarly, much of the work that managers do to help other staff members complete their work can be seen as customer service. For example, managers who make sure that their staff members are adequately trained and have enough time and resources to do their work are not just being good managers, they are being good customer service providers. Ultimately, all internal customer service eventually reaches, and has an effect on, external customers.

In a sense, the employees of a company are also its customers. They invest their time and effort with the company in exchange for the opportunity to earn a living. The chance for personal and financial growth, the level and quality of employee benefits offered by the company, the company's corporate culture, the professionalism and other attitudes exhibited by its management, and other facets of the company are the extra incentives, or value-added elements, that make these "employee/customers" want to continue doing business with (that is, working for) the company. Much of the work done in an insurance company consists of customer service transactions. How a company deals with its internal customers often indicates how it deals with its external customers.

Agents and Brokers

In addition to those groups of customers who can be classified strictly as either internal or external, there is a group of customers who can be *both* external and internal customers. These are the people who actually sell insurance products and who are compensated by an insurance company for making sales. This category includes career agents, agent-brokers, licensed brokers, home service agents, personal producing general agents (PPGAs), and salaried sales representatives. These people make up the insurance industry's distribution systems. Some work solely for one company and are considered the employees of that company. Others have contracts with several companies and are considered entirely independent entrepreneurs. Still others have contracts that make it hard to tell whether they are independent entrepreneurs or company employees. Whatever their exact relationship is to the insurance company, these agents and brokers (whom we will call *producers*) are among an insurance company's most important customers. If a producer becomes dissatisfied with the company's service, the company may lose hundreds of thousands of dollars in future income when the producer places business with a company that provides better service.

As you can see, insurance companies have a wide range of customers. And insurers must keep these customers satisfied to stay in business. Figure 1–1 shows various categories of customers and their relationships to an insurance company.

Figure 1–1
Insurance Company Customers

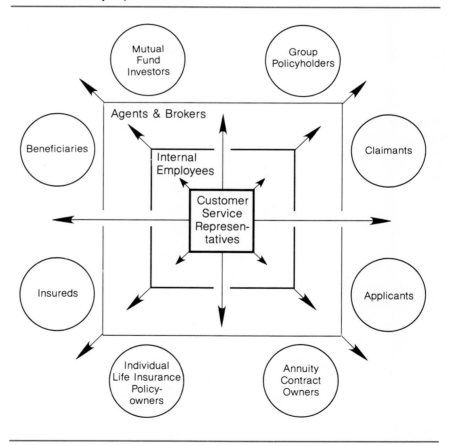

Who Provides Customer Service in Insurance Companies?

As we mentioned earlier, anyone in an insurance company may be called upon at any time to provide customer service. And every time there is contact between a company and a customer, a ***moment of truth*** occurs. The significance of each moment of truth is that any time a customer interacts with any part of a company—whether it's an agent, a customer service representative, or a recorded message—the company has an opportunity to create a good or bad impression in the mind of the customer. Look at Customer Service in Action 1–2, on the facing page, for an example of a moment of truth.

In the next few pages, we talk about some of the people who are involved in these moments of truth. We describe some of the most frequent customer service providers and some of the types of customer service they provide.

Customer Service Representatives

A customer service representative is usually the first person that comes to mind when we think of customer service. In many insurance companies, customer service representatives are employed in specific departments designed as centralized resources to help customers. These departments have a variety of names:

- Policyowner service
- Policyholder service
- Client services
- Financial services
- Customer service
- Policy administration
- Administrative services

Frequently, these departments have both an administrative and a customer service function. They are responsible for administering financial transactions that relate to contract values (such as policy loans and cash surrenders), maintaining and correcting policy records, informing policyowners of developments that affect their contracts, and processing simple coverage changes (such as adding riders and reinstating certain lapsed policies).

A Moment of Truth

Beth Hall, a customer service representative for Fidelity Union Life, recently received a telephone call from an elderly woman. The woman was weeping and obviously agitated.

"She seemed frightened," said Ms. Hall, "so I spoke with her for several minutes trying to comfort her. I assured her that no matter what the problem was, we were there to help her as much as possible.

"Gradually she told me that her daughter had stolen her wallet and checkbook and had overdrawn her checking account. She was proud that she had managed so well on Social Security and had never had an unpaid item before. But now, she was afraid that her preauthorized check (PAC) had bounced and her policy had lapsed."

The caller gave Ms. Hall the control number from an old draft so she could research the case. Ms. Hall searched for information about the policy, but there was nothing in the computer. The woman began weeping again, and Ms. Hall did her best to soothe her. She asked the woman to check the draft once more to make sure she had given her the correct control number.

"I'm sure I have," said the woman. "It shows it right here. United Fidelity control number 3800759-K."

There was a moment of silence. Then Ms. Hall cleared her throat and explained that the woman had called the wrong company. She had reached Fidelity Union Life, not United Fidelity.

"But I can get their number for you," said Ms. Hall.

She put the woman on hold and called information. She got the correct number and gave it to the woman.

"She thanked me," said Ms. Hall, "and told me she wished she had a daughter who would help her as much as I did. Maybe next time she'll buy a policy from Fidelity Union."

Source: Adapted with permission from Fidelity Union Life Insurance Company.

In the past, the nature of this work frequently required policyowner service representatives to concentrate primarily on administrative work — processing paperwork, making sure that documents were accurate, and moving papers quickly to the next person who needed to see them. In most instances, each employee was trained to do a specific task, such as processing policy loans, and did not know how to do other tasks in the department.

Because these types of services are part of what customers purchase when they buy insurance policies, performing such tasks will always be an important part of what customer service representatives do. However, a growing number of insurance companies are asking their customer service representatives to do more. They want their representatives to think not only of the specific request that a customer brings them, but to go beyond that request and consider the entire array of customer needs that the company can fill. Customer service representatives are being trained to understand the full range of a company's products and activities and to recognize marketing opportunities. At USAA Life Insurance Company, for example, the Sales Lead Program encourages customer service representatives to go beyond the customer's current request and suggest other insurance needs that the customer probably has but is unaware of.

Customer service representatives are also being given more intensive interpersonal-skills training and being taught how to process a wide variety of customer requests. They are being given more authority to make customer service decisions and are being encouraged to come up with creative solutions to customers' problems. In short, customer service representatives are being trained to provide sophisticated customer service, rather than being limited to administrative assistance.

Some customer service experts have suggested that customer service departments should not even exist. According to these experts, the very existence of customer service departments undermines the idea that everyone in a company should provide customer service. By having a customer service department, these experts say, a company gives its employees an excuse for avoiding customer service. It gives them an excuse to say, "I'm sorry. I don't handle that. You'll have to talk to someone in customer service."

Certainly, this danger exists when companies have a customer service department. However, even when all of a company's employees have a customer service attitude, customer service departments still serve a valuable function in most companies. By serving as the central location for information and aid for customers, customer service departments offer practical assistance not just to customers but to the company itself. A company's customers and its employees know that they can turn to the customer service department if they aren't sure how to handle a certain situation. For this reason, if for no other, it makes sense to have a customer service department. Such a department can offer customer service expertise, serve as a highly visible clearinghouse for customer service, and be an efficient and effective vehicle for helping customers.

Producers

For many consumers, the person who sells them an insurance policy *is* the insurance company.[1] As far as the consumer is concerned, the producer is the insurer. The consumer expects to be able to take all questions or problems to the person who sold the policy and say, "Here, take care of this for me." Quite often the consumer doesn't care where the insurance company's home office is and doesn't know (or even want to know) how to get in touch with it. They know the person who sold them their policies. They don't know anyone at the home office. Furthermore, many consumers see the producer as *their* agent and *their* customer service representative. They rely on the producer to represent their interests to the insurance company.

Every day, agents and brokers receive calls from consumers asking for some form of customer service. These producers (and the employees in their branch or agency offices) receive many of the same requests that customer service representatives at home offices receive. Producers are asked to change coverage on policies, add new beneficiaries, remove old beneficiaries, process claims, or explain contract wording. Some have even been asked to help a long-time client fill out an income tax form. The customer service provided by producers is varied and frequent. Some customer service requests are handled only by the producers; some are passed on to the home office to handle. But day in and day out, the producer is expected by both the consumer and the insurance company to play a major role in customer service.

The producer's role in customer service varies from insurer to insurer and from situation to situation. Many companies that use traditional agency or brokerage distribution systems tend to see the producer as a customer of at least equal importance to the actual consumer. Some companies even see the producer as being the company's primary customer. These companies concentrate on providing service to the producer, who in turn is expected to provide service to the consumer. Even direct-marketing insurance companies that use salaried sales representatives in the home office rather than commissioned producers see their sales force as a major link in the customer service process.

However, virtually all insurance companies, no matter which distribution systems they use, tend to see producers as a major service contact with consumers. The company encourages producers to field many customer service requests and to handle as many requests as possible in their own offices. In return for providing these services, the producers are treated as the company's valued customers. Home office employees (underwriters, claim examiners, customer service representatives, and so forth) are expected to provide producers with the highest possible level of customer service. These home office employees provide information, process claims, underwrite applications, and issue commission payments as quickly as they can. If a producer cannot provide the service that a consumer wants, then the employees at the home office are expected to take over where the producer leaves off.

The service that producers provide for consumers is in a sense a service to the home office, since the producer is helping to maintain the company's business relationship with the consumer. Conversely, whenever the home office provides the consumer with service, it is also serving the producer, since it is bolstering the producer-consumer relationship. All in all, the customer service relationship between an insurance company and its producers is an intricate dance, and the two partners (producer and company) take turns in the lead.

The next Customer Service in Action, number 1–3, should give you an idea of how important the producer is to insurance companies, both as a customer and as a provider of customer service.

CUSTOMER SERVICE IN ACTION 1–3

Focusing on Customers

To improve service to agents and policy-holders, Massachusetts Mutual Life is increasing communication between its agents and home office client service personnel through several new programs.

In addition to conducting focus group seminars that bring together home office and agency personnel to discuss policy-holder service issues, the insurer has instituted programs that send home office people to work in agencies for several weeks or months, "field trips" for home office employees to visit agencies, and a guest speaker program that brings agents into the home office to speak to groups of client service employees.

MassMutual has recognized the need for more open communication between home office service personnel and the company's 4,600 agents, said Paul D. Adornato, Senior Vice President, who heads the company's insurance and financial management client services division, which employs some 450 people.

Because the company's policyholders rely on its agents for financial planning and policy advice, MassMutual knows that if it doesn't understand its agents, it can't provide good service to policyholders, according to Mr. Adornato.

"MassMutual regards its field force as a primary client and as a valued research arm for determining the wants and needs of policyholders," he said. "Meaningful service improvements must be achieved with them."

Agents are "our primary focus," he said, adding that if MassMutual can better meet agents' expectations, agents as well

as the company will be able to provide better service to clients.

The shift in the industry's competitive battlefield from products to service also is a reason for the new programs, according to MassMutual.

"Ten years ago, 'competitiveness' was defined by new product development. But that era has largely passed, and now everyone is selling the same types of products," Mr. Adornato noted.

"Today it is as if everyone in the industry is selling Cadillacs, and so the next logical point of competition becomes whose dealership provides the best service."

Through the focus group seminars currently under way, home office personnel and agents are brought together to discuss methods for improving and streamlining elements of the company's policyholder service. The seminars are being conducted by one of MassMutual's longtime leading general agents, Ira E. Mogul, who is serving as a consultant to the company.

"We are structuring our home office/field service enhancement operation similar to the way we develop products. The first step is to develop an understanding of needs on both sides, and then take action to meet those needs," Mr. Mogul said.

It's the first time the field has been involved in working with home office service personnel on the company's service problems, according to Mr. Mogul. Client service people in the home office, even those who had been there for years, hadn't ever talked to the field, he noted.

Changes that are expected to be made

in MassMutual's client service program as a result of the process include: bringing general agents into the client service "loop," improved written communications for the field, and increased interaction among home office people and agents in the field so that the two groups are not antagonists, according to Mr. Mogul.

It sounds simple, but it hasn't been done in a lot of companies, he said.

A change that already has been made is that client service personnel are now participating in agent training classes. For the first time, service is part of the field training, he noted.

A goal of the process is to expand

agents' understanding of home office procedures, and vice versa, for improved communication between the two groups, he noted. In addition, increasing general agents' (GAs) understanding of client service issues will enable GAs to work better with agents, he said.

"One important benefit [of the process] is increasing the GAs' knowledge of service issues so that it is on a par with their expertise on product," Mr. Mogul said. As a result, "the GAs will be able to serve as troubleshooters and problem solvers for their agents in the service areas, as they now do with products."

Source: Adapted with permission from Sheril Arndt, "MassMutual Refocuses on the Field," *National Underwriter*, September 11, 1989, pp. 1, 39–40.

Claim Examiners

When consumers buy insurance, the most tangible return they typically expect to receive is the payment of a claim, either to themselves or some other beneficiary. Because of the importance of claims in insurance, the role of claim examiners (or anyone else in a claim administration department) is particularly critical to customer service. When consumers call the claim department, they want to know about money, *their* money. They want to know when they will get paid, how much they will get paid, why they weren't paid as much as they had expected to be paid, or why they aren't going to be paid anything at all. To the consumer, the person who sold the policy and the person who sends the claim check are probably the two most important people in the insurance company.

Because of its importance to consumers, claim processing is one of the primary measures of quality customer service: Was it accurate? Was it quick? Was it hassle free? Was it caring? The evaluation of claim payments is important at all times and in all areas of insurance. However, it is probably a more important measure of service in health insurance and property-casualty insurance than in life insurance. In life insurance, there is only one claim per insured, and that one is typically straightforward. In health insurance and property-casualty insurance, the insured can make many claims, some of which can be quite complicated.

Because of the critical nature of the claim administration process, claim examiners must be prompt and accurate in their work. Claim examiners also need thorough training in interpersonal skills, since they frequently deal with people who are worried about an illness or distraught over the loss of a loved one. Further, the manner in which a claim decision is made and communicated can expose the company to a lawsuit for bad faith. Should a court decide that the claim examiner acted improperly, the company's financial liability could be extremely high.

Underwriters

The customer service relationship between producers and underwriters is similar to the customer service relationship between consumers and claim examiners. In many ways, the underwriter holds the key to the producer's income. If an underwriter approves an application, the producer earns a commission; if the underwriter declines an application, the producer loses a commission. If an underwriter rates a policy (thus raising the premium), the producer may have to resell the policy to the customer or may lose the sale entirely. In fact, if an underwriter is simply slow in approving an application, the producer can lose a commission, because the consumer may get tired of waiting and choose to do business with another company. Furthermore, if a producer is not satisfied with the service provided by a company's underwriters, that producer may very well choose to do business with another company. Thus, the insurer would lose not only a potential policyowner but also a valued producer who will no longer be bringing business to the company.

The relationship between producers and underwriters has more variables in it than simply earning or losing a commission, but the purse-string variable is the most dramatic. If for no other reason than this one variable, underwriters need strong customer service skills as well as strong technical skills. But they must also be able to evaluate applications quickly and accurately so they can respond to agents as soon as possible. They must be able to explain their underwriting decisions clearly but without violating the applicant's legal right to privacy. They must also be able to educate producers about the guidelines on which their decisions are based.

In addition to their work with agents, underwriters also provide a number of customer service activities for other areas of the company. For example, they may develop and conduct training sessions and explain underwriting principles and guidelines to marketing and other company personnel. They may advise the marketing department on ways to improve agents' field underwriting. They may review requests for policy changes or reinstatements received by the policyowner service department. They may work with the claim administration department to reevaluate applications on policies that experience claims during their contestable periods. Each of these interactions requires the underwriting department to deal with other departments as its internal customers.

As with other personnel that provide a great deal of customer service, underwriters must weigh the needs of the company, the producer, and the consumer and come up with a solution that provides customer satisfaction in the most reasonable fashion possible.

Administrative Support Staff

In every insurance company, a large percentage of employees never interact directly with the company's external customers or producers. Mailroom personnel, systems programmers, trainers, and accountants, for example, work mainly with other insurance company employees, rather than with external clients. As support staff, these people provide customer service to internal customers, so those employees who work directly with customers can do so more effectively.

The Increasing Importance of Customer Service

Insurance companies have been providing customer service since the first policies were sold in the 1800s. Why then has customer service recently become such an important topic? Why is providing quality customer service on nearly all companies' lists of priorities? And why are service levels that were adequate a decade ago considered insufficient today?

One of the most important reasons that companies are trying to improve customer service is that consumers' expectations have increased over the years. Today's insurance consumers are better educated, more financially sophisticated, and increasingly aware that they have a greater number of choices when they decide where to spend their insurance dollars. As a result, many of these customers expect *value-added services* — services that provide customers with additional benefits (whether tangible or intangible) that do not routinely come with the product or service they have bought.

Moreover, companies in all industries — not just insurance and financial services — are placing greater emphasis on service. Consequently, consumers are beginning to expect more and better service from every company regardless of the industry in which it operates. As we will discuss more fully in later chapters, a company that wants to provide quality customer service must at least meet customer expectations. In such an environment, both the level of service and the quality of service provided take on added importance.

In today's economy, insurers must work harder to remain profitable in the face of declining returns on fiercely competitive products. If insurers expect to be profitable, they need adequate persistency rates on their products as well as repeat business from their producers. Excellent service — during and after each sale — is one way to keep customers.

As insurers work harder to attract and retain customers, they have come to realize that even the most casual contact between the company and the customer represents a moment of truth and has the potential for either improving or damaging the company's image. Every time one of a company's customer service providers or other representatives has an interaction with a customer, that representative is making an impression on the customer. That impression — whether good or bad — helps form the customer's opinion of the company and its service. In order to keep their customers, insurers are trying to make sure that such moments of truth are positive ones and that their customers are aware of the value of remaining with the company.

The relationship between customer satisfaction and corporate profitability has also become well documented in recent years, thus helping to dispel the view that customer service is a burdensome and expensive chore. Instead, research shows that customer service can be a strategic weapon for reducing the cost of sales by helping a company retain its policyowners, producers, and other customers. From its study of approximately 3,000 businesses, the Strategic Planning Institute has developed a data base called the Profit Impact of Market Strategies (PIMS). This data base shows a definite financial relationship between a business's profitability and the perception that its customers have of the quality of its products and services. In addition, research by Technical Assistance Research Programs (TARP) indicates that poor service is more damaging than most companies realize. According to TARP, 31 percent of customers who experience service problems never register complaints because it is "too much trouble" or because they believe no one at the company cares. Of the 31 percent who don't complain, most will never do business with that company again.[2]

In response to such information about the importance of customer service, many organizations are treating customer service as a marketable commodity. For example, many companies are trying to make their service more visible by marketing it as if it were a tangible product. Today's producers "sell" service, and marketing managers promote it as one of the features that make their companies stand out among the crowd. It's no wonder that customer service has suddenly become one of the most talked about functions in business.

For a further discussion of the importance of customer service, look at Issues in Customer Service 1–1, which describes the consumer movement and its effect on the insurance industry.

ISSUES IN CUSTOMER SERVICE 1–1

The Impact of a Growing Consumer Movement

Today's consumers expect more and better service, are more critical of companies and products that do not meet their needs, and are less loyal to traditional products and businesses with which they have relationships. Furthermore, leaders of today's consumer movement have become more knowledgeable about insurance and other business matters. They have also become more politically astute. As a result, an insurance company that plans to be successful in the 1990s must take the customer's perspective when it looks at its products, its customer service operations, and its corporate image.

It is important to note that the customer's perspective may be that of the actual consumer or that of professional consumerist organizations that survey the public, conduct consumer research and educational programs, and lobby for issues they feel are in the public interest. As the competition for insurance customers intensifies, consumers will take their business to the companies that serve them best. Moreover, if the industry fails to meet the consumerist challenge, it will likely be confronted with an increasingly contentious and negative political environment.

Three factors in particular are responsible for the growing consumer pressures on insurers. First, the growth of financial products and services has led to tremendous increases in both competition and consumer confusion. Competition and the higher costs of offering interest-sensitive products have contributed to reduced profit margins, fueling consumer concern about the soundness of many insurance and other financial service companies. Consumer confusion has contributed to dissatisfaction with financial service companies, as consumers become more suspicious of those who want to advise them on their financial service needs.

Second, the levels of service and responsiveness that previous generations of consumers found adequate are no longer acceptable. And this generation knows how to make its complaints heard. Although they may not be sufficiently informed to feel comfortable in the rapidly changing financial marketplace, today's consumers are more sophisticated about the obligations they believe financial institutions owe to them. They are also more demanding about their rights to receive those obligations.

The third factor responsible for growing consumer pressures is the evolution of the consumer movement. As consumer leaders have become more knowledgeable about business and more politically astute, they have greatly increased their power. They know how to gain media attention, and they are adept at mobilizing the public. Moreover, whether consumerists themselves or not, most consumers are more likely to trust consumer leaders, whom they consider to be on their side, rather than big business.

The increased sophistication of consumer groups was not a major challenge to life and health insurers as long as con-

sumer attention was focused on other industries. However, consumer interest is now turning toward the financial services industry—first banks, then savings and loans, then property/casualty insurers, and now life and health insurers. Consumer leaders distrust the industry, which they view as the last bastion of major unregulated (by the United States federal government) or poorly regulated (by the states) business. Consumerists view insurance as something most people need, something for which people have to pay a lot, and something most people don't understand.

Arcane policy language, perceived discriminatory underwriting, cost disclosure that seems inadequate, sales practices that seem misleading or unfair, poor service, and what consumerists see as uncompetitive, inefficient business practices are now high on their list for reform. They claim that lack of effective regulation has allowed the industry to withhold vital cost information from the buying public and has also allowed insurers to charge excessive premiums and perpetuate uncompetitive, unfair marketing practices and poor service. These are areas on which the industry can expect consumerists to focus their efforts during the 1990s.

To help address these problems, many insurers are hiring *consumer affairs professionals*. These staff members perform a number of customer service functions for their companies. For example, they

- interpret for their companies the key perspectives, sensitivities, needs, and expectations of consumers and advise companies about the effect this information can have on strategic business decisions;
- help make sure that a consumer orienta-

tion is built into companies' corporate mission statements;

- interact with marketing so that customer needs and sensitivities are incorporated into new product features and advertising and sales campaigns;
- work with the areas of a company responsible for external constituencies, including the media and regulators, so that the company maintains an accurate understanding of which consumer concerns are particularly troublesome and what regulatory actions are being proposed to Congress;
- consult with a company's operating areas on ways to improve customer service;
- sometimes run special programs, such as centralized complaint handling systems;
- conduct customer surveys and service audits to monitor the company's service quality;
- provide employees with customer service training; and
- build relationships with local and national consumer organizations to gather strategic information from consumer leaders about their ideas for improving the insurance business, which in turn may improve the industry's image.

Bringing the consumer-affairs perspective into top-level decision making and day-to-day operations adds value throughout the company. The consumer perspective stimulates cost-effective, practical approaches to product development, innovative marketing, and efficient service. The credibility and positive image earned through direct relationships with consumers also can differentiate and help distinguish the consumer-sensitive company from its competitors.

Consumer-affairs programs can play a major role in helping life and health insurance companies succeed in the decade ahead. Five areas in which companies can take action to give themselves a service advantage include:

- *Instituting comprehensive service improvements based on a solid core of customer information and top-level commitment.* Basically, this means conducting customer surveys and using focus groups and advisory panels to gather information about customer perceptions, needs, wants, and satisfaction. It also means that having a true commitment from top management is essential to any strategy for service improvement.
- *Engaging in proactive problem identification and prevention.* Simply responding to customers is no longer sufficient. Companies must anticipate customer needs and take action to prevent problems from occurring. Customer complaints, for example, provide companies with insights into areas in which they are weak on service. Yet many companies never use this information effectively. Instead they handle each complaint as if it were a separate, idiosyncratic situation. Insurers should use complaint trends to help identify problems with their products, their customer service systems, and their employees, and to take corrective actions based on such findings.
- *Developing consumer-oriented products and services.* Companies can use the consumer affairs perspective to design product features that customers need, develop innovative marketing ideas (such as teaming up with consumer groups), and create special service components for which customers are willing to pay. Following this perspective also helps companies avoid costly errors that might go undetected until customers complain to insurance regulators.

- *Developing working partnerships with consumer leaders*. With their finger on the public's pulse, consumer leaders are one of the best sources of strategic information about consumer needs and the economic and social factors that affect the insurance business. Jointly sponsored conferences and publications and collaborative research between companies and consumer groups encourage a healthy exchange of ideas.
- *Building relationships with customers and consumerists*. Building and improving relationships with customers and consumerists will become more important as new, more demanding consumers come to dominate the marketplace.

Two organizations that have taken the lead in improving insurers' relations with consumer groups are the Insurance Consumer Affairs Exchange (ICAE) and the American Council of Life Insurance (ACLI). The ICAE is the industry association of insurance consumer affairs professionals. It has been instrumental in helping companies improve their consumer affairs programs. The ACLI, concerned about the industry's image with the public, has also taken action in the consumer arena by stepping up its programs to help member companies provide consumers with improved service. The ACLI has drafted eight "Principles of Quality Service," and it recommends that each company in the industry should use these principles as a model for establishing and implementing its own principles of quality service. [See Figure 1–2 for the complete listing of the ACLI's Principles of Quality Service.] Finally, the ACLI recently joined with the Health Insurance Association of America (HIAA) and the Insurance Informa-

tion Institute (III) to establish a toll-free consumer insurance information hot line. [In Canada, the Canadian Life and Health Insurance Association (CLHIA) has developed and distributed a consumers' Code of Ethics to its 110 member companies. Compliance is encouraged. The CLHIA has provided consumers with a toll-free telephone line to its Information Centre since 1974.]

By understanding consumers and today's consumerist movement, insurance companies can develop the kinds of quality services that customers want and expect. And through these services insurers can improve their chances of success in the future.

Figure 1–2
The ACLI's Principles of Quality Service

- To help each buyer choose an insurance product appropriate to his or her financial needs and means.
- To develop fairly priced products that reflect a sound assessment of risk factors and respond to the changing needs of the public.
- To assist the buyer in understanding how various factors, including risk, relate to price.
- To guard the confidentiality of personal information about insureds and applicants.
- To provide a concise, readable policy and additional information that will be helpful to the policyholder.
- To communicate with the policyholder throughout the life of the contract, as appropriate, and to handle policy inquiries, changes, and claims quickly and courteously.
- To be honest and forthright in all advertisements and messages to the buying public and policyholders.
- To protect future policyholder benefits through sound company investments and efficient company and field office operations.

Source: Adapted with permission of the publisher from Sandra L. Willett, "The Battle for Customer Loyalty," *Best's Review*, May 1990, pp. 20–24, 199.

Benefits of Providing Quality Customer Service[3]

As we have already noted, providing quality customer service can be a powerful business strategy. Some of the major benefits an insurance company can reap by providing quality customer service are described below:

- *Building long-term customer loyalty.* Satisfied customers generally want to continue doing business with a company. Satisfied customers are more likely to renew or increase their coverages on products that they currently own. They are also more likely to buy additional products from the company. Thus, satisfied customers are excellent prospects for new sales, cross sales, and sales leads. According to *The 1987 Buyer Study*, published by the Life Insurance and Marketing Research Association (LIMRA), approximately one quarter of all individual life insurance sales in 1987 were made to consumers who already owned policies.[4] By continuously providing quality customer service, a company reassures its customers that it intends to meet their current and future financial needs. Superior service should increase the number of repeat sales to existing customers.

- *Attracting new customers.* When a company has a reputation for good service, attracting new customers is easier. A good reputation stays with a company for years and is one of those intangible attributes on which prospective customers base many of their purchase decisions. Furthermore, when a company does a good job of taking care of its current customers, those customers tell their friends about the good service "their" company has given them. In effect, the company turns these customers into an enthusiastic corps of voluntary salespeople who freely promote the company in exchange for the excellent customer service they receive.

- *Attracting and retaining producers.* Producers are more likely to do business with a company that has a reputation for good service. Thus, the quality of a company's customer service can be a key factor when producers are deciding which companies to represent. Service is also a key factor in keeping producers loyal to a company and encouraging them to continue distributing its products.

- *Attracting and retaining high-quality employees.* People in the work force are frequently aware of a company's reputation for providing service, and people are likely to want to work for a company that has a reputation for excellent service.

- *Differentiating a company and its products from the competition.* To the average consumer, insurance companies and their products tend to look much the same. By offering quality customer service, a company can differentiate itself from other insurers and create a unique, identifiable image that it can use to engender brand loyalty in its customers. As a result of their identification with the company, such customers will be more likely to return to the company — rather than go to some other insurer — when seeking additional products to meet their needs. Providing quality service helps give a company a competitive edge in the marketplace.

- *Improving the company's profitability.* When a company does not provide quality customer service, it loses customers — not only the consumers who decide not to renew or buy its products, but also the producers who decide not to sell its products. When policyowners leave a company, allowing the products they owned to lapse, the company may not have time to recover the costs of selling, underwriting, and issuing the products. When producers leave, the company not only loses the revenue that the producers would have generated, it also must spend more money on recruiting, training, and guiding new producers through their first few years on the job. These costs (for inexperienced producers) can run anywhere from $90,000 to $190,000 per person and can take the company 9 to 21 years to recover. [5]

- *Increasing productivity.* Although providing quality customer service initially involves a considerable investment in people and systems, it leads ultimately to more efficient operations. As the quality of customer service improves, productivity also increases, because customer complaints decline and the errors previously caused by poor service are minimized.

- *Improving the company's work environment.* When a company provides excellent customer service, its employees tend to be happier and more motivated. They have a high regard for their company and the work they do. They do not have to spend excessive amounts of time correcting mistakes or handling complaints. When complaints do occur, motivated employees are more likely to resolve the problems to their customers' satisfaction.

The Special Challenges of Customer Service in Insurance

In the last few pages, we've identified why customer service is so important to the insurance industry, and we've listed some of the major ways in which insurers benefit from providing quality service. With all the evidence we have presented, you would think that the value of customer service would be obvious and that most insurance companies would already have made sure that they provide the very best customer service possible. So why don't all companies provide excellent customer service? Why is the industry still struggling to find the solution to the customer service problem? There are a number of factors that make it difficult for companies to provide quality customer service. Some of these factors apply to all businesses, while others apply primarily to insurance companies. Listed below are six customer service issues that pose problems for most insurers:

1. The nature of customer service itself.
2. The nature of insurance products.
3. The present costs of service versus the possibility of future profits.
4. The reward system for customer service providers.
5. The difficulty of identifying the primary customer: Is it the consumer or the producer?
6. The manufacturing mentality in many insurance company home offices.

The Nature of Customer Service Itself

You can't touch or hold customer service. Customer service is experienced only as it is provided. Since almost nothing about customer service is tangible, customers often have few reference points on which to judge the value or quality of the service as it is being performed. In addition, insurance companies themselves find it difficult to test customer service or assess its quality before it is provided. Therefore, detecting customer service defects and fixing them is difficult.

Furthermore, customer service cannot be kept in inventory. A company cannot produce units of customer service and save them until they are needed. Producers and customer service representatives have only a certain number of hours in each day in which to provide customer service for their clients, and the hours available in one day cannot be carried forward to another day. Similarly, insurance companies cannot produce large quantities of address changes, claim checks, fund reallocations, or other customer services in advance and then send them out when customers request them. Instead, companies must be able to forecast accurately the number and timing of customer requests and allocate the resources needed to perform the necessary services.

Another problem faced by companies is that, by its nature, customer service is not consistent or homogeneous. Most customer services are performed by people, and no matter how skillful or well intentioned they are, people do not always perform consistently. They forget details, get delayed, show impatience, and sometimes are less than agreeable. The quality of customer service may vary from provider to provider, from customer to customer, from day to day. Sporadic bursts of excellent customer service may be easy to provide, but consistently excellent service is difficult.

Finally, customer service is consumed at the same time it is produced. The quality of the service is created and determined during the interaction between the service provider and the customer. In many cases, once the service has been completed, there is nothing left except the customer's perception of whether the service was good or bad.

The Nature of Insurance Products

Insurance products have a number of characteristics that pose problems for companies that want to provide quality customer service. Some of the most important of these characteristics are the intangibility of insurance products, the complexity of insurance products, and their association in the minds of customers with unpleasant circumstances.

The Intangibility of Insurance

Because insurance products are primarily services, they have all the intangibility of services and all the problems caused by that intangibility. Whereas a good is something you can lay your hands on, something you can grasp with your physical senses, a service is not.

Even though an insurance product has a policy contract that is tangible and physical, the product itself is intangible. An insurance product is a contractual financial obligation. It can't be seen or felt or smelled or heard or tasted. A customer can't take an insurance policy to the store, point to a damaged or ineffective part, and say, "It's broken. Here's the problem. Please fix it." Intangible products are generally more difficult for people to understand than tangible products. This lack of understanding can lead to distrust and anxiety on the part of the customer, which in turn can make the work of customer service representatives especially difficult.

Not only is the insurance product itself intangible, but in a sense the company that sells the product is also intangible. Although some customers meet directly with a producer when they need customer service and some may even visit their company's home office, most customer service for insurance is handled over the phone or through the mail. There is nothing wrong with providing service on the phone or through the mail, but it's not the same as going to a local department store and being surrounded by all the products available for purchase, or dealing face-to-face with the people who sell and service the products. The customer and the insurance company are distanced from one another, which can lead to anxiety and distrust on the part of the customer, and thus make customer service interactions more difficult.

The Complexity of Insurance

Most insurance products are complex. In their generic forms, they are legal documents in which an insurer promises to provide certain services under specified circumstances. Although most insurance companies are trying to simplify the wording of their contracts, legal requirements can still make the wording difficult to understand. And since consumers, by and large, don't understand the product they have bought, they frequently don't know exactly what they need when they ask for service. Because of the complexity of the product, the role of customer service becomes one of providing education as well as assistance. As part of this educational role, some insurance companies now offer buyer's guides and policy summaries to help consumers better understand insurance products.

The Circumstances Surrounding Insurance

A final characteristic of insurance products that makes them a customer service challenge involves the circumstances surrounding their use. Most people don't like to think about insurance, because it often involves dealing with unpleasant circumstances. The benefits of insurance are normally reaped when something bad has happened in the consumer's life — a sickness, an accident, or a death. For some people, even thinking about insurance is an unpleasant experience. Furthermore, when insurance customers have a claim, they are frequently under emotional or financial stress.

As a result, insurance company representatives who provide customer service must be prepared to deal with a great deal more than just the product. They must be prepared to help customers during emotional crises. And they must be prepared to ease the concerns and defensive attitudes of customers who need assistance. To meet these customer service challenges, many insurance companies are training their employees to handle a variety of interpersonal situations.

Present Costs versus Future Benefits

When we described the benefits of providing excellent customer service, we pointed out that there is a strong relationship between customer service and profitability. For both producers and insurers, providing quality service leads to additional sales. In most instances, however, the financial rewards of providing customer service are not realized when the service is being provided. Such rewards come later — for example, when a current customer needs more coverage and does business with the company, or when the customer refers a friend to the company. Initially, however, the company has to spend time and money on service, rather than on new sales, and many companies and producers are reluctant to forgo the income of immediate sales for the possibility of larger gains in the future.

The Reward System for Service Providers

A general principle in behavioral science states, "You get the behavior that you reward." If you do not reward a particular behavior, you are likely to see it less and less. For example, if an insurance company evaluates its customer service representatives primarily on the basis of the number of telephone calls they answer, the company is encouraging them to handle calls quickly but perhaps not effectively or courteously. In such a company, customer service representatives who spend enough time with a customer to understand and respond to the customer's needs will be rewarded less than representatives who provide cursory service. Because people want to be rewarded for their efforts, it's likely that the company's representatives will find ways, courteous or not, to shorten the length of their telephone calls, in effect reducing the quality of the customer service they provide.

Similarly, the traditional commission structure in the insurance industry is not designed to reward producers for providing customer service directly. Most producers receive the bulk of their income on ordinary life and health insurance products when they make a sale. A producer's initial commission on the sale of most ordinary products may range from 50 percent to 120 percent of the value of the first year's premium. The producer's commissions on renewal premiums received for that same product typically range from 5 percent to 20 percent of the premium. Critics of the traditional commission structure note that its very nature indicates to producers that sales, not service, is the primary goal of the companies they represent.

Insurance companies do, of course, emphasize to their producers the importance and rewards of customer service. And the best insurance agents and brokers have learned over the years that the long-term benefits of providing quality customer service are worth the time spent. Providing good customer service leads producers to future sales, renewal commissions, referrals, and a reputation for dependability. Most producers, however, have learned to provide customer service despite the traditional commission structure, not because of it.

Another problem with the reward system in the insurance industry — and in many other industries — is that customer service positions have not always been paid well. These lower salary levels can make it difficult to attract, motivate, and retain qualified employees. In recent years, however, the value of excellent customer service has become more apparent. And as companies realize the value of customer service and its effect on their bottom lines, they have increased the salary levels of customer service positions. Today, more people are finding it desirable to start their insurance careers in customer service. By working in customer service, employees get the opportunity to learn about their companies' products and to understand what customers need and how to work with them effectively.

The Who's-the-Customer Syndrome

As we mentioned earlier, many insurance companies see their two primary customers as the consumer and the producer — the person who buys the product and the person who sells the product. This two-tiered market occurs (except in direct-marketing companies) because a company has to convince producers to sell its products, while the producers, in turn, have to convince consumers to buy the products. Common sense tells us that the person who ultimately buys the product is the customer. For many companies, however, the only way to reach the customer is through the producer. So these companies have to treat the producer as the customer in order to continue making sales to the consumer. This situation does not always lead to problems, but the potential for problems is there.

For instance, if a company places too much stress on the producer as customer, thereby relying on the producer to provide most of the customer service for the consumer, then the company loses control of the customer service function. Since most producers are not employees of the company, the company cannot guarantee that producers are meeting company standards for customer service. Further, by placing the producer between itself and the consumer, the insurer runs the risk of cutting itself off from the consumer and, thus, appearing to be the cold, distant insurer that many consumers already imagine.

On the other hand, if the company tries to make direct contact with the consumer, producers may feel that the company is trying to usurp their role and perhaps deprive them of income-earning possibilities. In addition, producers may also feel that they are better qualified than home office personnel to provide customer service. They often take this position because they feel that they have a better understanding of the consumer's needs. After all, they made the original sales contact; they nurtured the business relationship with the consumer. Therefore, they want control of the customer service. Because of these factors, conflicts may arise between producers and the home office.

The best way for insurance companies to avoid potential problems in this area is to maintain clear and continuous communication to all of their customers. Companies should make it clear that they are available to assist consumers (either through the home office or the producer's office) in any way possible. Companies should also work with producers to establish clear guidelines about the level and type of customer service that the producer and the company will provide and exactly who at the home office or field office will provide these services.

The Manufacturing Mentality

Finally, many insurance company employees, especially home office employees, have a tendency to develop a "manufacturing mentality." As a result, they sometimes forget the real purpose of their work, which is to serve the customer. Such employees may concentrate so much on the functions and procedures of their day-to-day responsibilities that they forget about the customer. They simply "manufacture" paperwork. They get so involved in processing all the reports, files, forms, and letters that are such a large part of their daily routine that they start thinking that processing paperwork is their job, not serving customers. This problem, of course, is not unique to the insurance industry. It can occur in any kind of business, and as customers, we have all had to deal with it at one time or another. Most of us know the feeling of walking into a business and having to deal with a bureaucrat who looks at us with world-weary eyes and heaves a sigh of despair, knowing that we will be yet another interruption in the work routine.

One of the reasons that this manufacturing mentality takes hold is that, in many ways, it is easier to be a manufacturer than a server. A manufacturer controls all the variables. There are no outside factors, no customer interference. All a manufacturer has to concentrate on is speed, efficiency, and quality control. In effect, someone with a manufacturing mentality says, "Keep the customer out of my hair so I can get my work done."

In these types of situations, many employees often forget that there is a customer. They spend so much time out of direct contact with customers that, as far as they're concerned, the customer has disappeared. But without the customer, employees have no jobs. And that's what all companies and employees — especially those with manufacturing mentalities — have to be reminded of. Their corporate and personal livelihoods depend on the customer — on the satisfied customer.

Obviously, a company's employees cannot bear all the blame for falling into a manufacturing mentality. If a company puts a great deal of stress on completing paperwork and not on serving the customer, the company's employees will concentrate on paperwork. They will do what they are rewarded for doing. Any business can fall into this habit of forgetting the customer, but because of the nature of the work at a home office, insurance companies must be especially wary of it. As we will discuss in later chapters, employees learn to function within the system that their company establishes.

If the system encourages an inward-looking manufacturing mentality, that's the mentality that employees will develop. However, if the system is flexible and open to the customer, if it encourages employees to be outward looking, then the employees will be much more likely to adopt a customer service attitude.

Conclusion

In this chapter, we have presented some of the basic concepts of customer service, such as what customer service is, who the customer is, and who provides customer service. We have also discussed the importance of customer service, the rewards that insurance companies can reap by providing quality customer service, and the customer service challenges that are unique to the insurance industry. In the following chapters, we will expand on these ideas and answer some of the questions that these ideas have raised.

Key Terms

customer service	consumer movement
policyowner service	consumer affairs professionals
external customer	Principles of Quality Service
consumer	intangibility
internal customer	simultaneous production and
producer	consumption
moment of truth	who's-the-customer syndrome
value-added services	manufacturing mentality

Notes

1. See ICAE, *Building Policyholder Relationships: A Report on Four Focus Groups* (Hartford, CT: ICAE, 1989); and Albert J. Sheridan, *Understanding Customers: What Research Reveals about What Consumers Really Want* (Hartford, CT: LIMRA, 1989).
2. John A. Goodman, Ted Marra, and Liz Brigham, "Customer Service: Costly Nuisance or Low-Cost Profit Strategy," *Journal of Retail Banking*, Fall 1986.
3. Portions of this section are based on William A. Sherden, "The Erosion in Service Quality," *Best's Review*, September 1987, pp. 22–23, 148.
4. LIMRA, *The 1987 Buyer Study* (Hartford, CT: LIMRA, 1988), p. 2.
5. LIMRA, *Investing in New Agents* (Hartford, CT: LIMRA, 1985), pp. 11, 14.

CHAPTER 2

Building a Customer Service Culture

After studying this chapter, you should be able to

- Describe what corporate culture is and how it is formed
- Explain some of the major factors affecting corporate culture
- Describe the characteristics of various types of corporate cultures
- Explain why corporate culture is important to customer service
- Describe some of the challenges and fundamental changes involved in implementing a customer service culture

Introduction

In *Webster's New World Dictionary*, **culture** is defined as "the ideas, customs, skills, arts, etc. of a given people in a given period." This same definition of culture has been modified and carried over to the business world. Today, the phrase ***corporate culture*** (also called *organizational culture*) describes the attitudes, values, perceptions, beliefs, and experiences shared by the employees of an organization and instilled in new employees when they enter the organization. A company's corporate culture is, in effect, the company's personality, and it determines what the company deems important and how the company believes things should be done. Corporate culture gives employees a sense of what is expected of them on the job, how they ought to behave, and which types of behavior will be rewarded. A company's corporate culture also affects how well or how poorly the company provides customer service.

In this chapter, we will discuss how important it is for a company to have a customer service culture. We will discuss what a corporate culture means to a company, how a corporate culture is established, and how it affects the way customer service is provided in a company. We will describe different types of corporate cultures as well as some of the cultural characteristics that seem to encourage excellence in customer service. We will also describe some of the factors involved when a company changes from one type of culture to another. Finally, we will discuss the four elements that are essential for creating a truly customer-oriented organization.

Some Basics about Corporate Culture

Every organization has a distinct culture. For example, one company's corporate culture might be characterized as open, supportive, participative, and risk-taking. Another company's culture might be described as secretive, untrusting, unsupportive, and bureaucratic. A third company's culture might be a mixture of these. Furthermore, a company may have both a *dominant culture*, which is the culture that is most prominent throughout the organization, and a variety of *subcultures* within its operating units. Subcultures may be similar to the dominant culture or they may be totally different from it. Sometimes, a subculture may be so different that it appears to be at odds with the dominant culture. Such a subculture is unlikely to continue unless top management allows it to continue. And top management may allow it to continue because

- the subculture is seen as an experiment,
- top management wants the subculture to become dominant,
- the subculture is part of an important unit, such as a highly profitable revenue-producing unit,
- the subculture is part of an apparently insignificant unit that top management does not bother to change, or
- the subculture is influenced by a person who is respected in the company.

Major Factors Affecting Corporate Culture

Corporate culture is affected by many factors in an organization. Among the factors having the strongest influence are management, work groups, company characteristics, and systems and administrative procedures. (See Figure 2–1.)

Management

The managers of an organization, through their behavior, set an example for everyone else in the organization to follow. Whether anyone realizes it or not, the managers serve as role models for the rest of the employees. And the most influential role models are the executives of the company. If a company's executives are open to new ideas, if they encourage creativity and are willing to listen to honest critisism,

Figure 2–1
Factors that Affect Corporate Culture

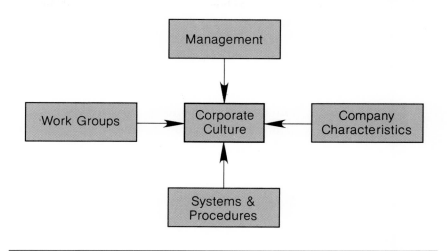

if they present an open, supportive attitude, these characteristics are likely to be imitated by the other employees, from middle managers to supervisors to frontline employees. On the other hand, if top managers appear secretive and distrusting of employees, if they threaten rather than encourage, if they demand obedience rather than inspire respect, these behaviors and characteristics will probably be imitated by most other employees in the company.

Work Groups

Work groups are small groups of employees who work together on a regular basis. The way in which the employees in these groups respond to each other, their work, and their environment affects the company's corporate culture. For example, if members of a work group are committed to their work, if they act as supportive members of a unified team, if their morale is high, if they see their work as important to the company's successful operation, and if they feel they are appropriately rewarded for their work, they are likely to have a positive view of themselves. And this positive outlook will become part of the company's corporate culture. On the other hand, if their attitudes are negative, these negative attitudes will also become part of the company's corporate culture.

Company Characteristics

By company characteristics, we mean such factors as a company's size, organizational structure, history, and even the type of work it does. For example, a large company may tend to be impersonal and bureaucratic, while a small company may encourage close working relationships between top management and frontline employees. Large, decentralized companies may have weak dominant cultures and strong subcultures, while a small, centralized company with a strong president may have a single corporate culture that very much reflects the president's personality.

Systems and Administrative Procedures

The systems and procedures a company establishes also affect its corporate culture. Consider a company that establishes a system that makes it easy for employees to communicate with one another, both between departments and between the various levels of employees. That company is likely to have a culture much different from that of a company that enforces a slow and highly bureaucratic system of communication. Similarly, a company with a performance-evaluation system that clearly links employees' performance with its reward system will probably not have the same culture as a company that does not tie performance to rewards.

All of these factors—management, work groups, company characteristics, and systems and procedures—interact to form a company's culture. And this culture, in turn, affects the way in which the company operates. If employees identify with, and like, the culture, they are more inclined to support it and, therefore, be more committed to the company. They will probably have higher levels of job satisfaction and be better performers. If they do not like the culture, they may fight it, try to change it, form opposing subcultures, or leave the company in search of a culture that is more compatible with their own personalities.

Types of Corporate Cultures

Because every business has its own unique personality, there are probably as many corporate cultures as there are corporations. However, there are certain characteristics that allow us to categorize some general types of corporate cultures. For the purpose of our discussion here, we will deal with four categories of cultures by borrowing from Rensis Likert's four systems of management.[1] These four corporate cultures are (1) exploitative autocratic, (2) benevolent autocratic, (3) consultative, and (4) participative team.

- *Exploitative autocratic.* In this type of culture, managers, especially top-level managers, make all decisions, maintaining a high degree of secrecy about the company's intentions. Management shows little confidence in the abilities of the company's employees. Strict, inflexible procedures control all activities. Productivity is maintained by threatening and punishing employees who do not meet standards. Managers give orders; employees take orders.
- *Benevolent autocratic.* In this culture, decision making still remains completely in the domain of management, indicating a lack of trust in employees. Procedures are still highly formalized, but the relationship between management and frontline employees is fairly cordial rather than antagonistic. Management takes a paternalistic interest in the company's employees, as if it were saying, "Do your job the way we say, and we'll take care of you."
- *Consultative.* A consultative culture is more open than the first two we discussed. Generally, top management shows a higher level of confidence in its employees. It is open to, and even seeks out, the opinions of employees when it makes decisions. It encourages suggestions that might improve the company's products and procedures.
- *Participative team.* In a participative team culture, employees at all levels are involved in making decisions. Companies with these cultures typically put a great deal of time and money into training their employees and increasing their skills and knowledge. Employees are encouraged to see themselves as essential members of a team that's committed to excellence. Employees are not just consulted by managers. In many cases, they are given the responsibility to make decisions. Employees work together to set goals, develop schedules, and even participate in the hiring process. Managers see themselves as coaches, counselors, and helpers as well as directors.

At the beginning of this century, most companies had autocratic cultures, either exploitative or benevolent. Many companies still have such cultures. The trend today, however, is toward the consultative and participative team cultures.

Traditional Organizational Structure

Autocratic cultures are the traditional cultures in business. They typically establish organizational structures with many layers of supervision between top management and frontline employees. These organizational structures are called **tall organizational pyramids** (see Figure 2–2). Autocratic businesses typically use a structure that is modeled on military organization and on the theoretical studies of early business experts, such as Henri Fayol (1841–1925), Frederick W. Taylor (1856–1915), Frank Gilbreth (1868–1924), Lillian Gilbreth (1878–1972), and Henry L. Gantt (1861–1919). The work of these experts formed the basis for what is called the classical theory of business management. Management based on the classical approach is generally characterized by a heavy stress on well-ordered activity, which theoretically leads to increased productivity. Productivity, in turn, is measured by how quickly and accurately tasks are carried out. Although classical management theory has a number of ideas that are essential for running a business well, it tends to have certain drawbacks, such as a rather mechanized attitude toward processing tasks and a rigid conformity to rules and procedures.

As Karl Albrecht says in *At America's Service*, the classical organization model has left business "still tool-and-task oriented; still structure oriented; still oriented to process and procedure rather than to human interaction. In a service management environment, we need to think in terms of workers having transactions with the customer, rather than in terms of workers performing predefined tasks."[2] Thus, although the classical approach to management may have worked quite well for manufacturing situations in which assembly-line employees were producing physical goods, this approach is much less effective in the management of customer service activities, such as those found in insurance companies.

Changing to a More Innovative Culture

In the insurance industry in particular, many companies are finding that they must change to meet the challenges posed by developments in the current business environment. Among other things, companies

Figure 2–2
Tall Organizational Pyramid

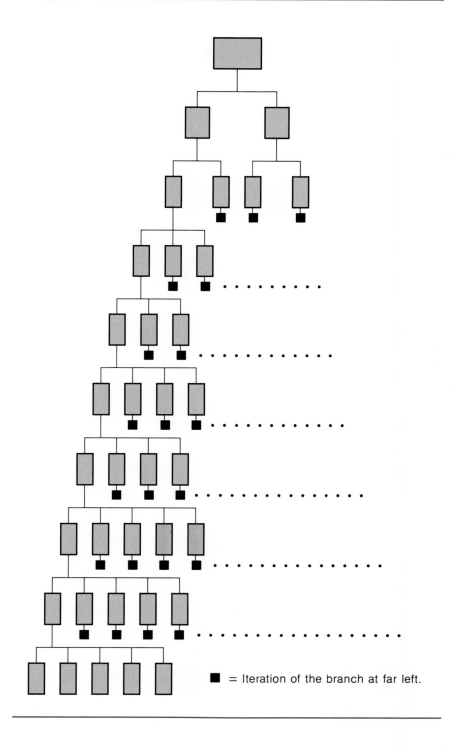

■ = Iteration of the branch at far left.

want to (1) improve the quality of their work, (2) become more flexible and responsive to the marketplace, (3) increase the creativity, skills, and professionalism of their employees, and (4) achieve excellence in customer service. They have found, however, as Karl Albrecht has indicated, that the traditional autocratic culture is not suited to the demands of a consumer-oriented marketplace. Therefore, more and more insurance companies are trying to move toward consultative and participative team cultures, which they believe will help them compete more effectively.

Flattening the Pyramid

One common characteristic of consultative and participative team cultures is that they usually occur in companies that have fewer layers of supervision between top management and frontline employees. These organizational structures are known as ***flat organizational pyramids***. And many companies today are trying to flatten their organizations, trying to reduce the number of layers in the pyramid. (See Figure 2–3.)

Figure 2–3
Flat Organizational Pyramid

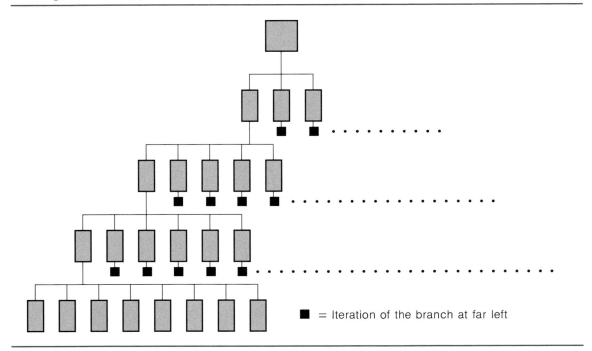

■ = Iteration of the branch at far left

Companies hope to achieve several goals by flattening the pyramid. First of all, they hope to make themselves operate more efficiently. By reducing the layers of employees between the top and the bottom, companies hope to decrease the time it takes to communicate and implement plans, commands, and ideas. Second, companies hope to push authority and responsibility to lower levels in the organization, to give the people who are closer to the consumer an enhanced ability to respond to the consumer's needs. Third, companies hope to improve relationships among all departments in a company. Companies theorize that, with fewer operational layers, it will be easier for people in the organization to communicate with one another—easier to communicate up and down the pyramid and back and forth between divisions.

For a description of what one company is doing to flatten its pyramid, look at Customer Service in Action 2–1.

CUSTOMER SERVICE IN ACTION 2–1

Allstate Restructuring Focuses on Service

Turning a product-driven insurance giant into a market-driven company with the customer as the guiding element was no simple task, according to William V. Henderson, Vice President, Sales for Allstate Insurance Company.

"Today," he told LIMRA, "people want more than top-notch products at a competitive price. They want service—personal service—and we at Allstate believe that the companies which provide extraordinary service will be the ones which excel in the marketplace of tomorrow."

To become a more market-oriented company, he said, Allstate needed to: streamline its organization, revise its management style, and change the agency force. The goal was "to increase sales opportunities and income, encourage entrepreneurship, incorporate some cost-sharing, and improve customer service," he said.

Allstate organizational restructuring began five years ago. "There were a number of aims," he said. Among them were: "to cut down on the layers of management that had developed over the years; to bring the management closer to our customers, to be able to anticipate their needs more quickly and more accurately; to streamline our operation in the interests of flexibility and speed; and to lower operating costs, since we wanted to continue to foster the reputation we had earned as a low-cost company which emphasized good value in its products."

In restructuring, Allstate cut down the layers of management in the home office and in 24 regional offices. Mr. Henderson said that operating expenses have been consolidated with the establishment of regional operating centers, each of which handles processing requirements for several regions.

"We recognized that there could be real differences within broad markets," he said, "so, instead of one sales manager for the entire region, there are now between two and five territorial sales managers, each in charge of developing their territories. The field sales manager position has been eliminated, and the district sales manager has become the market sales manager."

"This isn't just a change in title," he said. "Formerly, the district sales manager was concerned mainly with making sales. The new market sales managers have complete responsibility for the development of their markets, including identifying and staffing within those markets, building quality sales, and improving customer service."

One of Allstate's objectives was "to encourage decision-making at the lowest appropriate level," said Mr. Henderson. "Although Allstate has been evolving toward a participative management style for a number of years, the new structure has made this a necessity."

"As the regions began taking on a greater responsibility," he said, "we began to realize that our home office role had changed. From mainly a directive function, we shifted to more of a supportive function. Much of what the home office does today is to offer options to the regions which they can utilize or not, depending on their individual needs."

ALSTAR is the insurer's new agent computerized support system for the regions. "The system allows agents to give faster and more accurate service to their customers than ever before," he said. "It's also an outstanding sales tool, and has resulted in increased productivity wherever it's been introduced."

He said that eventually, ALSTAR will "enable agents to conduct all transactions by computerized hook-up with the regions and operating centers," producing "virtually a paperless operation." According to Mr. Henderson, ALSTAR will be available to "about 95 percent" of the agency force by year end.

"When you give people authority," he said, "they in turn tend to buy into the program and push authority down even further." He said Allstate's "growth teams" were a natural result of the reorganization. "These consist of rotating members of the agency force, sales management, underwriting, claims, the controller's department, and all the various functions in the regions."

Their purpose, he said, is "to find better ways to do business, to tap into human resources and, together, to look for solutions to their common problems: (the need for) quality business, (lower) loss ratios, and improved customer service. The interesting thing," he said, "is, this wasn't a part of the original design of the overall program. The growth team concept started in the field. They were so successful that they spread to other regions, and eventually became part of our strategy."

The good thing about the concept, he said, was that "by rubbing shoulders, each function learns all sides of the business, and the participants develop a give-and-take approach to problem solving. Because they deal first-hand with their local problems," said Mr. Henderson, "their solutions are often much more on target and effective.

"For instance," he said, "our agents

have come to appreciate more than ever before how their activities affect their rates. And just as pricing has more bottom-up input, so has product development," said the Allstate executive. "For example, our universal term policy came out of the needs we learned about from the local growth teams.

"Based on what they told us," he said, "we put together a package, went back to them in the form of focus groups, and refined the product based on their input."

Source: Adapted with permission of the publisher from Robert Knowles, "Allstate Restructuring Focuses on Service," *National Underwriter*, March 7, 1988, pp. 37–38.

Turning the Pyramid Upside Down

For companies to achieve a customer-oriented culture, flattening their organizational pyramid may not be enough. They may also need to change their attitudes about customers. They may need to turn their organizational pyramid upside down and put customers on top. So the organizational pyramid in a company that is truly dedicated to customer service would look something like Figure 2–4. Note that in Figure 2–4, customers are at the top of the pyramid. That is because they are the most important part of the organization. Next in line

Figure 2–4
Upside-Down Organizational Pyramid with Customers

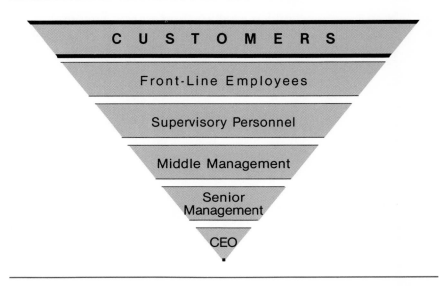

are frontline employees, the people who are most frequently in direct contact with customers. The supervisors, the managers, the vice presidents, and the president should see their roles as helping the frontline employees serve the customer in the best way possible.

This upside-down pyramid is, of course, only a symbol of how an organization should perceive itself in order to provide excellent customer service. Reality dictates that the final authority and responsibility for operating the company remain with the president and board of directors. But when a company is in the midst of change, especially when it is trying to establish a corporate culture that promotes excellent customer service, this upside-down pyramid can help everyone in the organization remember two important ideas:

1. A company doesn't stand alone. It must have customers to survive. Therefore, its organizational chart should include customers.
2. Turning the pyramid upside down reminds everyone of the absolute importance of customers and of the importance of the frontline employees who serve them. As far as customers are concerned, the frontline employees *are* the company.

In order to change its corporate culture, however, a company must do much more than flatten its organizational structure and add customers to its organizational chart. It must undertake a number of changes that, depending on the current culture of the company, can be difficult to make and quite stressful for everyone involved. Fortunately, there are a number of general guidelines that most companies can use to help them get through the change. Using these guidelines doesn't mean that changing a corporation's culture will be easy. But the guidelines should help reduce the stress involved and improve the chances that the change will be successful.

Before we go on to describe these guidelines, let's look at Customer Service in Action 2–2 to see how a mythical insurance company, Unfortunate Insurance Company, *failed* in its attempt to change to a customer service culture.

CUSTOMER SERVICE IN ACTION 2-2

Failed Culture Change at Unfortunate Insurance

In the spring of 1988, Joseph Ivy, President of Unfortunate Insurance Company, decided that some attitudes needed to be changed at The Unfortunate. He had read all the latest management bestsellers, and he decided that The Unfortunate needed to change its corporate culture. "It will improve productivity and make everybody happier," he told his top executives. So Mr. Ivy and his inner circle of top executives worked out a culture statement that outlined goals for improving staff attitudes at The Unfortunate. The statement said some very good things. It talked about instilling an attitude of teamwork between departments and among employees. It talked about encouraging creativity and flexibility among employees. It described how each and every employee and external customer was important to the company. And it talked about The Unfortunate's total commitment to quality. "Customers will be served in a prompt and courteous manner," was one of the many worthwhile positions taken in the culture statement.

The executive group then presented this statement to the company's middle managers and told them to circulate it to all employees. "This is the beginning of a new age and a new way of doing things at The Unfortunate," said Mr. Ivy.

Well, not quite—especially since the culture statement itself was not developed in a particularly new way. In fact, it was developed in the same way that Mr. Ivy had always done important things. He closeted himself in the board room with a few of his favorite top advisors and worked out a plan.

In this case, of course, it was not really a plan but rather a general statement of philosophy. But the philosophy was not matched by any action. Mr. Ivy had not asked any middle managers or other employees for input about the culture statement. He had not even asked them what their perceptions were of the present corporate culture. This lack of communication did not support the statement's assertion that all employees were important to The Unfortunate. Mr. Ivy's lack of concern for employee input on this issue only served to reinforce his employees' general belief that he felt they were unimportant to the company and that they had little impact on its success. In addition, the culture statement gave no concrete guidance about improving quality, nor did it provide for additional resources or training to help employees improve quality. In effect, it said that all employees should keep doing what they were doing with the resources they had, only they should start doing it better and with a smile.

Needless to say, the culture at The Unfortunate did not change. Mr. Ivy had a number of reactions. At first, he thought that things had changed. Banners were strung over office doors. Booklets describing the importance of customer service were sent to each employee. Programs to improve service quality were talked about for several months. Mr. Ivy was buoyed by the idea that he had done something positive for The Unfortunate and its customers and employees. Within a few months, however, he began to get the same complaints he used to get about bickering between departments. Productivity reports indicated a reversion to previous levels of quality. He fretted about this lack of change for a while, but then he became involved in other projects and other concerns and soon settled into his old attitudes. Later, when the topic of corporate culture came up in casual conversation, he would sigh and say that he himself had tried to improve customer service attitudes at The Unfortunate, "but the troops just weren't willing to accept it."

Guidelines for Implementing Change[3]

Corporate culture is a fundamental part of the character of an organization. It cannot be changed quickly or easily. Several companies that have deliberately changed their corporate culture to encourage a greater dedication to customer service (Travelers Insurance Company and Corning Glass are examples) note that it takes at least five years to implement a culture change. Such changes are not easily achieved, and to be successful they must be handled logically and with a great deal of patience. Many management experts have observed companies going through major changes, and these experts have identified a series of events that typically occurs in a successful change. This series of events is called the *change sequence* and includes the following steps:

1. Recognizing the need for change
2. Identifying methods to help the change occur
3. Making the change, which includes
   - Changing the old culture
   - Creating a new culture
   - Making the new culture permanent

Recognizing the Need for Change

Typically, a business finds that it needs to change its culture and the way it operates because

- its mode of operation does not fit the current business environment,
- its own industry is going through major changes and it must change to keep up, or

- its own industry is going through major changes and it must change to keep up, or
- it is growing and must change to accommodate that growth.

Of course, a company can recognize the need to change only by constantly monitoring its own environment. Any number of factors can be warnings of the need for change, such as (1) changes among the competition, (2) new demands from customers, (3) a decline in employee productivity or morale, or (4) a decline in the quality of work produced. All of these conditions may indicate that changes are in order.

Methods to Implement Change

Once the need for change is recognized, the company must decide how to implement the change. There is a wide variety of techniques that the company can use to help itself change, though none alone can guarantee a successful change. For example, surveys can be used to find out what customers and employees think about the company and how it ought to change. Consultants can be hired to help train employees in the new method of operating the company. Seminars in sensitivity training and team building can be offered to teach people how to work together and communicate more effectively. Employees can form task forces to determine the best ways to implement changes. Job enrichment can be used to make jobs more interesting and rewarding. Follow-up studies and training can be conducted to assure that customer service skills and attitudes are being maintained. In addition, employees themselves can be empowered. ***Empowerment*** means that the company gives them the authority and responsibility to make certain types of decisions without having to wait for approval.

No matter what methods a company uses to implement change, one important thing to keep in mind is that employees should be made an integral part of the change. Their advice should be sought, and they should be asked to help make the change become a reality. Unless employees buy into the change, it is unlikely that the change will be successful.

Making the Change

Actually making the change involves the next three steps in the process: changing the old culture, creating the new culture, and making the new culture permanent. All of these steps require a great deal of time and effort. Even when the people in an organization believe that change is necessary, those same people will probably feel uncomfortable, at least with certain portions of the change. They are likely to put up some resistance.

Overcoming Resistance to Change

Resistance to change can come from many areas of an organization, and the sources of resistance can be either individual employees or entire organizational units. Change is a difficult process, and whether employees like their company's culture or not, they will usually resist any attempt to change it. Change is upsetting. It challenges established authority and creates a mood of uncertainty and fear. Some employees resist change because they don't want to learn a new way of doing things, even if it is a better way. Some are afraid that they won't understand the new way of doing things, that they might not be able to keep up, and so they might lose their jobs. Other employees may feel that the change threatens their influence or even their social status. Still others have a certain emotional investment in the old ways. These employees might have helped develop the old way of doing things, so they might see a change as a personal affront to them and their previous hard work.

Because an organization is a system of interrelated parts, a change in one part of the organization may have unanticipated effects in another part of the organization. For example, some organizational changes might increase the power base of one unit in a company while reducing the power base of another unit. In such cases, those employees who work in the area that is losing its power base may come to resist the change although they know that it is best for the company as a whole and even though they may have supported it initially.

For these and other reasons, employees typically resist change and must be reassured and encouraged throughout the change process. They must be given workable techniques for actually implementing the change. They should be given all appropriate information about the change, and they should take an active part in helping the change come about. They should also be rewarded for their efforts in making the change. Furthermore, a change in corporate culture (in this case, a change to a customer service culture) cannot succeed unless the new culture is supported by the very way in which the company operates. Two important areas to consider when making the change to a culture that is oriented to customer service are management style and teamwork.

Management Style

Earlier in this chapter we noted that management is one of the major factors affecting corporate culture. All managers should commit themselves to the company's customer service goals and demonstrate by their own actions that the customer is the most important person to the company. Every manager — regardless of whether he or she is the head of underwriting, customer service, claims, accounting, personnel, or some other area of the company — plays an important role in building and maintaining a company's customer service image.

As we indicated earlier in the chapter, customer service cultures seem to flourish in certain corporate cultures. The overall corporate culture generally considered most conducive to the development of successful customer service is the participative team culture that we discussed earlier. Such a culture requires a ***participative management style***, which has the following characteristics:

- Encourages open communication and information sharing among employees and management
- Provides employees with considerate and supportive leadership
- Displays confidence and trust in employees
- Encourages teamwork and group approaches to problem solving
- Stresses employee autonomy and self-actualization
- Sets high goals for achievement and output

Most employees want to excel at whatever they do, and managers should provide an atmosphere in which employees are encouraged to do their best. After all, doing a good job not only boosts an employee's ego and self-esteem, but it also is good for the company. Often, however, doing a good job also means taking risks. To encourage employees to take risks and strive for excellence, participative management advocates that managers and employees work together to establish demanding goals that require employees to stretch their abilities in order to achieve those goals. Such employees should also be given assurance that they will not be punished if they occasionally fall short of their goals. Even when an employee does not perform up to his or her usual standards, steps generally can be taken to help the person improve performance. The company can provide more training or support or, if necessary, even help the person find a job that fits his or her abilities more closely.

Encouraging employees to excel at whatever they do, however, eventually necessitates adopting another characteristic of participative management. That characteristic involves empowering employees by giving them more independence and authority in their jobs.

When employees are challenged to do their best, they usually start thinking more about their work. As employees become more involved with, and committed to, their work, they begin to think of better ways to do their jobs and better ways to help their customers. They often respond to their newly found challenges with innovative suggestions and increased or extraordinary efforts. In conjunction with their increased interest in their jobs, such employees usually want the authority to take initiative and make improvements. Some of their ideas will be risky and some will fail. One of the most difficult aspects of participative management involves allowing employees to take risks and make mistakes. However, if managers operating under such circumstances want a fully productive staff, they must be willing to allow employees the freedom to try new ideas. Otherwise, they will stop trying to make any changes and will lose their initiative.

Empowering employees is a difficult thing for many managers to do. Giving employees authority means giving up control, and many managers do not like to give up control, which they have worked hard to attain. Control is closely intertwined with their own sense of self-worth and gives them a certain sense of security. However, successful managers usually discover that the control they give up, the authority they pass on to their staff, is not really important to their own work. In fact, managers usually find that giving up control of certain aspects of their jobs leaves them free to work on other matters that they did not have time to attend to before.

Developing a participative management style is not easy. Both employees and managers have to adjust to their new roles. Training employees to operate more autonomously takes time. Managers also need time to develop trust in their subordinates' abilities to handle their new autonomy. Furthermore, since not all employees want more responsibility or involvement in their jobs, management must also find a way to deal with the challenges posed by these employees' needs.

By assuming that the majority of employees want to do a good job, by giving employees more authority over their own work, by encouraging them to take more initiative in their professional lives, and by allowing them to fail on occasion, managers help create an atmosphere that leads to greater productivity, better employee morale, and ultimately improved customer service.

Figure 2–5 lists some of the many steps that a participative manager can take to help improve and maintain the quality of the customer service provided through his or her department.

Figure 2–5
Steps toward Participative Management

---

1. Create a positive environment for employees
2. Encourage teamwork
3. Empower employees (give them authority and responsibility)
4. Keep employees informed
5. Enrich their jobs by expanding their roles
6. Encourage employees to

   • Develop and improve work methods and procedures
   • Set goals
   • Develop schedules
   • Participate in the hiring process

Teamwork, Not Tribal Work

We have already mentioned that companies often contain one or more subcultures composed of people who work in various functional or regional areas of the company. We have also noted the important role that work groups play in influencing corporate culture. In many companies, each division, department, or section also has a tendency to identify its own agenda and isolate itself from other parts of the company. Part of the social behavior of human beings is that they tend to band together with the people with whom they spend most of their time. They tend to form self-contained units, or tribes. Once a group identifies itself as a unit, it tends to see other units as outsiders, rivals, or even enemies. Even the customer is sometimes seen as an enemy, someone who is interfering with the department's efficient and routine operation.

In the insurance industry, this tribal mentality often disrupts home and field office relations. In addition, it often affects the relationships between line and staff units. One of the most important roles of management is to dispel this air of isolation. Ideally, management should turn tribal attitudes into teamwork, encouraging the positive aspects they find, such as group cohesion and support, and discouraging the negative aspects, such as jealousy or elitism.

Customer Service in Action 2–3, which follows, describes how several insurance companies have encouraged teamwork and self-management among their employees. By reorganizing their systems and procedures and by stressing the importance of teamwork, these companies found that "a group of people pulling together to achieve a common goal is going to have more success than several individuals all trying to achieve goals of their own."[4]

CUSTOMER SERVICE IN ACTION 2–3

Tradition versus Teamwork

In a time when the insurance industry is growing more and more competitive, each insurance company looks for every edge that will help keep it ahead of the competition. What follows is a description of how life insurers have used the idea of teamwork to increase productivity, improve customer service, and raise morale.

Shenandoah Life Insurance Company

The transition to the team structure at Shenandoah was instigated from the top. At the end of the 1970s, when profits were stable but costs were rising, Shenandoah President William Battle asked the company's managers to study the company's operations and find ways to increase productivity and trim costs. With the help of John B. Myers, then Vice President of Human Resources, four "total processing teams" were established in the individual insurance services department.

Under the old structure, three separate departments were responsible for policy issue, premium accounting, and policyowner service. With the new system, each team is responsible for performing all three functions, and each team member now can individually perform all three functions. The 27 people across all four teams will each be able to do 17 different jobs. To reward those who learn additional skills, Shenandoah uses a pay-for-learning incentive program.

A five-person management team, led by an assistant vice president, supports the four full-service teams, with managers serving as advisers rather than bosses. The teams are expected to manage themselves —plan their own work flow and vacation time and address disciplinary matters within the team. This system leaves the managers free to perform such roles as developing new products, upgrading the computer system, and looking for ways to improve customer service.

Making the transition to a team structure was traumatic for many employees.

During the transition phase, many employees were intimidated by the prospect of expanding their duties and separating from friends in their old offices. In addition, some managers were worried about losing their jobs. In response, the company held numerous meetings to explain the process and diminish the fear factor.

The team system "is working very well" at Shenandoah, says Richard C. Wagner, Vice President of Individual Insurance Services. Since the teams were set up in 1985, Shenandoah has seen a 48 percent increase in productivity, based on the volume of business and the amount of time it takes to process that business. Claims once processed in four or five days can now be handled in just one day. In addition, the insurer's high employee turnover rate in the early 1980s has diminished to less than 1 percent under the new system. "Morale is very high today," says Mr. Wagner. "[The employees] say the new way is better, although it's not easy."

Aid Association for Lutherans (AAL)

Shenandoah's success attracted to Roanoke as many as 30 companies from various industries to take a first-hand look at the new structure. Among the early visitors was the Aid Association for Lutherans (AAL), which launched its own company-wide, self-directed teams in August 1987.

AAL President Richard L. Gunderson, elected in 1985, set out to improve efficiency through a corporate transformation. "Our purpose in doing it was really getting closer to the customer," says Jerry Laubenstein, Vice President of Individual Insurance Services. Mr. Laubenstein set up sixteen full-service teams, which handle all phases of the insurer's business, from underwriting to claims handling. Fifteen of the teams are responsible for a specific group of agencies. The sixteenth team communicates information from the AAL mainframe computer to agents in the field.

Each team has 20 to 35 employees, depending on the size of the agencies served. These teams are then divided into three or more functional self-managed teams of 6 to 10 people. An additional team of 10 policy specialists, who report to 4 regional managers, ensures that all four work teams are handling policies consistently. Each person is capable of handling any service that comes into the team.

The system allows employees to "grow in breadth as well as in depth," says Mr. Laubenstein. Traditional insurer work forces are set up on a production line basis and one job may pass through four or more people or divisions. In this situation, says Mr. Laubenstein, "no one person has responsibility for the whole service. The new concept is that the team has responsibility for the whole service."

According to AAL estimates, productivity has increased by 25 percent under the new system. This productivity is measured by comparing AAL's current volume of business and processing time with the company's 1978–1980 productivity rate. Quarterly customer service polls show that customer satisfaction has improved as well.

Blue Cross/Blue Shield of Virginia

Some consultants assert that the self-managed team structure is most successful when the change is instituted throughout the company, rather than on a limited basis. However, other consultants believe that large companies can successfully restructure into a team system one office at a time.

John Myers, who helped implement the teams at Shenandoah and now oversees three self-managed teams in an individual health insurance unit at Blue Cross/Blue Shield of Virginia, believes that the numerous offices and divisions in large insurers are like mini-companies. They can restructure relatively quickly. "Now, the bits and pieces you are dealing with are not as large as you think," says Mr. Myers.

Each team at Blue Cross/Blue Shield has 14 members whose responsibilities range from underwriting new policies to billing to claims processing. Improved customer service is the primary benefit of the team systems, Mr. Myers says. Customers may request a specific service representative for more personalized service, and each team member is capable of handling processes once handled by several people in several departments. Team members also make house calls to customers who are confined to their homes.

"You can't differentiate yourself in product and price" in the insurance industry, Mr. Myers says. "You differentiate in terms of how you deliver the product."

Source: Based on John Hoerr, "Work Teams Can Rev Up Paper Pushers, Too," *Business Week*, November 28, 1988, p. 64; Jill Conversano, "Self-Managed Teams Promote Productivity," *Resource*, LOMA, May/June 1988; and other articles.

Elements in Making a Service Culture Real

When an insurer decides to go through the changes that are necessary to create a customer service culture, it needs to understand the elements that are essential in making that culture work. As described by Karl Albrecht and Ron Zemke in their book *Service America!*, these elements are the customer, the service strategy, the systems, and the people.[5] In the next few pages we will discuss these elements and how they provide a framework for organizing the remaining chapters in this book.

In Chapter 3, we discuss strategic planning and the way in which companies incorporate customer service into their overall strategic plans. In addition, we will continue to refer to customer service strategy throughout the book.

The central element is, of course, the customer. Every decision, every strategy and tactic should be based on the wants, needs, perceptions, and expectations of the customer. A company must get to know its customers. It must consider its customers in all its plans and actions. It must listen to its customers—listen to the things they say, listen to the things they don't say—and try to get them to say more. We will talk more about the customer in Chapters 4 and 5.

The systems element does not refer only to computerized or electronic systems. It means all the procedures and technologies that a business uses to provide customer service. In Chapters 6 and 7, we will describe systems—their essential components, how they are established, how their performance is measured, and why they are so important for providing excellent customer service.

The last element we will discuss is people—the people that companies recruit, hire, and train to provide customers with the best service possible. In a sense we are saving the best for last, because without well-trained, highly motivated employees, no company can provide excellent customer service. The human resources required for excellent customer service are discussed in Chapter 8.

The Costs of Providing Quality Customer Service

In addition to the four elements identified above, there is another element that we will mention only briefly, even though it is enormously important. That element is money. Money is the glue that binds all this planning and culture changing together. Unless a company is willing to commit the money needed to make changes, nothing will change. Of course, simply throwing money at a problem isn't the answer either. But there has to be enough money to do the things that need to be done. There has to be money to pay adequate salaries, money to attract talented employees, money to pay for support systems that help customers and employees, and money to keep the lines of communication open between the company and its customers.

We won't discuss this element extensively in any one section of the book, but it is a key element, and it has to be considered in any attempt to develop a customer service strategy and run a customer service operation. It is the company's investment in its own future.

As we continue through this book, we will point out areas in which a company has to decide whether or not spending additional money will increase the benefits provided by customer service. For example, the amount of money a company spends on customer service is affected by

- the value its customers place on different levels of service,
- the level of service its customers are willing to pay for, and
- the costs that the company might incur by *not* providing a particular level of service.

Before going on to the next chapter, complete the quiz in Figure 2–6 to evaluate the customer service culture in your own company.

Figure 2–6
Test Your Company's Customer Service Culture

Rate each of the statements below on the following scale:

5=Always   4=Usually   3=Sometimes   2=Rarely   1=Never

_____ 1. We have a formal process in place to determine our customers' wants, needs, and expectations, now and for the future.

_____ 2. We encourage all employees to listen carefully to customer needs through informal systems and to act on this information.

_____ 3. Our repeat business exceeds the industry average.

_____ 4. When we lose a customer we know why, or we find out.

_____ 5. Management gives workers the responsibility and authority to take care of customers.

_____ 6. The predominant attitude in our company is risk-taking rather than defensive, and solving problems rather than laying blame.

_____ 7 We see ourselves as customers and suppliers in work relationships with one another.

_____ 8. Our systems make clear who has responsibilities for tasks.

_____ 9. Supervisors and managers in different departments work well together.

_____ 10. Very few things fall through the cracks because of miscommunication between departments.

_____ 11. We have clear measures and tracking systems to tell us how we are meeting our customers' requirements in every department.

_____ 12. What happens in the organization really matters to all our people, executives and frontline employees alike.

_____ 13. People feel responsible, needed, and empowered to do what needs to be done to take care of customers and keep them satisfied.

_____ 14. Managers and supervisors have the skills to influence others, communicate effectively, and motivate and lead subordinates.

_____ 15. Our focus is proactive. We try to prevent problems rather than simply waiting to fix them after the fact.

_____ 16. We concentrate on exceptional customer care, rather than cost-cutting, to increase earnings and profits.

_____   **Total**

If your score is 64–80 on the quiz, your corporate culture seems to be very customer-oriented. If you score 48–63, you may be personally committed to service excellence, but the systems that your company has established may not support quality customer service. A score of 32–47 indicates you may recognize the importance of customers, but your organization doesn't seem to be acting that way. And a score of 16–31 suggests that you and your organization seem to be interested in things other than service excellence.

Source: Adapted with permission of the publisher from Edward T. Cannie, "Developing a True Customer Service Focus," _National Underwriter_, June 26, 1989, pp. 5–6.

Key Terms

culture	flat organizational pyramid
corporate culture	change
dominant culture	change sequence
subculture	empowerment
organizational culture	resistance to change
work groups	participative management style
company characteristics	teamwork
exploitative autocratic culture	customer
benevolent autocratic culture	service strategy
consultative culture	systems
participative team culture	people
tall organizational pyramid	

Notes

1. Rensis Likert, *The Human Organization* (New York: McGraw-Hill, 1967).
2. Karl Albrecht, *At America's Service* (Homewood, IL: Dow Jones-Irwin, 1988), p. 89.
3. Much of this section was based on Judith R. Gordon, R. Wayne Moody, Arthur Sharplin, Shane R. Premeaux, *Management and Organizational Behavior* (Boston: Allyn and Bacon, 1990), pp. 634–47.
4. Bureau of Business Practice, *The BBP Customer Service Management Handbook* (Waterford, CT: Bureau of Business Practice, 1987), pp. 2–3.
5. Karl Albrecht and Ron Zemke, *Service America!* (Homewood, IL: Dow Jones-Irwin, 1985), pp. 40–43.

CHAPTER 3

Developing a Customer Service Strategy

After studying this chapter, you should be able to

- Explain the strategic planning process and the steps involved in establishing a corporate strategic plan
- Give some examples of what not to do when implementing a service strategy
- Describe the four primary sources of information about customer service
- Explain the development process for a corporate customer service strategic plan

Introduction

In order to provide quality customer service, an insurance company must go beyond merely establishing a customer service department or developing a customer service culture. It must establish a customer service strategy that makes customer service an integral part of the company's entire operation. This customer service strategy must be coordinated with the company's overall corporate strategy.

In this chapter, we will discuss some of the basics of strategic planning and the steps involved in establishing a corporate strategic plan. Next, we will describe a strategic plan for customer service and show how this plan should be coordinated with the overall corporate plan. Then, we will describe ways to develop a customer service plan, the important role that top management plays in making a customer service strategy work, and the steps needed to put a customer service strategy into effect.

Strategic Planning

Strategic planning is the process of determining an organization's long-term corporate objectives and deciding the overall course of action the company will follow to achieve those objectives. Most companies develop strategic plans that extend three to five years into the future. A strategic plan generally forms the basis for all other planning done by a company and establishes guidelines for everything the company does. Strategic planning typically involves four activities:

1. Conducting a situation analysis
2. Defining the company's mission
3. Establishing corporate objectives
4. Developing corporate strategies

We will describe each of these briefly and then show how developing a customer service strategy is tied to this process.

Situation Analysis

A situation analysis typically has three components: (1) an environmental analysis, (2) an environmental forecast, and (3) an internal assessment.

To conduct an ***environmental analysis***, a company gathers information about various ongoing events and relationships in its environment in an effort to understand how those events and relationships are likely to affect the company. From the information gained in its environmental analysis, a company develops an environmental forecast. The ***environmental forecast*** predicts the major trends that will affect the company's business activities and thereby provides many assumptions that will be needed to develop its strategic plans. Because it deals with future events, an environmental forecast is at best a well-educated guess. Typically, a company will look at trends it has observed in the past and try to forecast future developments based on those trends. By making an environmental forecast, a company establishes the assumptions on which to base its future plans.

The final component of a situation analysis is called an ***internal assessment***, which is an examination of the company's current activities and its ability to respond to potential threats and opportunities in the environment. Among other things, the internal assessment typically examines the company's current products and marketing systems, its organizational structure, its procedures for carrying out major activities, its technological resources, financial condition, corporate culture, and the skills and attitudes of the company's employees. Assessing a company's strengths and weaknesses in these and other areas allows the company to develop corporate objectives that are practical and realistic.

Defining the Company's Mission

The second activity in strategic planning involves defining the company's mission. A ***mission statement*** describes a company's fundamental purpose, defines the scope of its business activities, and answers a question that seems a lot simpler than it really is: "What business are we in?" It is not uncommon for a firm or an entire industry to misunderstand what business it is really in. Consider the railroad industry for example. In the early 20th century, the U.S. railroad business was booming. Railroad executives thought they were in the business of running railroads and moving trains from one place to another. But they were really in the business of transporting goods and people. When automobiles, trucking, and airlines became accepted modes of transportation, railroad companies did not understand the competition they were facing nor did they see the opportunities available to them if they would only participate in these newer means of transport. The railroad industry misjudged what business it was really in, and as a result its markets and profits were severely curtailed.

Two other questions can help a company understand its mission or the business it's in:

- Who are our customers?
- What exactly do we do for our customers?

In Chapter 1, we indicated how important it is for a company to be outward looking, to focus its attention on the customer. These two questions continue that idea and help guarantee that a company's mission statement has the proper orientation.

Even when a company develops a mission statement that presents an accurate description of its business, changes in the business environment may force the company to reassess its mission statement. Therefore, a company must be prepared to modify its mission statement as conditions require. Many insurance companies have recently changed their mission statements to reflect the changing environment. Whereas insurance companies may once have seen their mission as selling insurance, they now tend to define their mission in broader terms, that is, as offering financial products and services to help provide individuals and businesses with financial security.

Mission statements vary greatly from company to company. They may be short and general or long and detailed. Typically, though, a mission statement should be broad enough to encompass all the types of business in which a company is engaged but specific enough to provide a meaningful focus for the company's activities. Figure 3–1 provides several examples of brief company mission statements. Notice the variety in the statements and the fact that each statement

Figure 3–1
Mission Statements of Insurance Companies

Northwestern Mutual Life Insurance Company

The ambition of The Northwestern has been less to be large than to be safe; its aim is to rank first in benefits to its policy-owners rather than first in size. Valuing quality over quantity, it has preferred to secure its business under certain salutary restrictions and limitations rather than to write a much larger business at the possible sacrifice of those valuable points which have made The Northwestern pre-eminently the policyowner's company.

The Great-West Life Assurance Company

Our mission is to achieve excellence in the development and distribution of financial products and services for people, and to do so in a thoroughly responsible manner.

We will accomplish this mission through highly effective anticipation of and response to the challenging needs and preferences of our customers.

London Life Insurance Company

Our corporate mission is to be the leader in meeting the needs of Canadians for personalized financial security. We recognize that corporate integrity and superior service are essential in serving our individual and business customers. Everything we do supports our mission.

Source: All mission statements are reprinted with permission of the companies.

has a customer service component. One special note of interest: Typically, when we think of mission statements and strategic planning, we assume that these are current developments in business practices. This isn't necessarily true. Northwestern Mutual's mission statement was written in 1888. For an indication of how well Northwestern Mutual has fulfilled its mission, see Customer Service in Action 3–2 later in this chapter.

Since the mission statement in many ways defines a company's philosophy, a company that is committed to customer service should include the concept of customer service in its mission statement. Similarly, it should also include customer service in its corporate strategy. By weaving customer service into the fabric of its philosophy and strategy, a company helps assure that customer service will become an integral part of its day-to-day activities rather than a catch phrase that is often preached but seldom practiced.

Establishing Corporate Objectives and Strategies

After the mission statement is established, the company must develop the specific objectives that it hopes to achieve. ***Corporate objectives*** are statements that describe the long-term results a company intends to accomplish in carrying out its mission. Corporate objectives are established for the entire company. They should be clearly stated, realistic, specific, and measurable. Listed below are some examples of corporate objectives:

1. Increase new premium income 10 percent each year for the next five years.
2. Reduce the lapse rate of first-year policies by 25 percent during the next four years.
3. Reduce employee turnover rate to 5 percent per year within the next five years.
4. Increase sales leads produced by the customer service department by 20 percent over each of the next three years.
5. Increase customer satisfaction levels by 10 percent each year over the next six years.

After a company has established its corporate objectives, the next step is to develop strategies to achieve those objectives. ***Corporate strategies*** define the long-term methods by which a company intends to achieve its corporate objectives. For example, to increase the sales leads generated by the customer service department by 20 percent over each of the next three years (objective number 4 above), a company might develop the following strategies:

1. Train all customer service representatives to inquire about and recognize customers' additional financial needs.
2. Establish a bonus system to reward customer service representatives who identify leads that are later turned into sales.
3. Establish a system to improve communication between customer service representatives and producers.

To translate general strategies into specific tasks, companies develop annual plans. As its name suggests, an ***annual plan*** describes specific activities and programs that will be conducted during the year to meet corporate objectives. An annual plan is considered a tactical plan because it describes the specific methods a company will use to meet its objectives. The annual plan is generally developed at the same time that the annual budget is prepared, so that needed funds can be allocated for projects in the plan.

Now that we've discussed the basic concepts of strategic planning, let's see how these concepts can be applied to customer service.

Developing the Customer Service Strategic Plan

A customer service strategic plan establishes guidelines for providing customer service in the company. The plan states the philosophy behind the company's customer service, the objectives the company hopes to achieve by providing customer service, how the company intends to achieve those objectives, and the ways in which the company intends to measure the quality of its customer service. Having a formal customer service plan for the entire company gives everyone a common customer service goal and a common means for achieving that goal.

The customer service strategic plan takes its direction from the customer service component of the corporate strategic plan, just as the strategic plans for other company operations (such as finance or marketing) follow from the corporate strategic plan. In this way, the customer service strategic plan becomes a part of the company's overall strategy.

A major benefit of developing a formal customer service strategic plan is that such a plan gives customer service a legitimacy that it might otherwise lack. Typically, strategic plans are developed and approved by top management, and a customer service strategic plan that has been approved by top management helps assure the plan's success. The fact that a customer service strategic plan exists implies that top management has embraced the idea of customer service and intends to support it. In other words, top management has "bought into" the concept and the importance of customer service. Having top management buy into customer service is essential because top management must give its wholehearted support, including its financial support, to a customer service strategy if it is to succeed.

Although individual departments and individual employees often find ways to provide good customer service on their own, the overall level of a company's customer service cannot rise to its highest levels without the commitment of the company's executives. Individual initiative can only go so far. If company executives do not budget the funds needed to provide top-notch customer service, if they do not authorize the hiring of enough qualified personnel, if they do not encourage the company's internal culture to reflect a commitment to high quality customer service, then no amount of individual or departmental initiative will make the company truly customer-oriented.

Look at Customer Service in Action 3–1 to see how support from top management at The Travelers has led to concrete customer service strategies.

CUSTOMER SERVICE IN ACTION   3–1

Service at The Travelers

In 1986, Edward Budd, CEO and Chairman of The Travelers, wrote in an open letter to employees, "Quality is no longer an option or tradeoff in the marketplace. The competitive reality is that both low cost and quality are essential."

Like many companies, both in and out of the insurance and financial services industries, The Travelers believes that cultivating internal and external quality service is key—key to remaining competitive in the marketplace, key to retaining customers, and key to expanding the customer base. Budd's open letter marked a renewed emphasis on quality service at the Hartford-based company.

Its commitment to service excellence, says The Travelers, matured during the 1980s as the company focused its marketing thrust on market segments rather than on its products.

This shift from a product-driven to a customer-sensitive philosophy also saw The Travelers embark on a companywide program to "provide a level of service that is competitively superior in meeting customers' needs in our service-intensive business of insurance and financial services." This program included the creation of a Corporate Customer Service Officer position, a Customer Service Management Team, and a seven-step Quality Improvement Process.

Defining Barriers

In the mid-1980s, a task force looked at the major barriers to quality customer service at The Travelers. This task force found that the company

- concentrated on transactions rather than customers,
- needed to develop an internal and external customer service philosophy, and
- showed inconsistent levels of quality in its lines of business.

The task force recommended establishment of a position to oversee and coordinate The Travelers' quality improvement strategy. In mid-1987, John Maxwell assumed the role of Corporate Customer Service Officer and began developing the company's commitment to customer service.

"One thing I am not," Maxwell notes, "and that is accountable for customer service." Instead, Maxwell sees his position as responsible for establishing a sense of urgency to quality service. "My position," he clarifies, "is to work on the awareness, the mechanics, and logistics of putting the process in place, to help The Travelers better manage its operation, which is driven more by customer expectation and satisfaction than by transactions."

The Service Process

In 1987, The Travelers formed a Customer Service Management Team that reported to CEO Budd and to Maxwell, who served as chairman of the team. (The team has since been replaced by the Quality Council, a group of 14 managers from all departments in the company.) The Customer Service Management Team provided the impetus behind the company's customer service initiatives, including the Quality Improvement Process.

The goal of the Quality Improvement Process, states the company, "is to assist each business group in achieving a level of customer service excellence that differentiates the company from [its] competitors." The strategy involves four integrated areas.

1. *Cost effectiveness.* Costs associated with redoing tasks, correcting errors, and performing unnecessary work are examples of how poor service quality affects a company's bottom line. Estimates show that poor quality reduces a company's revenue by 25 percent to 35 percent.

2. *People development.* To understand how all jobs in an organization fit into the internal and external service continuum, employees throughout the organization require training and education. Specifically, employees benefit from training in problem-solving, participatory management, and teamwork skills. Recognition and rewards are given for achieving quality objectives.

3. *Technology.* Technology provides the tools and information to satisfy customer needs. Technology allows a faster response time to inquiries, enhances communication between service providers and customers, and provides measurement and tracking systems to spot trends and resolve problems.

4. *Customer satisfaction.* Assessing performance from the customer's point of view is the focal point of service quality. Seeing service through the customer's eyes enables a company to improve procedures and systems, meet customer needs, perform the job correctly the first time, and be more cost efficient. Internal customer satisfaction is as important as external customer satisfaction.

The Quality Improvement Process consists of seven steps. The steps guide each business unit toward achieving a level of customer service excellence.

Step One: A Commitment to Service Quality.

This step focuses on understanding the impact of service quality and making a commitment to improve it. A commitment from leadership helps employees make the same commitment. Commitments from both management and employees are necessary to develop a service quality organization.

Step Two: Assessing Customer Expectations and Perceptions.

An organization must know who its customers are and identify their expectations. Customers measure service quality by asking questions like the following: Are my expectations being met? Is the organization's service responsive to my needs? Am I being treated fairly, promptly, and courteously?

Step Three: Competitive Analysis and Benchmarking.

Comparing service provided by direct competitors and leaders in quality service enables a company to measure its performance against the competition. Knowing the competition helps an organization develop a service strategy and position itself in the marketplace.

Step Four: Performance Evaluation.

After defining customer expectations and the competition's level of service, an organization can see how it "measures up" to other companies. A workflow analysis can assess service delivery. By listing the steps from customer contact to fulfillment of the request, a company can identify areas in the delivery process that need improvement.

Step Five: Strategic Service Vision.

An organization develops a service strategy once it knows its strengths and weaknesses, defines its customers' expectations, and understands service quality in the marketplace. The strategic service vision establishes goals and objectives to reach service excellence and should be integrated into the organization's business plan.

Step Six: Implementing the Strategy.

Set performance standards to achieve the quality strategy. Train employees in service skills. As the strategy is implemented, integrate these performance standards into each employee's performance appraisal.

Step Seven: Monitoring Performance.

Monitor performance against standards to see how well the organization meets customer expectations. Based on the findings of the company's monitoring efforts, strategy and performance standards should be reassessed to improve quality. Service excellence is the result of an ongoing process of quality improvement.

Incorporating Service

At The Travelers, a business unit internalizes the Quality Improvement Process to its needs and environment. As a company, Maxwell says, "we look for an emphasis on customer service to be part of each business group." For example, each unit is at a different stage in the Quality Improvement Process. All units have surveyed their customer bases and have defined customer expectations. About one-third have developed strategies to overcome customer service barriers. Maxwell continues, "The only corporate thrust is to be able to trade information and to look at success stories."

Examples of service quality success stories include:

• The Financial Services Division (individual life, health, and annuity products) surveyed its agents and consumers. The division then established a central service unit with toll-free phones to serve consumers, field staff, and agents. Division staff underwent extensive service and product training. Recognition programs reward employees for outstanding service.

- The Moneytrac Division (integrated banking, insurance, and mortgage products) developed an information file and tracking system. This system provided information for each customer product and contact. One phone call handled questions and changes.
- The Private Placement Division (investment loans) surveyed investment bankers. Based on survey results, the division improved its responsiveness and increased its business with investment bankers.

Maxwell believes that in today's competitive business environment, a company's future survival depends on its current commitment to service quality. He is not optimistic about the fate of those companies who don't emphasize service quality.

He also acknowledges that making a commitment to service quality can challenge a company's method of operation and its corporate culture. "Often," he says, "the difficult part is getting the organization to accept and embrace what it must do to make the commitment to service quality."

"This doesn't happen overnight," he continues. "A company is kidding itself if it thinks it can revamp the organization's service quality in a year's time. It's a process that takes three to five years and is ongoing after that."

Source: Adapted with permission of the publisher from Chris Breston, "At Travelers, Quality Is No Longer an Option," *Resource*, LOMA, November/December 1988, pp. 38–39, 54.

Developing a Service Strategy

Once top management decides that a company will commit itself to customer service and decides to support it, a major hurdle is overcome. However, there are several steps still to be taken if customer service is to become a well-coordinated companywide strategy. Just as we discussed in the sections on corporate strategic planning, a strategic plan for customer service should have certain components: a situation analysis, a statement of the service mission, customer service objectives, strategies for accomplishing quality customer service, and specific tactical plans.

But before we describe the steps that ought to be taken to implement a service strategy, let's talk about steps that some companies have mistakenly taken and why those steps didn't work.

How *Not* to Implement a Service Strategy

One of the reasons that many well-intentioned customer service commitments do not work is that companies never develop them into plans or strategies. What often happens is that top management adopts the idea of improving customer service, decides it will commit itself and the company to the idea, and then develops a catch phrase or slogan, such as "Take the Lead in Customer Service," to demonstrate its commitment. Throwing around catch phrases, however, does little to achieve their intended goals. If improving customer service is to be a strategy, it must be treated as such. Goals must be stated, plans for achieving the goals must be developed, procedures for implementing the plans must be established, training must be provided so that employees know how to follow the procedures, and systems support must be integrated with procedures so employees provide customer service in the most efficient and effective way possible.

The following scenario describes one of the biggest implementation mistakes that companies typically make. In its enthusiasm for improving customer service, top management informs its middle managers: "We *will* be committed to customer service." This command from the top is then followed by a few pep rallies in which the staff is addressed by management and told how important customer service is. These events might then be followed by company-sponsored seminars designed to teach employees some of the skills needed to get along with other people. To reinforce their training, employees are given buttons or balloons or banners or coffee mugs (depending on the publicity budget), and every item is emblazoned with slogans like "The Customer Comes First" or "You're Number One" or "Customer Service Is Our Top Priority."

The company's employees are then sent back to their jobs and told to give better service. The employees aren't given new procedures to provide service. Nor are they given the authority or support they need to do anything new or different regarding service. They're just told to give better service.

This kind of campaign might be effective for a month or two while the initial enthusiasm lasts, but it isn't effective for long. The company has no infrastructure to support such a campaign. Procedures for doing jobs or handling customer service interactions have not been modified. Systems that support the employees' work activities have not been improved. The criteria that managers use to evaluate their employees' work have not been changed. Rewards for motivating employees to provide better customer service have not been changed.

Everything remains the same—except now there are buttons and cups and banners scattered around the office.

Now, let's be clear about something. There is nothing wrong with campaigns and buttons and banners. They can build morale and enthusiasm. But if they are not supported by a real customer service strategy, including improvements in a company's policies and procedures, then such campaigns will yield only limited short-term improvements. In effect, they can end up being nothing more than publicity stunts. And it doesn't take long for employees and customers to see through publicity stunts.

Actually, this sort of service campaign without substance is not the worst thing that can happen in a company. An even worse thing would be for a company to conduct such a campaign more than once. Every time a company conducts a campaign without a supporting strategy, service improves for a little while and then declines. But after each campaign, the improvement lasts for a shorter time and the decline is steeper. In fact, morale and service are likely to get progressively worse after each such campaign. Typically, the company's employees will feel misused. They'll feel angry and betrayed. They'll feel that management is all talk and no action. And further attempts to improve service will be met with cynicism and perhaps even outright resistance. When a company has a habit of announcing new plans with a big fanfare and then failing to follow up such announcements with concrete plans or actions for their implementation, the company's employees are likely to become wary of embracing any kind of change enthusiastically.

In the next few pages, we will talk about ways to establish a real customer service strategy and not just a happy-face campaign. Notice that although we will deviate somewhat from the format of a typical corporate strategic plan (in order to meet the particular demands of customer service), the general framework of strategic planning for customer service is still similar to the overall strategic planning process.

In Issues in Customer Service 3–1, Jim Clemmer points out important differences between two approaches that companies can take to make themselves service leaders.

ISSUES IN CUSTOMER SERVICE 3-1

A Critical Choice at the Service Quality Crossroad

The only North American managers not concerned about improving service quality today are either badly out of touch or don't care about their organizations' well-being. In large corporations, small companies, government and public sector institutions, service quality has become a serious issue. For the weak, it will become deadly serious. Many executives are adopting the position CEO James D. Robinson recently stated: "Customer service is American Express' patent protection. Our goal, simply stated, is to be the best in the service industry."

But identifying where an organization has to go and getting it there are two very different things. As anyone who ever made a new year's resolution, started a fitness program, or prepared a strategic plan knows only too well, "There's many a slip 'twixt cup and lip."

Executives who want to make their organizations more service-driven stand at a critical crossroad almost as soon as they identify that destination. Too many fail to make a conscious choice about the road they will travel to service-quality improvement. Not surprisingly, most end up on dead-end routes, or only part-way to their destination.

While there are many routes that head toward improved service, they can be reduced to essentially two:

1. Service improvement as a training program

2. Service improvement as a corporate strategy

At first glance, the two roads appear deceptively similar. However, around the first bend the terrain and direction gradually differ. Eventually the two roads fan out to a series of pathways, thoroughfares, avenues, and dead ends that are as radically different as the destinations to which they ultimately lead.

The "service as a corporate strategy" road is clearly the longest and most difficult. At times it parallels the training road. Often it splits into a series of tricky twists and turns that the organization must travel simultaneously. The energy and commitment to stay the course is enormous. But then so is the payoff. If this road were quick and easy, it would be as crowded as the training route has become. As it is, traffic is light and virtually disappears further along the route. Those rare organizations who press on become members of an elite group of exemplary performers. They are miles ahead of their industry. They have set a performance pace so brutal, many of their contemporaries struggle just to keep them in sight.

Mapping Out the Terrain

The following tabulation identifies the main areas where service improvement through corporate strategy differs from service as a training program:

Service as a Training Program	Service as a Corporate Strategy
Employees are taught how to use what exists more efficiently	Existing systems are redesigned to support superb service delivery.
Frontline employees and their supervisors are "fixed" to give better service	Hiring, training, supervision, and rewards are directed toward creating high service quality.
Senior management makes guest appearances and gives its blessing to training	Senior management visibly and relentlessly focuses all activities toward building a service-driven culture.
Service is added to the existing structure and duties of selected people	Service determines strategies, systems, structures, skill development, and accountabilities of *everyone*.
Employees are told by management how to meet customer needs	Employees uncover customers' expectations and plan how to exceed them.

Many Aspire, Few Arrive

A woman rushed up to famed violinist Fritz Kreisler after a concert and cried, "I'd give my life to play as beautifully as you do."

Kreisler replied, "I did."

There's commitment and then there's commitment. Many senior managers are *interested* in improving service quality, but not really *committed* to it. Making service-quality improvement a corporate strategy can only come from an intense commitment to the cause from the entire senior management team. Anything less inevitably leads to service improvement as a training program.

Source: Adapted with permission from Chapter 5 of *Firing on All Cylinders: The Service/Quality System for High-Powered Performance* (Toronto: Macmillan of Canada, 1990), by Jim Clemmer, President of the Achieve Group.

Situation Analysis: Measuring Current Levels of Service

Before a company can decide how to establish a service strategy and provide better customer service, it needs to find out what kind of service it is already providing. It also needs to find out what kind of service other companies are providing. There are a number of techniques for measuring customer service, and we will describe these techniques extensively in Chapters 4 and 5. In the next few pages, however, we will offer a broad overview of the steps a company should take in measuring customer service. The three primary sources of information about customer service are (1) the company's customers, (2) the company's employees, and (3) acknowledged leaders in customer service.

The Company's Customers

The customer is certainly the most obvious, and probably the most important, source of information about customer service. According to Peters and Waterman in their book *In Search of Excellence*, excellent companies stay close to their customers and learn from them. Insurance companies can contact customers (both producers and consumers) directly from the home office by using written surveys, telephone surveys, focus groups, advisory panels made up of the company's customers, and other methods. In this manner, insurers can find out how consumers and producers feel about the service they are receiving and what other services they would like to have. An insurer can also use its contacts with producers and consumerist organizations to find out what consumers think of the company's customer service.

The Company's Employees

As we discussed earlier, consumers and producers aren't the only customers an insurance company has. A company also has internal customers. Every insurance company employee either serves, or is served by, another employee in the company. Companies can ask their employees what they need in terms of internal service and have them identify areas in which the company is falling short of meeting their needs. Moreover, a company's employees often reflect the feelings of a company's customers. By dealing with customers day after day, company employees find out what customers want. They may not have statistical data about customers' attitudes, but they certainly have anecdotal evidence of how customers feel. This information can be used to develop more accurate surveys of customer satisfaction. As we discussed in Chapter 1, consumer-affairs professionals and the service activities they perform are also good sources of information about customer service.

In addition, the attitudes and perceptions that employees have about their work offer a good indication of the kind of service the company provides as a whole. If morale is low, and the service that employees offer to internal customers is not good, then external customers are probably not receiving the best possible service either.

The Company's Competitors

Surprisingly, one good source of ideas on how to improve customer service is often a company's competitors. Although companies consider some information proprietary and will not share it with other companies, many companies are willing to share a certain amount of information about their customer service activities. They do this in the interest of better serving the public. Such information exchanges regarding how to provide more effective customer service may take place between individual companies or through networking activities provided by industry trade associations. Organizations such as LOMA (Life Office Management Association), LIMRA (Life Insurance Marketing and Research Association), ICA (International Claim Association), ACLI (American Council of Life Insurance), HIAA (Health Insurance Association of America), and ICAE (Insurance Consumer Affairs Exchange) serve as forums to facilitate the exchange of information on how companies can operate more efficiently to serve the needs of their customers. This sharing may be available in the form of published reports or through seminars and conferences.

Acknowledged Leaders in Customer Service

Finally, insurance companies should look to companies that are acknowledged leaders in customer service. These companies might be in any kind of business — insurance, retailing, entertainment, or manufacturing. The one thing such companies have in common is a commitment to excellent customer service. Many of these companies are well known. Companies like McDonald's, Disney, and IBM have been closely studied and lauded as examples of good service providers for years. Numerous books and articles have been written about these and other companies that are considered excellent, not only in customer service but also in many other aspects of their work. Managers and other insurance company employees can study and learn from these leading companies' activities. Some of these acknowledged leaders even present seminars in which they teach other companies the customer service lessons that they have learned over the years.

Look at Customer Service in Action 3–2 for the profile of an insurer that is considered one of the best service providers in the industry.

CUSTOMER SERVICE IN ACTION 3-2

Northwestern Mutual Life

Each year, five policyholders of this Milwaukee-based company are selected by the board of trustees to make, at the company's expense, an unrestricted, independent review of operations from headquarters to the front lines. They go over records, investigate consumer complaints and requests, and have carte blanche to question anyone from CEO Don Schuenke to agents in the field. A summary of their report is incorporated into the company's annual report. More substantively, their insights have resulted in numerous changes and improvements in the 70 years that the program has been in existence.

When *Fortune* polled business executives, outside directors, and financial analysts in 1987 for its sixth annual Corporate Reputations Survey (reported in January 1988), the name at the top of the list of life insurance companies was Northwestern Mutual Life. The year before, Northwestern also led the list. And the year before that. In fact, every year since the survey began in 1983, Northwestern has been number one. As one insurance industry analyst told *Forbes* in 1988, "The perception [that] Northwestern is genuinely concerned for policyholders is universal in the industry."

All of this didn't start in the 1980s, however. It actually traces back to the 1880s. As related by Frederick G. Harmon and Garry Jacobs in their book *The Vital Difference*, "The company's agency field force developed a high reputation for professional skill and an intense loyalty to the company. Northwestern Mutual's agents became noted for high ethical standards and an almost religious zeal for serving the customer."

Today, service at Northwestern Mutual is an attitude that saturates the entire personality and atmosphere of the company and has become institutionalized as a self-perpetuating custom or culture of the organization.

Stability has a lot to do with that culture. In 1987, agent turnover was about half the industry average, while home office employee turnover was about a quarter of the industry average (about 4.5 percent compared to approximately 20 percent).

Productivity benefits from that stability, and in turn encourages it. Northwestern has the industry's lowest ratio of employees per $100 million of life insurance in force, about half the industry average. In return for productivity, employees are compensated well. Company salaries for administrative support staff rank in the top 10 percent of the industry.

Sales agents are supported with streamlined administrative systems and sophisticated computers that can profile each individual policyholder in a matter of keystrokes. The company's training catalog includes literally hundreds of seminars and courses, all of them designed to improve the performance of frontline salespeople by helping them improve their selling and business management skills. Evidence of the value the company's agents place on that support becomes visible every July, when thousands of members of the field sales force pay their own way to Milwaukee for a four-day sales meeting. There they share information and techniques, discuss market trends and issues, and meet the administrative staff that supports them in the field.

They also interact constantly with the home office, both informally and through three formal associations of agents. Agent representatives are included on joint committees that review new products and procedures, modify existing offerings, and help the company stay in touch with conditions in the marketplace.

In the end, it still comes back to how well or how poorly a company serves its customers. Northwestern prides itself on interpreting the fine print in the policyholder's

favor. One of the stories Northwesterners tell is the one about the student pilot who purchased a $50,000 life insurance policy. The policy had an aviation exclusion that said no benefits were payable if he died as a result of a flying accident while he was a pilot or crew member. Several years later, he did indeed die when the plane he was piloting crashed. In the wreckage, investigators found his logbook, which showed that just before the crash he had logged his hundredth hour at the controls, making him eligible to apply for a removal of the exclusion. Even though he hadn't applied for the removal, Northwestern paid off on the policy.

Source: From THE SERVICE EDGE by Ron Zemke and Dick Schaff. Copyright © 1989 by Ron Zemke and Dick Schaff. Used by permission of New American Library, a division of Penguin Books USA Inc.

Drafting a Customer Service Mission Statement

After analyzing its own customer service, the customer service provided by other companies, and the needs and perspectives of consumers, an insurance company is ready to begin to develop its customer service mission statement. The *customer service mission statement* tells why a company is providing customer service and how customer service relates to the company's goals. The mission statement helps give employees a sense of direction and purpose. But at this point, the mission statement should not be considered permanent. It should be a working document that can be changed as the company's service strategy is clarified. In its initial draft, however, the customer service mission statement should at least make it clear that the company has made a commitment to providing quality customer service.

Like corporate mission statements, customer service mission statements can vary greatly in their length and detail, depending on the company's needs. For example, a long, detailed statement may provide the company with specific direction and may be a document that employees can turn to for specific guidance and clarification. On the other hand, a short statement may be easier to remember. And because it is less detailed than a long statement, it may give the company more flexibility and fewer restrictions in setting its course of action.

Figure 3–2 provides several examples of customer service mission statements used by divisions within various insurance companies.

Establishing and Achieving Service Objectives

Although a mission statement is intended to provide direction and guidance to company management and employees, in reality the mission statement is nothing more than words if it is not backed by objectives, a strategy to fulfill its mission and achieve its objectives, and tactical plans (including programs and procedures) for implementing its strategy.

Service objectives define the specific goals that the company must meet to fulfill its customer service mission. They define the measurements for determining whether or not the company is fulfilling its mission. For example, assume that the company's service mission refers to prompt, courteous, accurate service. How will the company know if it is fulfilling this mission? The answer is by establishing goals that, when met, will ensure that the service given by the company meets its definitions of "prompt," "courteous," and "accurate." Thus, objectives in such a situation could read as follows:

- Respond to all customer requests within 48 hours.
- Provide convenient telephone access to home office staff.
- Reduce customer service processing errors by 15 percent annually during the next four years.
- Create opportunities for open and regular dialogue between the company and its customer groups.
- Establish formal policies regarding communicating with customers.

Note that each of these objectives describes a concrete action that the company believes it needs to take to fulfill its mission. Such objectives, then, provide the company with a yardstick to measure its progress. Furthermore, the company can use these objectives to set the performance standards it uses to evaluate its customer service system.

Figure 3–2
Customer Service Mission Statements of Insurance Companies

Great-West Life Assurance Company

Our Client Service Mission:

1. Deal with people not policies.
2. Work as a team with head office and field staff.
3. Provide personal service whenever possible.
4. Treat every *client* with respect.
5. Remember, agents are our biggest clients.
6. Do things right the first time.
7. Continue to upgrade skills and product knowledge.
8. Remember, *you* are Great-West Life.

Fidelity Union Life Insurance Company

The mission of the Client Services Division is to provide timely, accurate, and courteous service to our clients (agents and policyholders) in a cost-effective manner which encourages personal development for our home office associates.

New York Life Insurance Company
Individual Policy Services Department

The IPS Team is committed to being the industry service leader. We take pride in providing customers and each other with excellence in service through "personal attention". For us, that kind of service team is a dynamic one which is concerned and responsive, accurate and prompt, professional and dependable.
    In our crusade to Be The Best, we are committed to:

• Support company goals and objectives in service and sales.
• Develop and maintain practices and procedures to foster policyholder and agent loyalty and growth.
• Provide prompt, courteous, high-quality service through personal attention to internal and external customers.
• Continue to recognize people as our most important asset and enrich their careers through challenge and fair treatment in hiring, training, and promotional practices.

Source: All mission statements are reprinted with permission of the companies.

Service Strategies

Although objectives are more concrete than mission statements, they still do not describe exactly *how* the company plans to accomplish its goals. For this, the company develops service strategies, which it implements through programs and procedures. Through its **service strategies** a company establishes its general plans for achieving its service objectives. For an example, look at Figure 3–3, where we show two service objectives and the strategies that a company might use to achieve those objectives.

Note that, whenever possible, both objectives and strategies are stated in quantifiable terms, and there is a time frame for ac-

Figure 3–3
Objectives and Strategies

Objective:

Provide customers with convenient telephone access to home office staff.

Strategies:

- Install toll-free customer service hotline for each major product line within two years; inform all customers about the new service within two months of its availability.
- Ensure that customers in all U.S. and Canadian time zones can reach the home office between the hours of 10 a.m. and 4 p.m., local time.
- Maintain sufficient staff in key customer service areas so that all telephone calls can be answered within 10 rings, with the average number of rings fewer than 5.

Objective:

Reduce customer service processing errors by 15 percent annually over the next four years.

Strategies:

- Install systems with error-checking features in all areas, where feasible, within four years.
- Within two years, train all staff people who handle particular functions to detect common errors.
- Within three years, cross-train 50 percent of the staff to handle functions in three distinct areas.
- Establish quality circles in each area to identify problems and develop solutions; each area should hold at least three meetings during the next year.

---

complishing them. In this way, the company can plan accurately to accomplish specific goals. Plus, it can determine if, and to what extent, it is actually achieving its goals.

Operational Plans

While strategies establish the general plans for achieving goals, more detailed plans are needed to make the strategies work. These detailed business plans, which outline the actual steps needed to implement a strategy, are called *operational plans* (or tactical plans). Two of the most important components of operational plans are programs and procedures. A *program* establishes the activities that are needed to achieve a specific objective. For example, assume that a company has a strategy, as mentioned in Figure 3–3, to make sure that customer service is available for all U.S. and Canadian time zones at least between 10 a.m. and 4 p.m. The program for implementing that strategy might call for (1) a budget to hire new employees or buy new telephone equipment, (2) training for new employees, and (3) a promotional campaign to let customers know about the new customer service hours.

On an even more detailed level than programs are procedures. *Procedures* are the step-by-step actions that must be taken in order to complete the specific tasks or jobs that make up day-to-day activities. For example, the procedures for training new employees in customer skills would identify the actual skills to be taught, the number of hours needed to teach them, and the sequence of steps needed to complete the training. Procedures are discussed in greater detail in Chapter 6 when we describe customer service systems.

Although operational plans get their direction from the strategic plan, they can frequently have a dramatic impact on the strategic plan itself. For example, when developing specific programs to implement a strategy, the company may determine that these programs will not achieve the objectives originally stated. Perhaps the costs are much higher than anticipated or company employees find a conflict in the objectives, where achieving one objective will prevent the company from achieving another objective. This information is then used to reevaluate the company's objectives and, possibly, to modify the strategic plan itself. Although strategic plans are long-range plans, usually covering three to five years, they need to be reviewed periodically (generally once a year) to ensure that they continue to provide accurate direction for the company. Information obtained during the operational planning process is essential for such reevaluation.

Implementing the Customer Service Strategy

When discussing strategic planning and especially the customer service strategic plan, it is easy to get the impression that a plan is created and then everyone in the company simultaneously puts the plan into effect. This seldom happens. Often, the very size of a company gets in the way. In very large companies, individual divisions operate much like separate companies, and it is not always easy to coordinate their activities. Even in medium-sized companies, each department has different constraints (such as budgeting, staffing, or management style) that prevent them from implementing the customer service strategic plan on the same schedule throughout the company. Therefore, many companies implement their customer service plans in a more sequential manner. For example, a company might begin by introducing its customer service plan in a particular department or regional office. The company can observe the manner in which the plan is implemented, noting successes and failures, then modify the plan to improve its chances for success. Next, the plan might be introduced to several other departments or regions and then to the company as a whole. Such a process allows the company to test its customer service plans and procedures on a small scale, so it can learn from its mistakes and have a better chance of success on the large scale.

Smaller, less diverse companies may find they have fewer difficulties implementing a customer service plan simultaneously throughout the company. But even they may find that testing the plan on a small scale can help assure later success.

Key Terms

strategic planning	corporate customer service officer
environmental analysis	quality improvement process
environmental forecast	customer service mission statement
internal assessment	service objectives
mission statement	service strategies
corporate objectives	operational plans
corporate strategies	programs
annual plan	procedures

CHAPTER 4

Customer Expectations and Perceptions

After studying this chapter you should be able to

- Define the concepts of perception and expectation and explain their importance to customer service
- Describe gap analysis and the five gaps in customer service
- Explain how companies reduce or overcome service gaps
- Describe the service dimensions that customers use to evaluate service quality

Introduction

An insurance company cannot successfully serve its customers if it does not know what kind of service they expect and what they think of the service they are already getting. In this chapter, we discuss the concepts of perception and expectation, the effect that perceptions and expectations have on customers' attitudes toward service, some of the areas in which expectations often are not met, and the factors that most customers find important when judging service quality.

Perception and Expectation

In Chapter 1, we defined customer service as the broad range of activities that a company and its employees undertake to keep customers satisfied. One of the most important of these activities involves learning what sort of service customers want. To find this out, an insurer must first learn how its customers perceive the service they are now receiving and what they expect from that service.

Perception

Perception is the process by which people select, organize, and interpret information in order to give it meaning. As such, perception is a person's view of reality. Sometimes what is objectively real and what we perceive to be real are one and the same. At other times, objective reality and perception are two different things. And depending on the circumstances, perceived reality can be more believable—and consequently more important—than objective reality.

As an example, let's consider our view of the world. It is mathematically accurate to say that the earth is a slightly egg-shaped sphere 24,901.55 miles in circumference, hurtling through space at a speed of 66,636 miles per hour, and revolving around a medium-sized star that is 93 million miles away. That's the objective reality. For most of us, though, our perception tells us that the earth we live on does not move because we can't feel it move. The sun goes around the earth, not vice versa, because we see the sun travel across the sky every day. And the earth can't be round because if it were, the people in Australia would be walking around upside down.

From a customer service perspective, it is more important to find out what customers (both internal and external) perceive to be real rather than what *is* real. Customers judge products, companies, agents, customer service providers, and customer service interactions based on their perception of reality. For example, suppose a company is providing what it perceives to be excellent service based on industry standards. When it surveys its customers, however, the company discovers that they perceive its service to be lousy. In reality, the company is meeting and even surpassing industry standards. But should it berate its customers for not appreciating the excellent job it is doing? Not if the company wants to stay in business. It should try to find out why its customers perceive its service to be bad. Perhaps one element of the service process causes customers to view the entire service as inadequate. Perhaps customers are comparing the insurance company's service to the service provided by a company in an entirely different industry. Whatever the reason, if the company's customers perceive the service to be poor, the insurer will need to change that perception if it wants to keep its customers.

Expectation

An *expectation* is what people believe is likely or certain to happen. Sometimes expectations involve what people believe to be reasonable or due. Sometimes they involve what people consider obligatory or required. Most customers have expectations of what specific future events or business encounters will bring. These expectations are based on what customers have been told is likely to happen and on what they perceive to have happened in the past. Customers develop their expectations through (1) listening to, or reading about, the experiences that other people have had; (2) promotional materials, such as advertising and other forms of marketing communication, which have been designed to tell customers what to expect; (3) their own previous personal experiences with similar or related events. For example, if customers perceive that they are treated with indifference or even rudeness every time they go into the post office, they will expect to be treated that way. On the other hand, if they perceive that they are treated well and get good service in the post office, they will expect the same treatment until something happens to change their expectations.

Just as perceptions affect expectations, customers' expectations also affect their perceptions. For example, if a customer expects the post office to deliver a letter in three days, but it delivers the letter in two days, the customer will probably have a better perception of the postal service than if the customer had expected next-day delivery.

As another example, consider the time it takes Bravo Life Insurance Company to process customers' requests for information about their policy values. The average time to process such requests in the insurance industry is four days.[1] Bravo typically meets this standard or may even beat it by a day or two. Bravo, therefore, thinks it is doing a pretty good job. But a number of Bravo's policyowners have developed expectations on the basis of the service they receive from their mutual funds. To find out the value of their mutual fund accounts, all these customers have to do is call their funds on a touch-tone telephone. Using an automated assistance service, they can enter their account numbers and find out instantly the value of their accounts. Therefore, although Bravo's perception is that it is providing good to superior service, the perception of at least some of its customers is that it provides surprisingly slow service. This difference between customer expectations and customer perceptions amounts to a *service gap* that the insurance company should try to reduce if it wants to maintain customer satisfaction.

The Service Gap

Quality customer service is not measured by how impressive, how personalized, or how costly a service is. Instead, the quality of the customer service provided is measured in terms of how well the service matches customer expectations. Research indicates that delivering quality service means that a company meets customer expectations on a consistent basis. One of the primary goals of any service provider is to reduce the gap between customers' expectations and their perceptions.

When customers evaluate the quality of the service they have received from a company, they compare the **expected service**, which is the quality of the service they expected to get, with the **perceived service**, which is the quality of the service they believe they actually received.[2] Therefore, in order to satisfy customers, a company must match the perceived quality of its service with its customers' expectations regarding the service. To achieve this match, a company must manage its customers' expectations and perceptions. Successful service providers consistently meet their customers' expectations. Excellent service providers consistently exceed their customers' expectations. Excellent service providers also make sure that their customers know that the company is exceeding their expectations. Exceeding customers' expectations enhances a company's reputation and leads to satisfied customers who are repeat buyers. Therefore, a company that provides excellent service should make sure that the quality of its service is highly visible to its present and potential customers.[3]

A Model of Service Quality [4]

The study *A Conceptual Model of Service Quality and Its Implications for Future Research* by Parasuraman, Zeithaml, and Berry presents one of the most comprehensive models now available for examining service quality. This model identifies

- *Five gaps* — including the service gap — that can prevent businesses from providing service that consumers "perceive as being of high quality" and
- *Five criteria of service quality* that are of greatest importance to consumers. These criteria are called service dimensions.

In the sections that follow, we will describe this model and some of the ways insurance companies try to influence customer expectations.

Gap Analysis

The process of identifying and studying the differences between expected service and perceived service is called **gap analysis**. It is much like situation analysis, which we described earlier in our discussion of strategic planning. The purpose of gap analysis is to find any gaps that exist between customer service performance and customer service expectations, so that companies can develop tactics to overcome or remove those gaps. The five gaps in customer service identified in the service quality model include:

Gap 1: customer expectations versus management perceptions
Gap 2: management perceptions versus service specifications
Gap 3: service specifications versus service delivery
Gap 4: actual service levels versus advertised service levels
Gap 5: expected service versus perceived service

Of these five gaps, only two — the first and the last — directly concern the external customer. The other three gaps occur within the service company itself. Each of these gaps within the company (internal gaps), however, increases the likelihood that Gap 5 — the most critical gap — will exist. Figure 4–1 illustrates where each of the five gaps typically occurs in a company and in a company's relationship with its customers. We will discuss each gap individually.

Gap 1: Customer Expectations versus Management Perceptions

Gap 1 represents the difference between what customers want and what the company thinks they want. In the insurance industry, Gap 1 can occur at several levels. It can occur between home office executives and consumers, between producers and consumers, between home office executives and producers, between internal service providers and external customers, and between internal service providers and internal customers.

Many companies believe they know what their customers want, though they have never done any quantifiable research on the topic. The attitude in these companies follows this logic:

We've been in this business for years. We talk to our top salespeople. We know what services our competitors offer. All in all, we have our ear to the ground and our finger on the pulse of the customer. We know what our customers want.

These companies base their beliefs on hunches and on the intuition their senior managers have gained through years of experience. And quite often hunches and intuition lead to correct assumptions. But

Figure 4–1
The Five Gaps in Customer Service

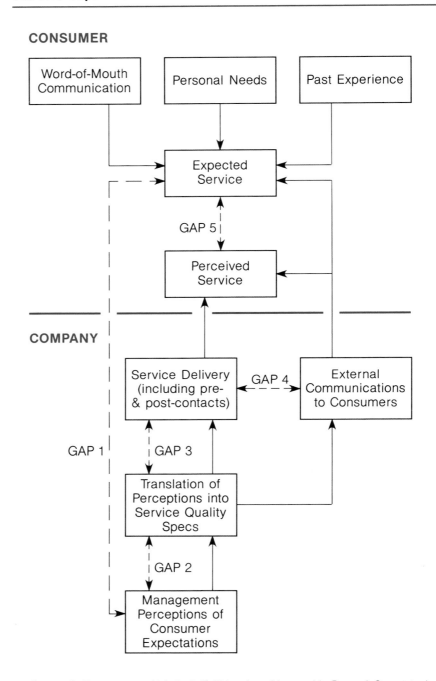

Source: A. Parasuraman, Valarie A. Zeithhaml, and Leonard L. Berry, *A Conceptual Model of Service Quality and Its Implications for Future Research* (Cambridge, MA: Marketing Science Institute, 1984), p. 7.

there's little certainty in hunches, and it's risky to rely on intuition. There is no substitute for good solid research.

Gap 1 usually occurs for one reason: The people responsible for providing service neither talk to, nor listen to, their customers. They don't find out what their customers really want. The only way to prevent this gap from opening is to go to customers and ask them what they want. And the best way to ask customers what they want is by using well-constructed and thorough research tools, which we will discuss in Chapter 5.

By not gathering accurate information about their customers' expectations, insurance companies run the risk of not meeting those expectations. They also run the risk of spending millions of dollars on services that customers don't really value, on training that doesn't really help employees provide the service that is wanted, and on technology that doesn't meet the real service needs. A misinformed company, in effect, could position itself to provide the wrong service with the wrong people through the wrong technology, wasting millions of dollars in the process and losing the opportunity to provide the right service.

Gap 2: Management Perceptions versus Service Specifications

Gap 2 represents the difference between what a company's management believes that customers want and the specifications that management sets for the work that its employees do. Although an insurance company may understand the kinds of service and the levels of service that its customers want, it may decide not to deliver that level of service.

Generally, discrepancies between what customers want and what a company delivers exist for two reasons. First, the company may not be able to provide the service that customers want. For example, in order to provide the level of turnaround on policy loan requests that its customers want, a company may have to invest more money in technology or hire more staff than it can afford or feels is worth the cost. Second, the company's top management simply may not be committed to quality customer service. Top management may still maintain the attitude that service is of marginal value, that customer service is in fact a chore and an unjustifiable expense, rather than a strategy for increasing profits. If management is not committed to service, it will not be willing to spend the money on personnel, training, and technology to provide the service that customers want.

By learning what kind of service customers expect and setting job and performance specifications that allow employees to provide the expected service, insurance companies can help close Gap 2.

Gap 3: Service Specifications versus Service Delivery

Gap 3 represents the difference between the service specifications set by the company and the service that it actually delivers. Even when a company establishes adequate procedures and appropriate job-performance specifications, the company's employees may not perform at the level set by those specifications. There could be several reasons why employee performance falls short of company expectations:

- *Lack of the right people.* The company may not have the right people providing service. During the hiring process an insurance company must look for people who have the personal characteristics that will make them likely to succeed as service providers. If the company does not make the effort to determine what those characteristics are or to look for them when interviewing applicants for customer service positions (as well as other types of jobs), then the company can hardly expect its employees to be good service providers.
- *Lack of training.* The company's service people may not be properly trained. As we have mentioned before, even a person who has a great talent for providing service must be trained to do the job properly. A company must be willing to educate and train its employees. It must be willing to teach its employees about its products and help them develop the skills they need (such as listening skills, writing skills, and telephone communication skills) to serve the customer. If the company does not train its employees properly, then it can hardly expect its employees to be good service providers.
- *Lack of resources.* Service providers may not have the resources they need. There may not be enough staff to handle the volume of customer service interactions required or enough staff to handle the other types of customer service activities (such as research, training, media and consumer group relations, service audits, and so forth) that need to be performed. The company may not have given its service providers the technology and procedures (in other words, the systems) they need to provide excellent service.

- *Lack of well-defined jobs and standards.* The company may have defined the jobs of its service employees so poorly that they do not know how to perform all their roles and still meet service standards. Companies must clearly define service employees' jobs, establish realistic and attainable performance standards for those jobs, and clarify job performance goals with employees so that they know what is expected of them in their roles as service providers. Feedback must also be provided in order to reward and encourage desired behavior.

- *Lack of motivation.* The company's service providers may simply choose not to provide the level of service that specifications call for. For one reason or another, motivation may be lacking, and employees may choose not to meet service standards. Employees may not be convinced of the importance (to the company and to their continuing employment) of providing quality customer service. Or they may not be rewarded well enough to feel that it is worth their effort to meet specifications. In addition, the reward system may inadvertently encourage employees to ignore the standards. For example, the company may have told service employees that answering customers' telephone calls is their most important function. However, if the company's evaluation and reward system measures only the number of forms processed, the service employees may be more likely to let the phones ring while they finish their paperwork.

Gap 4: Actual Service Levels versus Advertised Service Levels

Gap 4 represents the discrepancy between the service a company advertises that it will provide and the service that it actually does provide. From the customer's point of view, this gap can be the most glaring and damaging. It is also one of the most common.

Earlier in the book we talked about the smile campaigns that companies too often use in place of customer service strategies. We also talked about the disillusionment that employees feel if they conclude that the company is not serious about its commitment to service. Customers feel the same anger and sense of betrayal when a company advertises a certain kind or level of service and then does not deliver it. A company must be especially careful not to promise its customers higher-quality service than it can provide. When the quality of service provided by a company does not match the quality of service promised by the company—and thus expected by its customers—its customers are more likely to be dissatisfied than they would be if no promise of high-quality service had been made. Companies that promise quality service but do not provide it are going to create customer dissatisfaction.

"Underpromise; overdeliver." That's the rule. But many businesses do the opposite. They advertise the high quality of their service without making sure that they have the mechanisms in place to provide that service. Then, when customers discover the gap between what was promised and what was delivered, they are disappointed with the service. Instead of closing a gap, companies can, in fact, create one. They raise their customers' expectations, and then they cannot meet those expectations. A company must make certain it can deliver whatever level or quality of service it advertises. It must either raise its service to the level of its promises, or it must promise no more than it can deliver.

Consider what happened at Lumbago Insurance Company recently. John Philips, manager of broker relations, conducted some research and found out that brokers hate waiting for customer service representatives to return their calls. In an effort to attract brokerage business, Mr. Philips initiated an advertising campaign that promised same-day call backs to all of its brokers. Unfortunately, Lumbago customer service reps found out about the promise when they called brokers back—a day or two after the brokers called them. Brokers who previously had found next-day call backs acceptable were suddenly surly and angry. More complaints than ever before flooded Mr. Philips's desk. Mr. Philips promptly canceled the campaign, grumbling about unreasonable producers and slow employees.

Gap 5: Expected Service versus Perceived Service

The purpose of identifying and reducing gaps 1 through 4 is to reduce the gap that is always most apparent to the customer: Gap 5, which is the difference between the expected service, the service that customers expect to get, and the perceived service, the service that they feel they actually receive. This gap is the *service gap* and can be viewed as the culmination of the four preceding gaps. By reducing or eliminating gaps 1 through 4, an insurance company can reduce or eliminate the service gap. An insurance company can also reduce this gap by changing customer expectations.

Influencing Customer Expectations

Many companies have a policy of actively educating their customers about the level of service to expect from the company. This **consumer education** influences customer expectations and reduces the gap between customers' perceptions and expectations.

Most consumers expect to be educated about insurance by the producer, by "their agent." Consumers tend to think of the person who sold them their most recent policy as "their" agent. This "agent" may be a broker, a captive agent, a personal producing general agent, a salaried sales representative, or a financial planning consultant. In general, customers rely on their agents for information and advice. They expect their agents to explain the products they are selling and the services that come with them. A customer's need to understand what he or she is buying provides the agent (and the company) with an excellent opportunity to educate the customer, to explain as clearly and as positively as possible the product features and the kinds of services that the company offers.

In addition to providing education through agents, companies can reach customers through newsletters, brochures, fulfillment kits, and other types of marketing communications. Many companies publish newsletters for producers, and a few have developed them for consumers. Brief, appealing, and informative newsletters can be excellent vehicles for customer education, and especially useful for informing them about new services. Customers don't want fluff or news that is really of no importance to them. They don't want a company wasting their time with what they regard as junk mail. When customers receive a newsletter from a business, they want something that will provide them with information that will help them make good use of the services that the business provides. Look at Figure 4–2 for an example of the kind of newsletter published by insurance companies.

Fulfillment kits and customer service brochures can be extremely helpful when they are designed to explain a company's services and the procedures for making inquiries, registering complaints, or exercising various policy rights and options. An additional benefit of such materials is that they help reduce some of the problems customers experience after a sale because they tell the customer where to go for help and what steps to follow for particular types of service. Some companies even include photographs of their customer service personnel to give their materials a more personal touch. Customers like to associate a face with the voice they hear on the

Figure 4–2
A Customer Newsletter Produced by an Insurer

The TIAA-CREF

A quarterly
newsletter for
TIAA-CREF
participants

Participant

November 1990

THE CREF MONEY MARKET ACCOUNT AND TIAA: STEADY PERFORMERS IN UNCERTAIN TIMES

Is recession on the horizon? Is inflation rising? Are the bears devouring Wall Street? At a time like this, it's natural to wonder how the uncertain economy might affect your CREF stock accumulations. The answer depends somewhat on how long a view you're taking. So far, this hasn't been a banner year for stocks. But over time, the stock market has outperformed many other types of investments; you just have to be able to stay the course and wait out its downturns.

(continued on page 3)

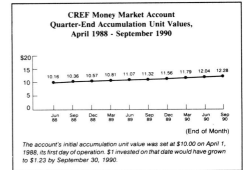

CREF Money Market Account
Quarter-End Accumulation Unit Values,
April 1988 - September 1990

$20
15
10
5
0

10.16 10.36 10.57 10.81 11.07 11.32 11.56 11.79 12.04 12.28

Jun Sep Dec Mar Jun Sep Dec Mar Jun Sep
88   88   88   89   89   89   89   90   90   90

(End of Month)

The account's initial accumulation unit value was set at $10.00 on April 1, 1988, its first day of operation. $1 invested on that date would have grown to $1.23 by September 30, 1990.

TIAA INVESTMENTS: SAFETY AND SECURITY COME FIRST

Failures in the savings and loan industry, a slump in some once-robust real estate markets, and lingering doubts about junk bonds have disquieted many Americans. Some commentators are fanning fears with speculation that the insurance industry may become the nation's next S&L crisis.

In this atmosphere, and in view of TIAA's consistently high participant dividends in

addition to its guarantees, it's natural for TIAA participants to ask, "How safe are TIAA's investments?" The answer is, "Very safe, indeed."

TIAA takes seriously its responsibility to stay in sound financial health for generations to come, while providing lifetime benefits you can count on absolutely. So in selecting new investments and monitoring its portfolio, TIAA's investment professionals and trustees first

consider the risk appropriate for long-term pension commitments. Then TIAA seeks the highest long-term return compatible with acceptable risk.

TIAA's strategy has paid off for participants. TIAA has declared dividends every year for the last 41 years. Moreover, TIAA has beaten the insurance industry average net rate of return in every one of those 41 years.

(continued on page 4)

Figure 4–2   (Continued)

ARE YOU UNDERESTIMATING YOUR LIFE SPAN?

How Long Can You Expect to Live?
Once you reach age 65, here are your
chances of living to ages 85, 90, and 95

It's said that some people need a healthy respect for mortality to stay out of trouble. But sometimes it's possible to get into trouble because you think you're more mortal than you really are. If you underestimate your longevity when you're making retirement financing decisions, you might find yourself long on life but short on money.

True, Social Security benefits will last your lifetime. And so will the payments from a lifetime annuity. But if you'll also be tapping into personal savings, be sure to consider for how long you need to plan.

The table at left offers some idea of what to expect. A 65-year-old who retires today has almost a 60% chance of living 20 or more years, and a 20% chance of living to age 95.

Just think what 20 or 30 years mean in terms of car repairs and purchases . . . furnaces, refrigerators, and sofabeds . . . vacation travel and family visits!

And it's a safe bet that, because of improving health care, someone retiring a decade or more from now can expect to live even longer after retirement. That's good news. But it also means that you'll have to consider long-term care costs more seriously. ❏

RESEARCH NOTEBOOK

TIAA-CREF conducts research on a wide range of important issues. We take frequent surveys to help us understand your needs and retirement goals. We also study retirement planning, pension plan design, and the future of Social Security. In addition, we sponsor independent researchers studying career- and retirement-related issues in higher education.

Some of these studies are reported in *Research Dialogues*, a TIAA-CREF publication written primarily for benefit plan administrators. The studies are often technical in nature — so here are capsule reviews of recent issues. If you wish, you can request a copy of any issue of *Research Dialogues* by calling 1 800 842-2733, ext. 5509. Ask for an issue by its number, and please keep in mind that supplies are limited.

- The present health care system in the U.S. is characterized by high cost, limited access for the uninsured, inadequate insurance for others, and increasing administrative complexity. Any public policy response to the health care crisis will affect both employers and individuals, whether they have health care coverage or not.

  To provide a perspective on pressing health care issues, *Research Dialogues* No. 27, October 1990, describes the development of our present health care financing structure (based principally on employer-sponsored group insurance plans), its current status, and recent proposals to improve health care access and lower costs.

- We surveyed over 1,900 TIAA-CREF participants

between ages 55 and 70 about their plans and expectations for retirement. The study was spurred by a 1986 federal law eliminating mandatory retirement because of age. (An exception, under which tenured employees of colleges and universities may be required to retire at age 70, expires December 31, 1993.) Participants were asked about their attitudes toward work, about how they were preparing for retirement, and at what age they expected to retire.

Most people reported that eliminating mandatory retirement didn't affect their career plans. The age at which these participants stop working will depend primarily on their expected retirement income and health. After years of high inflation and rising

(continued on page 7)

Source: Reprinted with permission of Teachers Insurance and Annuity Association and College Retirement Equities Fund.

phone or the name they see at the bottom of a letter. As an additional measure to get the customer service relationship started, some companies call each customer who has recently purchased one of their products. Such calls generate goodwill and provide the company with feedback about common questions that new customers have. Such materials and practices help educate as well as reassure customers that the company cares about their needs and that someone is there to help answer questions or solve problems they may encounter.

Newsletters, fulfillment kits, and brochures aren't the only types of marketing communications used to educate consumers. Look at Issues in Customer Service 4–1 to find out what American Family Insurance Group has done to understand the effects of education on customer expectations.

ISSUES IN CUSTOMER SERVICE 4–1

Consumer Education: Strategies that Work

Concerned that consumers' attitudes toward insurance have recently taken a turn for the worse, two researchers at American Family Insurance (Annette Zacher and Nancy M. Johnson) decided to study the effects of education on insurance customers.

Zacher and Johnson selected 3,500 American Family customers as the sample for the study. The demographics of the sample mirrored the demographics of American Family's customer base. The researchers began by mailing a survey that determined the customers' current understanding of insurance in general, American Family products in particular, and the customers' attitudes toward insurance. About 30 percent of the sample responded to the survey. These respondents were then divided into four equal groups. One group received a catalog that described insur-

ance products. Another group received a videotape with the same content as the catalog. A third group received both the catalog and the videotape. The final group received no information.

Zacher and Johnson used the catalog format because of the current popularity of catalog shopping. They felt that consumers would be more likely to read a catalog than something that looked more like junk mail. Even if the respondents didn't read the catalog right away, they might throw it in a basket with their other catalogs and read it later.

The videotape format was chosen because of its obvious popularity, and because the researchers assumed that many of the respondents would have videocassette players in their homes.

To choose the topics for the catalog

and the videotape, Zacher and Johnson conducted focus group research with claim representatives, underwriters, and receptionists—frontline employees who are close to the customer. Zacher and Johnson asked the focus groups three questions: "What do customers think that they know about insurance that they are right about?" "What do customers think that they know about insurance that they are wrong about?" and "What insurance concepts are customers confused about?" The focus groups discussed the areas covered by the three questions, and the educational material was developed based on their discussions.

The material begins with an overview of how insurance fits into an individual's financial plan. Then comes a section on each line of insurance, including products offered by American Family. The material also contains tips on how to reduce premiums, how to file a claim, even on how to increase your life expectancy.

The results of the study showed that both the catalog and the videotape im- proved the respondents' understanding of insurance, with the videotape being slightly more effective. After receiving the educational material

- 12 percent more of the respondents understood the basic definition of insurance, up to 66 percent from 54 percent,
- 16 percent more understood term insurance, up to 91 percent from 75 percent,
- 21 percent more understood whole life insurance, up to 88 percent from 67 percent, and
- 27 percent more understood universal life insurance, up to 78 percent from 51 percent.

In addition, the respondents who received either the catalog or the tape had a better attitude toward American Family and the insurance industry in general than respondents who received no educational materials.

Source: Adapted with permission of the publisher from Annette Zacher and Nancy M. Johnson, "Consumer Education: Strategies that Work," *Resource,* LOMA, March 1990, pp. 24–27.

Another excellent way to educate consumers is through local colleges, universities, and civic groups. These institutions sometimes ask financial-services experts to conduct brief seminars on financial products such as insurance, annuities, stocks, or bonds. Insurance companies can use these types of public service seminars as objective forums to educate consumers about the various types of products that insurance companies offer.

By educating customers in an objective, sincere manner, insurance companies create a credible image for themselves. In addition, they help to make sure that their customers have realistic expectations and an accurate perception of the services that insurance companies provide.

On the other hand, companies cannot reduce the gap between customer expectations and customer perceptions through education alone. Competitors are constantly seeking ways to improve their own level of service, and insurers will have to follow suit or fall behind. All insurance companies must be prepared to improve their service on a continuing basis, because what seemed like exceptional service last year will appear to be standard service two years from now, and four years from now may even appear to be substandard. Customer expectations will rise as the overall level of service provided by all businesses rises, and insurance companies must be prepared to meet those expectations.

Service Dimensions

Businesses that understand the five gaps in customer service are more prepared to avoid or overcome the problems encountered in areas where service typically breaks down. Companies can use their knowledge of these gaps as a framework for structuring customer service research designed to gather information needed to solve or avoid potential service problems. To gather the necessary information, however, companies need to know the criteria that customers generally use to judge the quality of all the services they receive. Companies can use these service criteria to structure research that helps them understand their own customers' attitudes, perceptions, and expectations.

In their model of service quality, Parasuraman, Zeithaml, and Berry have identified a number of criteria that customers typically use to judge the quality of the service they receive. These five criteria are referred to by the researchers as *service dimensions*:[5]

- Reliability
- Assurance
- Empathy
- Responsiveness
- Tangible factors

In the sections that follow, we will discuss these dimensions and the effect that they have on how customers perceive service.

Reliability

Reliability means performing the promised service dependably and accurately. Reliable companies provide customers with the level and quality of service promised. Most customers do not want to conduct business with a company they cannot rely on. They want a level and quality of service that they know they can expect time after time. They want service they can depend on, service designed to fulfill their needs, and service that doesn't cause them unexpected problems. Companies can enhance the perception of their reliability by maintaining accurate records, paying claims quickly and correctly, and billing customers accurately.

In the financial services industry, reliability is especially important. When an insurance company makes a mistake, hundreds or thousands of dollars can be involved. A damaged item, such as a shirt with a flawed collar or a toaster oven that won't work, can be replaced easily enough, and the customer usually can be given satisfaction. But when an insurance company errs with someone's money, the damage to the company's image can be much more difficult to repair.

Assurance

Assurance refers to the competence and credibility of service personnel, their ability to convey trust and confidence, and the courtesy they show to customers. A company's employees must have the necessary knowledge and skills to perform required services. Plus, they must be empowered to handle difficult customer situations when they occur. Employees must also treat customers in a polite, considerate, and friendly manner. The level of assurance displayed by customer service providers and other company employees strongly affects the amount of trust and confidence that customers develop in a company. The two qualities of courtesy and competence must be combined. Most customers do not expect to be treated like royalty, but they do expect common courtesy, and courtesy can make up for a number of shortcomings. Courtesy, however, cannot stand alone. A customer may appreciate a company employee who is polite. But after that employee has given the customer incorrect information for the third time in as many days, courtesy will start to lose its shine. A courteous employee must also be competent and knowledgeable about the company's products and procedures if the customer is to be satisfied.

As consumers have become better educated and more sophisticated, and as the level and quality of service required by nontraditional products have increased, the degree and level of competence needed by customer service providers have changed correspondingly. Educated, well-trained service personnel are a key factor in a company's ability to provide quality customer service. Companies must set high educational and professional standards for their customer service and other employees. Employee education and training is an ongoing process that should be viewed as an investment in a company's future ability to compete.

Empathy

In some organizations, employees view a customer with a problem as an annoyance. Such negative attitudes are often communicated to customers (either knowingly or unknowingly) and are counterproductive to offering quality service. Employees should regard the process of solving problems not only as a way to serve the customer and strengthen customer loyalty but as an opportunity to gain information on ways to improve service. *Empathy* is the process of understanding the customer's emotional state and imagining how you would feel in a similar situation. Empathy means putting yourself in the customer's shoes. Customers prefer dealing with service providers who seem to care about their needs and concerns. To make customers feel comfortable dealing with a company, employees need to have a sincere interest in customers and their needs. Empathy can be especially important in dealing with an unhappy or emotionally distraught customer. An employee who can empathize with a dissatisfied customer's problems has made an important step in recovering that customer's confidence and loyalty.

Empathy also entails a strong commitment to customer communication. Empathetic companies listen to customers and keep them informed about products and services *in language they can understand*. For example, a company that's committed to customer service trains its representatives not to use jargon or technical language that could confuse customers. And if the company knows that it has significant numbers of customers who speak a foreign language, the company hires at least some customer service representatives who are fluent in that language.

Responsiveness

Responsiveness implies a willingness to help customers and an ability to provide them with prompt service. Customers want fast, dependable service. Responsiveness requires a positive attitude on the part of the person who is providing service and a level of support from the company (in staffing, training, procedures, and technology) that allows the employee to be responsive.

Note that responsiveness is not passive. It is proactive; it requires initiative by the company or the customer service representative. A responsive customer service representative goes beyond giving the customer what is asked for and, instead, asks questions to make sure that a full solution to the customer's needs is provided. Careful listening and probing questions are necessary to understand the full implications of a service problem. A responsive company looks for ways to improve customer service before being presented with the need to make an improvement.

For insurance companies, responsiveness entails the prompt issuance of policies, the prompt payment of claims or commissions, returning customers' calls as quickly as possible, and being flexible and competent when responding to customers' requests. Most insurers, for example, establish standard turnaround times for issuing policies and processing claims, give customers' calls priority over other tasks, and make sure all customer requests are handled within a specified time period. In some states, insurers must handle certain policyowner and beneficiary requests within legislatively defined time standards.

Flexibility and the authority to take action are two additional aspects of responsiveness. Since different customers have different service needs, a company's customer service system should be flexible enough to meet those needs. When a company's rules for serving customers are too rigid and service is handled in a bureaucratic manner, the customer service effort is impeded. Customers expect a company's contact personnel to be able to think for themselves and to have the flexibility and authority to address problems that may not fit a company's procedures manuals. As we discussed in Chapter 3, customer service providers and other employees need to be empowered to perform the work that customers expect of them. Through careful hiring and training, some insurers are finding they can push their decision-making authority down the chain of command, allowing frontline employees to make decisions that only their supervisors had previously been allowed to make. Through such empowerment, customer service representatives gain the flexibility to make on-the-spot decisions that can improve the quality and speed of service.

Insurers use many different methods to improve their responsiveness, including

- changing from policy-oriented data bases to customer-oriented data bases,
- providing toll-free 800 telephone numbers for producers, policyowners, and other customers,
- allowing producers access to home office computerized information networks through which they can get information about submitted applications, outstanding policy loans, billing information, and underwriting status,
- making customer services available for longer hours,
- placing company listings in telephone books and yellow pages in areas in which the company still has customers but no longer maintains an agency, and
- allowing customers to conduct as many transactions as possible over the telephone rather than requiring them to spend additional time writing to the company.

We will discuss two of the most important of these ways of increasing responsiveness: customer-oriented data bases and toll-free 800 numbers.

Customer-Oriented Data Bases

To improve their responsiveness, many insurers are changing from policy-oriented data bases to customer-oriented data bases. With a *policy-oriented data base*, the representative can call up information only on one particular policy at a time and, therefore, has a fragmentary understanding of the customer's needs. When a company uses a *customer-oriented data base*, each service representative can use just a few computer key strokes to call up all the pertinent information available about a particular customer, such as the company products that the customer currently owns, products that the customer may have owned in the past, and various information about the customer's recent dealings with the company. By having this information so readily available, the customer service representative can understand a customer's needs more quickly.

Using a customer-oriented data base, a business can attach a detailed personal transaction history to the names of its customers. This service history then becomes the cornerstone on which to build a more personal relationship with the customer. No longer will the customer's relationship with the company be fragmented and departmentalized. One central ledger can include all of the customer's accounts. A financial-services organization, whose different divisions handle a single customer's different accounts — mortgage, annuities, insurance policies, mutual fund investments, and so on — can now centralize that customer's service. The customer won't have to receive a separate statement for each account or call different divisions to get information on different accounts. Further, when a change occurs in one account area, the change can be reflected instantly in the customer's total record.

In the hands of frontline employees, complete customer information presents a powerful service and sales tool. Employees can let a repeat customer know about new products or services that the customer's past purchasing history indicates might be of special interest to him or her. Furthermore, since current technology allows customer files to be called up from many different locations, service representatives in regional offices and agencies can often provide customers with the same information they would normally get only from the home office. Through the use of customer-oriented data bases, a record of each service transaction can be added to an existing customer file with little difficulty. These updates help sketch an increasingly detailed profile of each customer's preferences. The files can be used to diagnose problems, identify unstated needs, and sell additional products and services. Unlike some corporate assets, these customer files appreciate rather than depreciate in value.[6]

Toll-Free Numbers

Responsive companies also make sure that (1) telephone access to their services is readily available, (2) the waiting time to receive service is short, and (3) their services are available at hours and locations that are convenient for their customers. Insurers, for example, often provide toll-free 800 telephone numbers for producers, policyowners, and other customers, and print these numbers on premium notices and other customer communications to encourage customers to use these numbers. Some companies use several toll-free lines. Along with a general toll-free line for the entire company, many companies use special toll-free numbers to handle specific inquiries regarding such topics as retirement benefits, survivor benefits, various types of annuity services, and group major medical benefits. By providing such telephone lines, the company can ensure that specially trained people are available to answer technical questions and to provide specific services to agents and consumers.

Besides improving service to their customers, companies also benefit in other ways from being responsive to customers' needs. For example, the availability of a toll-free telephone number is a positive selling point with customers, because transactions can be handled much more quickly on the telephone than through the mail. By solving problems quickly, before they get out of hand, insurers increase customer satisfaction and save themselves unnecessary headaches. Furthermore, use of the telephone often means less paperwork, lower costs, and reduced duplication of effort among consumers, producers, field offices, and the home office. Finally, customers who can easily contact the company about problems are less likely to seek assistance from regulatory authorities.

Take a look at Customer Service in Action 4–1 to find out how some insurance companies and insurance associations are using toll-free numbers. In Chapter 6, you can learn more about the benefits and the difficulties associated with toll-free numbers by reading Issues in Customer Service 6–1.

CUSTOMER SERVICE IN ACTION 4–1

Hello, Hotline?

The call that came in one afternoon put the consumer relations department into high gear. After all, the staff was supposed to be able to answer any question about Kemper Group insurance, and this caller was no different. "I have to know where to find one of those buckskin jackets the actors wear on the Kemper Insurance commercial," she said. It took some doing, but when she hung up, she had her answer.

Although her insurance question was unorthodox, her research method was not. She simply had dialed one of the thousands of insurance information hotlines proliferating across the country.

Called Action Lines, Customer Response Numbers, Help Lines, and a host of other names, toll-free 800 numbers are growing in importance among concerned corporations and associations trying to market products, handle complaints, and answer questions.

Use of such 800 numbers is much more than just a short-lived trend. Customer reaction to them generally has ranged from excellent to spectacular. A Detroit auto manufacturer received so many responses the day after it publicized its 800 number that a central telephone switching system blew a fuse. Some Silicon Valley computer firms have received so many calls for information that some have begun charging callers for the privilege of speaking with their experts. And Kellogg Company had to stop publicizing a toll-free number for Sugar Frosted Flakes when it was inundated with young callers wanting to talk with Tony the Tiger.

In 1989, AT&T telephone directories contained 200,000 toll-free numbers, almost double the number in 1987. In 1974, consumers made 234 million interstate toll-free calls over AT&T's 800 lines. In 1985, they made 3 billion such calls, and in 1989, they made 8 billion toll-free calls.

Says Ralph Dobriner, a spokesperson for AT&T, "800 numbers are one of the company's fastest growing services."

There's no question that hotlines are hot news. But how good are they? Here's how several insurance companies and agencies answer that question.

Insurance Companies

AT&T directories in 1985 listed about 680 toll-free numbers to insurers and insurance organizations. The number of lines, the staffing and the role they play in each company vary widely.

A number of insurance companies use their hotlines to field a broad range of inquiries, mainly concerning claims, billing, and the company's products. For instance, in 1971 The Travelers started its first consumer-information line by offering generic information to consumers. In 1972, 12,400 customers called. By 1985, that number had risen to 48,700. And in 1989, 157,000 customers used the line.

The telephone lines are manned by young homemakers and by retirees, nearly all working on a part-time basis. Using retired employees has worked especially well for the company because they are familiar with the product line and do not

need to learn new terminology. Using part-time workers also is an excellent way to combat burnout—a major problem among employees who operate toll-free telephone lines.

John Hancock Group, with 62 lines at its corporate headquarters in Boston handling 10,000 to 12,000 calls a week, is one of the busiest hotlines in the industry. John Hancock recently activated eight 800 lines in San Mateo, California, to help establish Hancock Property and Casualty's West Coast presence, particularly since its property/casualty field offices are not automated. About half of the calls on these lines are from agents; the remainder from customers.

Some insurance companies activated hotlines for specific purposes, and some are seeking ways to put them to new uses. CIGNA Corporation uses its Action Line to react to emergency claims, such as late-night auto accidents or fires. The hotline at the headquarters of the Utica National Group is dedicated to receiving policyholders' accident reports. The Chubb Group lists an 800 number in its personal lines advertisements so potential customers can locate an agent in their area or ask for information on the company's personal lines coverage and service. The Hartford Insurance Group offers toll-free lines for its customers who are billed directly. Liberty Mutual Insurance publicized toll-free numbers in an attempt to solicit information about traffic accidents. John Hancock service representatives answer auto policyholders' questions and then launch into a pitch about homeowner's insurance; the promotion has proved quite successful.

Aetna Life and Casualty originally planned to use its hotline, called Telefast, as an emergency claim contact number, but found that consumers began using it for just about everything else. The 10 lines, which operate 24 hours a day, seven days a week, take about 15,000 calls a month, some 750 each day. But when the unexpected occurs, the number of calls soars. When Hurricane Gloria hit in September 1985, the company received 650 hurricane-related calls in only two days. Aetna considers Telefast an adjunct to the information dissemination done by its independent agents.

Problems on the Line

Answering questions and responding to complaints are two of the biggest functions of any hotline. To do the job well, hotline staffers need a knowledge of business, finance, current events, and a wide background in insurance. Much more than telephone operators, these people have to know how to soothe an irate person while searching through vast files of complex insurance information. The job requires people with a calm, upbeat disposition, people who are interested in and want to help customers.

"You never know who's going to be at the other end of the phone," says Arlene Lilly, who oversees the hotline as manager of information services at the American Council of Life Insurance (ACLI). "There's always something different coming at you."

Robin DiNatale, a hotline manager for the Independent Insurance Agents of America (IIAA), says, "You have to enjoy talking, and you have to be able to deal with people who demand service."

Mary Viveiros, supervisor of consumer information at The Travelers, says, "You have to learn how to defuse the customer's anger when necessary."

Hotline operators aren't cut from any one bolt of cloth. Says Brian Zibuda, customer service manager for the property/casualty division of the John Hancock Group, "We've got mothers returning to the work force, recent college grads, waitresses —they can withstand pressure real well— and even drama majors."

Source: Adapted with permission of the publisher from Gauri Bhatia, "Hello, Hotline?" *Insurance Review*, November 1986, pp. 27–29.

Tangible Factors

Tangible factors are the physical aspects of a company and its employees. Tangible factors include (1) the appearance of a company's buildings, offices, and other physical facilities; (2) the appearance of company personnel; and (3) the quality and appearance of any supplies, equipment, or other items used to provide service, such as the company's stationery, policy forms, policy statements, and so forth. Physical appearance is frequently a critical factor when customers judge the service they receive. Customers notice whether offices are neat and well organized, whether stationery is appealing. They notice whether employees are well groomed and well spoken. They notice whether letters are well written and present a warm, caring manner. They notice whether forms are easy to read and fill out. Although tangible factors may seem superficial, they create an impression that can attract or repel a customer.

The Purpose of the Model

The purpose of analyzing customer service using the model developed by Parasuraman, Zeithaml, and Berry is to find out what service customers expect and what service they perceive they are getting in relation to the five dimensions. Companies can also use the model to measure customers' perceptions of their major competitors. Customer Service in Action 4–2, which concludes this chapter, presents a brief description of the way that Metropolitan Life Insurance Company used the model to measure the quality of its customer service. By conducting the type of research done by Metropolitan, companies can locate potential problems in customers' perceptions of the service they are provided and make corrections to those problems.

CUSTOMER SERVICE IN ACTION 4–2

Metropolitan's Customer Service Surveys

In 1985, Metropolitan Life Insurance Company began a corporate-wide effort to improve the quality of its customer service. One of the steps that Metropolitan took in this improvement effort was to use Parasuraman, Zeithaml, and Berry's SERVQUAL model to conduct customer satisfaction research. Examples of how this model was used include: (1) a survey of internal customers, employees who used the company's information systems, and (2) a survey of external customers, consumers who dealt with the company's group health insurance claims operations.

The Information Systems survey is a specific application of the SERVQUAL approach. It consists of 32 pairs of expectation/perception statements like the pair below, which asks about the responsiveness dimension.

	◀Strongly Agree					Strongly Disagree▶
Expectation Statement The availability of on-line computer networks should meet customer business needs.	7	6	5	4	3	2	1
Perception Statement The availability of on-line computer networks provided by the Information Systems Department meets my business needs.	7	6	5	4	3	2	1

From its internal survey, Metropolitan found that its customers were pleased with the confidentiality provided by the Information Systems Department, the equipment that the company provided, the personalized care received from contact personnel, and the expertise provided by the Information Systems Department. On the other hand, the survey also found that the Information Systems Department could improve in the following areas: soliciting customer feedback, pricing its services, response time, communications, training its customers, operating hours, and its responsiveness to unexpected requests for assistance.

The results of the feedback survey were given to everyone who responded to the survey. The Information Systems Department established customer advisory groups to help develop solutions to problems identified in the survey. Metropolitan now repeats the survey annually.

In the example of an external survey, Metropolitan not only measured customer evaluations of service quality, it also ana-

lyzed the results in light of internal and industry-wide standards. The results of the survey showed that the following four things were most important to Metropolitan's group health insurance customers: accurate claim settlement, prompt service, understandable explanation of benefits paid, and "quality" telephone service.

The comparison of customer evaluations to industry standards raised a number of interesting questions. For example, consider the concept of prompt service. In the insurance industry, a generally accepted standard is to process 80 percent of health insurance claims within 10 working days after the claim reaches the insurer's offices. Customers, however, begin counting processing time from the moment they submit their claims to their employer, and since employers may sometimes take several days to verify a claim, Metropolitan was not meeting its customers' expectations. From Metropolitan's perspective, it was meeting standards. From its customers' perspective, it was not.

Source: Adapted from seminar papers presented by Mary LoSardo of Metropolitan Life. Adapted with permission of Metropolitan Life.

Key Terms

perception
expectation
service gap
expected service
perceived service
gap analysis
customer expectations
management perceptions
service specifications
service delivery
actual service levels
advertised service levels

consumer education
service dimensions
reliability
assurance
empathy
responsiveness
policy-oriented data base
customer-oriented data base
toll-free 800 numbers
tangible factors
action lines
hotlines

Notes

1. Stephanie C. Consie, "Survey Measures Service Times," *Resource*, LOMA, April 1991.

2. Christian Gronoos, "Innovative Marketing Strategies and Organization Structures for Service Firms," in *Emerging Perspectives on Services Marketing*, ed. Leonard L. Berry, G. Lynn Shostack, and Gregory D. Upah (Chicago: American Marketing Association, 1983), p. 9.

3. A. Parasuraman, Valarie A. Zeithaml, and Leonard L. Berry, *A Conceptual Model of Service Quality and Its Implications for Future Research* (Cambridge, MA: Marketing Science Institute, 1984), pp. 3, 11.

4. The sections on gap analysis and the five dimensions of customer service are based primarily on three sources: A. Parasuraman, Valarie A. Zeithaml, and Leonard L. Berry, *A Conceptual Model of Service Quality and Its Implications for Future Research* (Cambridge, MA: Marketing Science Institute, 1984); Leonard L. Berry, David R. Bennett, and Carter W. Brown, *Service Quality: A Profit Strategy for Financial Institutions* (Homewood, IL: Dow Jones-Irwin, 1989); Jan Carlson, *Customer Focus Research: Building Customer Loyalty as a Strategic Weapon* (Atlanta: TouchStone Marketing Research, 1989).

5. During their research, Parasuraman, Zeithaml, and Berry identified ten criteria (called dimensions) that customers typically use to judge the quality of service they receive. Because some overlap existed among the original ten dimensions, the researchers later condensed them to five dimensions.

6. W. Earl Sasser and William E. Fulmer, "Creating Personalized Service Delivery Systems," in *Service Management Effectiveness*, ed. David E. Bowen, Richard B. Chase, and Thomas G. Cummings and Associates (San Francisco: Jossey-Bass, Inc., Publishers, 1990), pp. 220–21.

CHAPTER 5

Customer Service Research

After studying this chapter, you should be able to

- Describe the qualitative and quantitative phases of customer service research
- Describe qualitative and quantitative research techniques, such as focus group interviews and surveys
- Explain the concept of sampling and its use in research
- Identify and discuss the different types and sources of research data

Introduction

In Chapter 4, we presented a model for understanding customers and described the expectations and perceptions that affect the way in which customers judge customer service. We described the gaps that commonly cause the quality of customer service to be less than what customers had expected. And we discussed the service dimensions that customers believe are most important when they evaluate the quality of service they receive.

In Chapter 5, we will describe customer service research itself, including various categories of research and techniques for conducting that research. As we discussed in the last chapter, only by conducting research can a company accurately determine its customers' expectations and whether its customers perceive that their expectations are being met.

Typically, customer service research can be divided into the qualitative phase and the quantitative phase. In the qualitative phase, the insurance company gathers information from individuals and from small, fairly informal groups of customers. This information can then be used to identify the subjects and issues that should be examined in the quantitative research phase. The quantitative phase typically investigates a larger, more representative sample than the qualitative research phase and usually produces results that are more generally applicable to particular market segments of customers.

The Qualitative Research Phase

The purpose of *qualitative research* is to examine what people think and how they feel about a subject, so the researcher can learn about the general nature of a problem, including its causes and solutions and the factors that need to be considered in addressing the problem. Qualitative research, which is often referred to as *exploratory research*, is not intended to provide conclusions. Instead, it is used to investigate a situation and provide direction for further research. For example, insurance companies don't always know what kind of customer service information they need. Usually, they'll see the symptoms of a problem (such as increasing customer complaints) rather than the problem itself. When companies can only identify symptoms and are not sure how to define a problem, they often conduct qualitative research, which frequently leads to more specific research.

Typically, qualitative research is highly flexible and unstructured. It is usually conducted using a relatively small number of people in group sessions, although it can also be conducted using in-depth interviews with individuals. Some common forms of qualitative research that are most useful in customer service research are

- focus group interviews,
- advisory panel discussions,
- in-depth interviews,
- company visits,
- employee interviews, and
- examination of customer complaints.

Focus Group Interviews

Focus group interviews are unstructured, informal sessions during which six to ten participants are asked to discuss their opinions about a certain topic. Focus groups, which are normally led by a professional group moderator, help companies understand consumers' general perceptions, expectations, attitudes, and opinions about specific topics. Insurers also use focus groups to help them generate ideas for new services and modifications for current services. Focus groups are not made up of consumers only. Insurance companies also gather valuable information from focus groups made up of producers, field office employees, or home office employees.

Researchers use focus group interviews for several reasons:

- Focus group discussions usually last for several hours, thus providing an opportunity to gather a good deal of in-depth anecdotal information from participants.

- Focus group discussions are an excellent source of qualitative research data regarding what people think and how they feel about a particular subject.
- Focus group interviews allow for a great deal of flexibility. Although the moderator will have certain topics for focus group participants to discuss, the agenda can be modified as needed to uncover additional insights as the discussion progresses.
- Focus group participants are usually highly motivated. Although most group members are offered an incentive for participating (such as a meal or a small amount of money), the real incentive for many participants is a chance to air their opinions about a particular subject.

Focus groups require well-trained moderators who can keep the discussion lively and on target without dominating the group. Moderators must be careful to keep any one member from monopolizing the discussion and must draw out members who are reluctant to state their opinions.

While focus group interviews are excellent sources of qualitative data, they have some distinct limitations: the attitudes and opinions of the participants involved in the focus groups may not be truly representative of the overall population that the company is trying to research. Therefore, companies must be careful about generalizing the information they gain from focus group interviews. In addition, some of the participants' comments may appear to be contradictory or hard to interpret. On the other hand, focus group interviews can give companies a sense of the general issues that concern their customers. And companies can then use the information obtained from the focus groups to develop more accurate and quantifiable research.

Both the Life Insurance Marketing and Research Association (LIMRA) and the Insurance Consumer Affairs Exchange (ICAE) conduct focus group interviews with insurance consumers. Issues in Customer Service numbers 5–1 and 5–2 present some of the conclusions and recommendations that these two organizations have presented in reports developed from their qualitative research. Many, though not all, of these conclusions were substantiated by later quantifiable research.

Conclusions from
Building Policyholder Relations: A Report on Four Focus Groups

Consumers tend to see the insurance industry as insensitive and inaccessible.

> Customer: "I had to deal with the life insurance company two days ago because of my retirement. And I talked to seven different people before I got the person I wanted, and I told every single person exactly what I wanted. 'Oh, we don't handle that, I don't handle that, we'll send you something.'"

> Customer: "Seems like they're such a big bureaucracy. 'You need to talk to so-and-so. I'll get back to you.' All that stuff. They're just a maze of bureaucracy, and they're trying to wear you down, say to hell with it and hang up."

The perception that the life insurance industry is highly competitive bolsters consumers' satisfaction with the industry.

Many focus group participants believe that most life insurance companies and agents do not provide satisfactory service after the sale is made. They fail to keep their clients informed of changes in their insurance needs and the availability of new products and services.

Consumers feel they have the right to expect five key qualities from insurance companies:

1. A policy with understandable provisions
2. Fairness in dealing with customers
3. Presentation of the rationale for changes affecting policyholders

4. Responsiveness to questions and complaints
5. Rewards for long-term, loyal customers

> Customer: "The first couple of years are critical to keep someone with you. Give your good customers a discount at three years."

Consumers expect their agent to play a key role in inquiries and complaint-handling.

Focus group participants see the role of the home office as providing information to educate the policyholder, while the role of the agent is to analyze the policyholder's particular needs and make the sale.

> Customer: "Outside the fact of somebody selling you something, there should be a customer representative, whose job is to mediate between the consumer and the company."

Participants also pointed out four key steps insurance companies can take to improve their relationships with consumers:

1. Provide help in using the policy
2. Review policies to assure they are up-to-date
3. Maintain a clear division between informational and sales activity
4. Avoid gimmicks or other insincere programs

Among the other things that participants said they would like were: an owner's manual that explains in simple language what a policy covers, a toll-free number to contact the company, a directory of company services, and the address and phone number of the state insurance commissioner (or provincial superintendent of insurance) as a resource for complaint resolution.

> Customer: "Given the choice between one insurance company that had an 800 number and one that didn't, I'd take the one with the 800 number. Although, I called [a company] about a mortgage product I was interested in. And I got 45 minutes of a tape, the same tape, over and over again. That was really infuriating."

Source: Adapted with permission of the publisher from *Building Policyholder Relations: A Report on Four Focus Groups*, prepared by Mathew Greenwald & Associates for the Insurance Consumer Affairs Exchange (ICAE), April 1989.

ISSUES IN CUSTOMER SERVICE 5-2

Conclusions from *Understanding Customers: What Research Reveals about What Consumers Really Want*

What do customers want from insurance companies?

1. *Purchase information*

   > Customer: "I consider myself educated, but I don't know about insurance. The main reason for that is because you can't read the policy. I just have to trust my agent. I hope he's got me covered."

2. *Post-sale information*

   Customers want information on a regular basis about the current status of their insurance and whether or not it is continuing to meet their needs. Customers also want someone to tell them about new insurance products and what these new products mean for their current insurance program.

3. *Personal touch*

   Customers want to be treated as individuals, important individuals.

   > Customer: "I have one person that I can ask for and talk to. When I call I just mention my name and she knows who I am. She just takes care of everything right away."

What do customers want regarding transactions?

1. *Accessibility*

   Customers want to know who they should contact when they need something done, and they would like it to be one person, not a whole series of people.

2. *Performance*

Customers want things done right, and they want them done quickly.

> Customer: "I'm not expecting the world, but I want them to do something reasonable to solve the problem."

3. *Ease of handling*

Customers want transactions to be simple.

What do customers want from agents?

1. *Contact*

Customers want agents to keep in touch with them after the sale. When agents keep in touch, customers consider them to be their personal agents, and they are less likely to buy additional insurance from other agents or other companies.

2. *Regular checkups*

Customers want agents to check with them on a regular basis to make sure that their insurance coverage is up-to-date.

> Customer: "I wanted to review my

life insurance—this was about 15 years ago. I had to call them to review it. Never since I became a client and customer, never did they suggest that they review my insurance by 5-year increments, 10-year increments, or whatever."

3. *Help in dealing with the company*

Because most policyholders don't understand insurance or insurance company operations, they are uncomfortable when dealing with an insurance company. They would much rather call their agent and have the agent deal with the company.

4. *Unexpected service*

Customers expect certain things with their insurance, such as the right to take out policy loans. And when they ask for and receive the services that they feel are their due, the insurance company keeps them from being unhappy with its service. But to make customers positively happy with a company's service, the company must do the little things that raise service above the norm: little gifts on birthdays or policy anniversaries, unexpected phone calls just to see if everything is going okay.

Source: Adapted with permission of the publisher from Albert J. Sheridan, *Understanding Customers: What Research Reveals About What Consumers Really Want* (Hartford: LIMRA, 1989), pp. 18–32.

Advisory Panels

In addition to using focus groups to gather information, many insurance companies have standing ***advisory panels*** that help them stay close to their customers. These advisory panels may consist of the company's producers, the company's policyowners and contract holders, field office employees, or home office employees. Like focus groups, these panels provide a company with useful qualitative information about the services that the company provides and suggestions for improving those services. Unlike focus groups, however, advisory panels meet on a regular basis and provide companies with a continuous flow of qualitative information. In exchange, the company should report back to the advisory panel concerning their suggestions. Otherwise, the panel members may view the company's interest as insincere and stop participating.

The Travelers has an advisory panel called the Mature Market Advisory Board, which advises the company about the concerns and perspectives of older consumers. The board consists of six retired people and meets every three months. The meetings are highly focused, with representatives from The Travelers asking the members for their opinions about specific issues, such as a particular product or advertising campaign. The Travelers has gained a number of valuable insights from this advisory board.

In-Depth Interviews

In-depth interviews concentrate on a few respondents who are interviewed individually. The interview questions are loosely structured and may consist of only a checklist of topics relevant to the research study. This research technique is most often used when a company needs a great deal of information from important customers in a geographically dispersed market. Respondents in these situations typically have little to do with each other. They may even be competitors. Therefore, they might be reluctant to answer questions in a group setting. Although time-consuming and expensive to conduct, in-depth interviews can be extremely useful for providing complex and technical customer information. In customer service, in-depth interviews are most commonly used in business-to-business customer service situations, such as providing service to commercial clients with large group policies or to independent property/casualty firms, such as national brokerage houses.

Informal Qualitative Research

In addition to formal processes, such as using focus groups and advisory panels, insurance companies also use less formal means of gathering qualitative information. Many companies bring producers and field office employees into the home office to let them observe home office operations. In turn, home office employees visit field offices and observe their operations. This process allows both groups to get to know each other's particular concerns, perceptions, and expectations and allows each group to give and receive recommendations for improvements in service. Moreover, by providing a mechanism to allow various groups of service providers to get to know one another, communication among these groups is improved, thus helping to avert service problems in the future. Whenever possible, these types of visits should be extended to consumers as well, thus giving them a chance to air their concerns and gain a more accurate perception of company operations. For example, a number of insurance companies offer public tours of their home office operations.

Another informal means of gathering qualitative information is through *job rotation*. By moving people through various jobs, a company can gain fresh perspectives on its operations and services. Several insurance companies have their senior executives work periodically in frontline service jobs, answering the phones and responding to complaints. By seeing operational problems and service demands from a frontline perspective, company executives get a better idea of the practical modifications needed in order to allow their companies to provide service that will satisfy their customers. During one such session at CUNA Mutual Insurance Society, for example, senior executives spent several weeks performing customer service duties. One executive, after helping a customer go through the 39 steps required to file a claim, saw to it that the number of steps was cut in half.[1]

Another means of gathering information on internal customer service satisfaction is exit interviewing. In *exit interviews*, employees who are leaving the company are asked to give their impressions of the company. These departing employees can often provide valuable insights into the factors that help or hinder the delivery of quality service in the company.

Finally, companies can gather qualitative information by monitoring complaints. Complaints are free of charge. Complaints come over the phone and through the mail, via word of mouth, and by interoffice memoranda. They come from consumers, producers, field office employees, home office employees, regulatory agencies, and consumer groups.

Complaints can lead to important insights about the specific services that insurance companies offer. Based on such complaints, insurance companies can make adjustments in their services or products so that they better fit the needs of their customers. According to a study of the scientific instruments and machine tool industries, 80 percent of all product innovations are initiated by customers making inquiries and complaints.[2] If these industries can find such profitable use for complaints, certainly the insurance industry can too.

For many businesses, access to valuable complaint information is difficult because no central records are kept concerning consumer complaints. However, this is not a problem for insurance companies. All life insurance companies in the United States maintain centralized complaint logs describing every written consumer complaint received by the company. These logs are required by state statutes and must be available for periodic review by market conduct examiners. Although state regulations vary with respect to the specific information that must be logged and the information that must be reported to the state, the complaint log typically indicates the

- name of the individual making the complaint and the policyowner (if the policyowner is a different person),
- policy number and type of policy,
- date the complaint was received,
- nature of the complaint,
- action taken,
- date of resolution,
- state in which the complaint originated, and
- agent, field office, or home office department involved.

In most states, the insurance company must respond to the consumer within 10 days of receiving the complaint, though in some cases the response can simply indicate that the complaint has been received and describe the preliminary actions being taken. If the complaint has been referred to the insurance company by a state insurance department, then the state insurance department must receive copies of the correspondence. Insurance department regulations also specify the information that must be included on the annual or quarterly reports on complaints that companies must submit to the insurance departments.

Many insurance companies use such centralized complaint information as a basis for various internal reports describing common consumer complaints and suggesting methods of changing operations to avoid such complaints in the future. For example, Aetna Life and Casualty's complaint registration and recording system is used to give the company early warning about negative service trends and perceptions. Other companies also use complaint information to develop reports for regional marketing directors concerning common complaints received from consumers in their areas.

Note that the complaint logs required by statute describe only consumer complaints. Thus, complaints made by another company or by other customers (such as producers) are generally not handled in as organized a fashion. If a company wants to ensure that complaints by these customers are responded to, then it must establish a system that makes it easy for its customers to register complaints and that ensures that all complaints are given appropriate attention.

For an enlightening discussion of what happens to businesses when they don't listen to complaints or don't make it easy for customers to complain, look at Issues in Customer Service 5–3.

ISSUES IN CUSTOMER SERVICE 5–3

Strategies for Improving the Satisfaction of Business Customers

Attention: Unhappy users of Burroughs B-800 and similar Burroughs computer hardware and software.

Our firm is preparing to sue the Burroughs Corporation. We would like to find other firms who, like us, feel that overly zealous computer salespeople may have misrepresented the Burroughs B-800 or similar product lines to them. We wish to combine our information in efforts to seek a solution to our problems using all available legal remedies. All responses will be treated confidentially.

The Wall Street Journal, July 19, 1980

This advertisement suggests that at least one customer of a major computer manufacturer was dissatisfied. The 350 responses to the ad and a subsequent lawsuit provided evidence of widespread dissatisfaction. The incident brings into focus a question seldom addressed: How do businesses react to problems with products and services used in their operations?

The complaint behavior of businesses using products and services purchased from other businesses has not been subjected to careful scrutiny. Apparently, management often assumes that salespeople or service representatives will resolve the overwhelming majority of problems. Our experience suggests that few companies solicit complaints from their business customers. Preliminary results from a survey of corporate accounts of an automobile rental company and anecdotal evidence from four additional companies indicate that most companies do not escalate complaints beyond the customer contact representative but, instead, take market action, such as nonrenewal of contracts and brand switching.

Three recent major studies of individual consumer complaint behavior have indicated that many consumers who encounter unsatisfactory products or services do not complain because they do not consider it worth their time, or they do not believe the organization is interested in solving their problems. Those who do complain tend to be more brand loyal than those who do not. Interestingly, business customers seem to behave in a similar manner. Since most business depends on loyal customers, effective complaint handling is vital to successful business strategy.

Little attention has been devoted by researchers to the reactions of business executives to product or service deficiencies. But the following assumptions seem to be common:

- Companies assume that business customers will voice complaints if a defective product or service is encountered.
- Executives assume (because a salesperson or service representative is on the scene) that the problem will either be solved at that level or that the representative will request his or her management to provide a referral to the appropriate person.
- The company often assumes that if the salesperson or service representative is not responsive, the purchaser will escalate the complaint.
- Service is seldom blamed for a loss of business. The company assumes that when most business customers discontinue using a product, it is because of price.

Our experience, working with private clients in five industries, indicates that in repeated instances none of the aforementioned assumptions hold true.

In one instance, we assisted a major car-rental company in surveying almost 1,000 of its small- and medium-sized corporate accounts. We received 189 replies for a response rate of 18.9 percent. Of those responding, 81 companies reported unsatisfactory service in at least some area —that is, auto performance, counter personnel, reservations, and so forth. Fully 39 percent of those who had encountered inadequate service had not complained to any employee of the rental company. The most often cited reasons were, "it would not do any good" and "it was not worth the time or hassle."

The next set of questions addressed the relationships between complaint behavior and repurchase intention. Of those companies that did not complain, 33 percent had reduced the number of rentals from the rental-car company. In other words, these customers consciously switched brands. Of those who did complain but were not satisfied, almost three-quarters (74 percent) used the company less than before the inadequate service occurred. This implies that if a customer goes to the trouble of complaining and then is not satisfied, the tendency to switch brands is even higher. Finally, of those corporate accounts that did complain and were satisfied, only 26 percent were using the company services less than before.

The vice-president for administration of a major mailing house indicated the organization had received unsatisfactory service from the company that had installed its internal communications hardware. The hardware—including telephones, call directors, and data transmission equipment—often malfunctioned. Also, service was slow and ineffective. The account generated approximately $300,000 per year in rental fees.

When asked if complaints had been filed, the vice-president responded, "Certainly, we complained every time the service people came out to fix the equipment." When asked if the complaint had been escalated to a senior executive, the vice-president said, "No, we simply were dissatisfied with service, so we didn't renew their contract. We switched to another company."

A small consulting firm reported it was renting word-processing equipment for approximately $1,000 per month. The office manager was under pressure because of excessive down times due to machine malfunction. At the end of the one-year lease, she decided to switch to a different brand of word-processing equipment even though it was 10 percent more expensive. When asked whether she had filed complaints, she stated, "We complained to the serviceman each time he came out, and we complained to the local marketing representative. The representative stated that they had been having problems with the equipment, but there was nothing more which could be done other than expediting service." Note that the office manager complained only to the marketing representative, not directly to the manufacturer.

A commercial lines insurance agent has a strong incentive to maintain satisfied policyholders, since renewed accounts lead to higher levels of personal income. However, when one insurance executive was asked why approximately 6,000 small accounts had cancelled group policies in the previous year, he indicated that no research had been done because they were relatively small accounts (group policies of less than 10 persons). Earlier, we discussed business-complaint behavior with the president of a small company that had cancelled its policy. The small company had complained to the agent about claims and other administrative problems but had received an unsatisfactory response. The insurance executive explained that incentives were not as strong for small accounts because salespeople were paid a substantial portion of the first-year premium "up front" and a lesser amount for subsequent years. Another insurance executive acknowledged that the health benefits officer in a company may discourage the employees from choosing a group health plan if the company has had administrative difficulties with or previous complaints about a particular insurance company. The health-benefits officer can avoid future complaints and problems by doing this. Therefore, an insurance company may lose market share to competing health plans due to previous problems and be unaware of the reasons.

In addition to the foregoing industries, we have witnessed cases where the experience of a corporate executive has drastically affected the company's purchasing behavior. For example, an executive of a trade association had severe difficulties with a major airline. This executive specified that the airline be avoided unless no other alternative existed. As a result, more than $100,000 per year in air travel (out of approximately $300,000 per year spent by the company's staff) was lost by the airline.

Source: Adapted with permission of the publisher from John A. Goodman and Larry M. Robinson, "Strategies for Improving the Satisfaction of Business Customers," *Business,* April–June 1982, pp. 40–44.

Quantitative Research

The results of a company's qualitative research give a company a good idea of the nature of a problem, but in most cases, the information is not sufficiently complete or reliable to be used by itself. Instead, the company uses such results to provide direction for developing and conducting more extensive, structured research. Thus, the next phase of research is quantitative research. In order for its quantitative research to be effective, however, a company must include enough of the right kinds of customers in its research base in order to reduce the chances that the information that is gathered will be misleading or inaccurate. To gather information that best represents the overall views of a company's customers, it is necessary to use a technique called sampling.

Sampling means examining a portion of a group in order to develop conclusions about the entire group. The entire group is called the *population*, and the portion, or subset, of the population that is studied in order to develop conclusions about the total population is called the *sample*. The sample may be selected at random from the entire population, or it may be chosen in accordance with specific, well-defined criteria. Researchers use samples for several reasons:

- Statistically, researchers have found that the information gathered from a well-chosen sample is just as accurate as, and frequently more useful than, information gathered from an entire population.
- Researchers have also found that examining an entire population is time-consuming and expensive, usually too time-consuming and too expensive for most companies to afford. For many customer research projects, for example, the potential number of customers from whom data could be gathered might number in the thousands or millions. Because questioning all customers is neither practical nor necessary in most cases, researchers generally collect data from only a part of the total group of customers.
- Because some customers view marketing research or customer service research as an aggravation or intrusion into their lives, companies want to reduce the potential for such intrusions. By using sampling, companies contact only a portion of their customers and thus are able to reduce the potential for intrusion and the amount of their customers' time that they take up with research.

- The larger the amount of data collected, the more difficult it is to analyze and the easier it is to make mistakes and miss significant information. The use of sampling allows researchers to reduce the number of errors they are likely to make.

Once a sample is chosen, the company can begin to gather quantitative data. The quantitative research phase allows companies to use more structured data-collection methods and larger samples than those used in the qualitative phase. Information obtained during the quantitative phase can be quantified or summarized statistically. The most frequently used method for conducting quantitative research about customer service is the survey.

Surveys are data-collection methods that use structured data-collection forms, such as questionnaires, to gather data directly from the population being studied. The three major survey methods are personal interviews, mail surveys, and telephone surveys. Figure 5–1 describes the relative strengths and weaknesses of each method.

In most situations, researchers gather data from a representative sample of a total population, analyze the data (including the relationships between the factors or variables being studied), and then develop conclusions about the population as a whole. In other situations, the company surveys all its customers. For example, an insurance company may include a survey with all newly issued policies, or a company may send a short survey along with premium notices. Although all customers will not take the time to complete the survey, all will have been given the opportunity to let the company know how they perceive the service the company provides. LOMA conducts several surveys relating to customer service: *Consumer Focus*, *Producer Focus*, and the *Service Turnaround Times Survey*. The first two are opinion surveys that help a company find out what its policyholders and producers think of its customer service. The third survey gathers information on how long it takes insurance companies to provide specific services.

One insurance company that has been a leader in using surveys to gather information about customer satisfaction is USAA. Once a month USAA Life Insurance Company's Work in Process (WIP) system produces an activity report of completed transactions. Customers who have completed transactions with the company are chosen randomly from the activity report and are sent a satisfaction survey. Surveys are returned to the Quality Assurance Department, which sees that the results of the surveys are distributed to the appropriate departments to correct any recurring problems. In addition, USAA

Figure 5–1
Pros and Cons of the Three Major Survey Methods

	Personal Interview	Mail Survey	Telephone Survey
Versatility of questioning	High—interviewer can adapt questions based on what transpires during the interview	Little—uses highly standardized format limited to simple, clearly worded questions	Moderate—more versatile than mail, less versatile than personal interview
Amount of data that can be collected from each respondent	Large amount	Small, moderate, or large amount	Moderate amount
Time required	Moderate amount—depends on size of sample	Can be slow—questionaire development time, mailing time, and analysis time can be long	Quite fast
Cost	Usually most expensive because of interviewer's time and travel	Usually least expensive, assuming response rate is adequate	Inexpensive
Accuracy	Varies—least accurate on sensitive questions	Varies—most accurate on sensitive questions	Varies—moderate on sensitive questions
	Potential for misunderstood questions is low because interviewer can clarify them	Potential for misunderstood questions is high	Potential for misunderstood questions is moderate
	Potential for interviewer to influence answers is high	No potential for interviewer to influence answers, though phrasing of questions can influence answers	Potential fo interviewer to influence answers is moderate

sends out another more extensive service questionnaire every six months to gather more information about customers' perceptions of the quality of customer service at USAA.

Look at Figure 5–2 for an example of some types of questions that might be asked on a customer service survey. Such survey questions are designed to provide quantitative data that can be analyzed statistically. The first group of questions seeks quantitative inform-

Figure 5–2
Excerpt from the SERVQUAL Multiple-Item Scale.

Instructions and Statements for Measuring Consumer Expectations and Perceptions

Directions: This survey deals with your opinions of _____ services. Please show the extent to which you think firms offering _____ services should possess the features described by each statement. If you strongly agree that these firms should possess a feature, circle the number 7. If you strongly disagree that these firms should possess a feature, circle the number 1. If your feelings are not strong, circle one of the numbers in the middle. There are no right or wrong answers. All we are interested in is a number that best shows your expectations about firms offering _____ services.

E1. They should have up-to-date equipment.
E5. When these companies promise to do something by a certain time, they should do so.
E7. These firms should be dependable.
E13. It is okay if they are too busy to respond to customer requests promptly.
E19. Customers should be able to trust employees of these firms.
E23. Their employees should be polite.
E30. They shouldn't be expected to have operating hours convenient to all their customers.

Directions: The following set of statements relates your feelings about XYZ. For each statement, please show the extent to which you think XYZ has the feature described by each statement. Once again, circling a 7 means that you strongly agree that XYZ has that feature, and circling a 1 means you strongly disagree. You may circle any of the numbers in the middle that show how strong your feelings are. There are no right or wrong answers. All we are interested in is a number that best shows your perceptions of XYZ.

P1. XYZ has up-to-date equipment.
P5. When XYZ promises to do something by a certain time, it does.
P7. XYZ is dependable.
P13. Employees of XYZ are too busy to respond to your requests promptly.
P19. You can trust employees of XYZ.
P23. XYZ employees are polite.
P30. XYZ does not have operating hours convenient to all its customers.

Source: Adapted from A. Parasuraman, Valarie Zeithaml, and Leonard L. Berry, *SERVQUAL: A Multiple-Item Scale for Measuring Customer Perceptions of Service Quality* (Cambridge, MA: Marketing Science Institute, 1986), pp. 31–34.

ation about customers' *expectations*; the second group seeks quantitative information about customers' *preferences*.

In Customer Service in Action 5–1, you can see the results of a telephone survey conducted by Massachusetts Mutual Life Insurance Company. The purpose of this survey was to gather general information about customers' preferences, rather than about their satisfaction with specific services.

CUSTOMER SERVICE IN ACTION 5–1

Clients Want Service; They Value Agents

Life insurance policyholders require frequent service on their policies, and they want that service to be provided by their agent, not through the local general agency or home office, a recent Massachusetts Mutual national telephone survey found.

The 411 policyholders surveyed were primarily middle-aged with household incomes over $50,000 and averaged 2.4 MassMutual policies per household. Seventy-six percent were male and 24 percent were female.

"Our survey demonstrates that the agent plays a major role in the policyholder's satisfaction with company service," said MassMutual Senior Vice President Donald D. Cameron, who heads the Insurance & Financial Management Marketing division. "There is a very strong correlation between the agent-client relationship and the policyholder's attitude toward company service."

The most important service that agents provide, according to survey results, is information. Policyholders want their agents to review their insurance coverage with them at regular intervals and provide retirement planning information on the fifth and tenth policy anniversaries.

An overwhelming majority surveyed (66 percent) said that they request service by contacting their agent directly, as opposed to contacting the local general agency (which 18 percent did) or the home office (which 12 percent did).

The survey also showed that 70 percent of the policyholders had requested service in the last three years. In addition, cross-selling to existing clients may prove to be the most efficient avenue to growth for agents, according to the survey results, because households with multiple policies don't request proportionately more service.

"Overall, the policyholder survey demonstrates that good service is an extension of the sales process, and as such may enhance the agent's ability to generate new sales," Cameron said.

Source: Adapted with permission of the publisher from "Clients Want Service, Value Agents," *Life Association News*, December 1989, p. 28.

Types and Sources of Research Data

When a company starts planning its research, it often considers developing its own research instruments and preparing its own list(s) of people to survey. However, these steps are not always necessary, since there are many sources of information that can help reduce the time and money that a company must spend on its research. Rather than conduct its own research, sometimes a company can use the results of research that has already been done or hire another organization to conduct research for it. For example, as we noted earlier, the ICAE and LIMRA have already conducted focus group interviews with customers and published the results of these interviews. In the next few pages, we will discuss different sources of research data and the types of data each source provides.

An insurance company typically gets research information from two types of data: primary data and secondary data. *Primary data* is new research that is gathered to help a company understand a specific problem, such as the reason for an increase in customer complaints about certain products or services. It is not necessary, however, for an insurance company to use only primary data to help it deal with a specific research problem. Companies can also use *secondary data*, which is data that has already been collected for some other purpose, either by the insurance company itself or by some other organization.

Insurance companies can get primary and secondary data from a variety of sources. These sources can be divided into two broad categories: internal sources and external sources. *Internal sources* of data are located within the company itself. Internal sources may provide primary data (such as research conducted on a particular issue by the company's research department) or secondary data (such as complaint logs routinely maintained to comply with insurance department regulations). *External sources* of data are located outside the company and include a variety of research firms, advertising agencies, and professional and trade associations. As with internal sources of data, external sources may provide either primary or secondary data. In the next few pages, we will talk about these different types and sources of data, their uses, and their advantages and disadvantages.

Primary Data

Typically, when we think of an insurance company gathering information about its customers, we think of the company going directly to the customer and getting just the information it needs on a specific topic. By gathering primary data, insurance companies usually reap several benefits. They know that the information is up-to-date, because they have just gathered it. They can also decide how the research should be designed, exactly what kind of data it should gather, the specific sources of the data, and how the final results of the research should be presented. Thus, the company can ensure that the research data is relevant to its situation and the information will be useful in developing their plans and strategies.

However, for all its advantages, primary data has two big disadvantages: it can be expensive and time-consuming to gather. Gathering primary data requires a company to spend time and money on staff to develop and conduct the research and on computer technology to organize the results of the research so it can be analyzed. In addition, if the research is in the form of a written survey, the company must pay printing and mailing costs. If the company uses an external source, like a research firm, to collect the primary data, the company will also have to pay consulting fees. The very cost of gathering primary data often leads companies to look for usable secondary data.

Secondary Data

Researchers usually investigate the availability of secondary data before trying to collect primary data. When secondary data is available, its use normally reduces the cost and the amount of time needed to complete a research study. Much secondary data, such as data available from internal reports or provided in government publications, is available free or at a nominal charge. Other secondary data, called *syndicated data*, is collected by commercial marketing research firms, who sell it to their clients, or by industry associations, which also collect marketing research and other types of information for distribution or sale to their member companies. In many cases, an individual company cannot afford the costs of collecting information. Therefore, it seeks out data that is already available from government or industry associations. In some cases, secondary data may be the only feasible source of data for a research project.

The usefulness of secondary data depends on a company's situation and needs. Therefore, secondary data must be evaluated carefully to make sure it will provide the kind of information that the company is looking for. Otherwise, the company might find it has obtained information that is of no real value. For example, a research study that requires data listing the number of customer telephone calls per product line per month may not be able to use secondary data that does not break down telephone calls by product. Also, especially in markets undergoing rapid change, secondary data may become outdated soon after it is collected. Finally, while external secondary data can give a fairly accurate general picture of the industry, it cannot describe the perceptions of one particular company's customers.

Types and Sources of Secondary Data

Secondary data is classified as either internal or external, depending on its source. As its name implies, **internal secondary data** is data that has already been collected by the company for some purpose other than the current research study. A firm's accounting and sales records, its customer files, and the results of its previous research studies are all examples of an organization's sources of internal secondary data. When seeking secondary data, companies usually investigate the internal secondary data available before going to external sources. Although internal secondary data may not always be suitable or adequate for a current research project, it is usually less expensive, less time-consuming to obtain, and perhaps more pertinent to the research situation since it is based on information from inside the organization.

   External secondary data is data collected and initially processed by sources outside the organization. Generally, these sources can be grouped into four categories: government sources, syndicated sources, marketing research firms, and industry and trade associations.

- *Government sources*, such as agencies in federal, state, provincial, and local governments, provide more external secondary data than any other source. Much of the information they provide is free of charge. Census data is one example of external secondary data that is readily available. The U.S. Census Bureau is the most important government source of external secondary data in the United States. In Canada, the most important source is Statistics Canada.
- *Syndicated services research firms*, such as A.C. Nielsen, Arbitron, Gallup, MarketFacts, and the Stanford Research In-

stitute (SRI), gather information about consumers and sell the information to businesses. These firms collect data for a number of client firms and spread the cost of gathering the data among the companies for whom it is gathered. Because data provided by syndicated sources has been developed especially for the use of business clients, syndicated data is more likely to address business needs than government data. Syndicated data is also usually updated more frequently than government data. Many firms that provide syndicated data services also provide primary data collection and other types of customer research services to client companies.

- *Non-syndicated marketing research firms* offer customized research services that provide both primary and secondary data for business clients on a special-project basis. Some of these firms conduct multi-sponsored studies that are jointly funded by participating companies. Some marketing research firms concentrate on serving the research needs of particular industries. Others focus on conducting research in specific areas of marketing, such as customer service. For example, because of its extensive research about complaint handling in North America, Technical Assistance Research Programs (TARP) is well known for its customer service research.

- *Professional and trade associations* frequently provide customer research services. These associations include the Life Insurance Marketing and Research Association (LIMRA), the Life Office Management Association (LOMA), the American Council of Life Insurers (ACLI), the Canadian Life and Health Insurance Association (CLHIA), the Insurance Consumer Affairs Exchange (ICAE), the Health Insurance Association of America (HIAA), the Society of Actuaries, the National Association of Life Underwriters (NALU), and the Million Dollar Round Table (MDRT). One example of external secondary data provided by the ACLI is the *Monitoring Attitudes of the Public (MAP)* survey. Conducted annually since 1967, the *MAP survey* questions representative samples of the adult U.S. population to provide the industry with information on consumers' changing viewpoints toward life and health insurance products, the insurance industry itself, insurance agents, and various aspects of the major external environments.

Conducting research is a crucial part of a successful company's customer service activities. Only by regularly talking to an adequate number of people whose behaviors, attitudes, perceptions, and expectations are representative of its customers can a company be reasonably assured that it knows what will satisfy its customers' service needs. However, gathering this information is only the first step. The information must be taken into consideration by the company when developing standards and procedures. Further, to be really valuable to the people who interact directly with customers, the results of research analysis need to be communicated to all levels of the company. In this way, the needs of the customers will guide the company as it develops its customer service systems.

Key Terms

qualitative research	surveys
exploratory research	personal interview
focus group interviews	mail survey
advisory panels	telephone survey
in-depth interviews	primary data
company visits	secondary data
job rotation	internal data sources
employee interview	external data sources
exit interviews	syndicated services research firms
examination of customer complaints	syndicated data
quantitative research	non-syndicated marketing research firms
sampling	professional and trade associations
sample	Monitoring Attitudes of the Public
population	(MAP) survey

Notes

1. Amanda Bennett and Carol Hymowitz, "For Customers, More than Lip Service," *The Wall Street Journal*, October 6, 1989, p. B1.
2. R. T. Pascale, "Perspective on Strategy: The Real Story Behind Honda's Success," *California Management Review* (Spring 1981), p. 70.

Establishing a Customer Service System

After studying this chapter, you should be able to

- Explain the differences between efficiency and effectiveness
- Define and explain what a system is
- Describe the different parts of a system
- Explain the importance of systems to businesses
- Explain the importance of systems to customer service
- Define systems analysis and the steps involved
- Describe what a performance standard is
- Identify the elements of an effective performance standard
- Explain the importance of resource analysis
- Define work-flow analysis and the steps involved

Introduction

The Straight-Ahead Insurance Company has just completed an extensive customer satisfaction study, and the results indicate that its customers are not happy with Straight-Ahead's service. The company's agents are dissatisfied with the service provided by the home office, the company's clients are unhappy with the company's responses to their customer service requests, and the company's employees are grumbling about each other. The company's internal reports, however, indicate that all systems are functioning just the way they should: proper procedures are being followed, the company's computer systems are operating satisfactorily, and employees are competently performing their assigned jobs. By all accounts, everything is being done right.

So why is everyone unhappy with the service they are receiving? Apparently, Straight-Ahead is doing things right, but it's not doing the right things. It is being efficient without being effective. As described by Peter Drucker, [1] *efficiency* (doing things right) is the ability to achieve objectives with a minimum of waste. For example, an efficient customer service system is one in which there are no errors and all work is done according to the established schedule. *Effectiveness* (doing the right things), on the other hand, is the ability to establish and achieve *appropriate* objectives. For example, an effective customer service system is one through which customers receive the service they expect. A customer service system is effective when customers are satisfied. Unfortunately, it is possible to have a customer service system that is highly efficient but not effective. Straight-Ahead's customer service is just such a system. It is efficient but not effective. And according to Peter Drucker, "Effectiveness is the foundation of success—efficiency is a minimum condition for survival after success has been achieved."[2] "The pertinent question is not how to do things right, but how to find the right things to do, and to concentrate resources and efforts on doing them."[3]

To find the root cause of its problems and to do something about them, Straight-Ahead needs to evaluate its customer service system and first make sure that the system is effective and then that it is run efficiently.

In this chapter, we will discuss what a system is and how businesses and their customer service operations function as systems. We will describe systems analysis and why it is necessary for companies to monitor their systems on a regular basis. Finally, we will describe the steps involved in systems analysis, including analysis of services, performance standards, resources, and work flow.

What Is a System?

A *system* is a group of elements that work together to perform a specific function or to achieve one or more desired objectives. For example, an internal combustion engine is a system of intake valves, pistons, spark plugs, and exhaust valves that work together to create the power needed to run an automobile. Similarly, the earth's atmosphere is a system that circulates certain chemicals, such as oxygen and carbon dioxide, that are necessary for the earth to sustain life. In fact, each one of us is a system that operates within the larger system of the earth's environment. In much the same way, a business is also a system. It is a system that

- *receives* information, money, and materials from a larger system (the economic environment),
- *transforms* the information, money, and materials into products or services, which it then
- *sends* out for use in the economic environment.

These three components of receiving, transforming, and sending are known in systems theory as input, processing, and output, and all systems have these three components.

An *input* is something that needs to be worked on by the system in order to achieve the system's objective. *Processing*, also called the *process step*, is the work performed by the system on the input. The *output* is the final result produced by the system. (In this chapter, we are concerned with the performance output of providing quality customer service.) A system also has a fourth component known as control. The *control* mechanism monitors the system to ensure that it is functioning properly, and then it provides feedback to the system, so that the system can adjust its operation as needed. Later in this chapter, we will discuss work-flow analysis, and the terms *input, output*, and *process step* will be described in more detail. [4]

In systems theory, the basic system model is often presented as shown in Figure 6–1. Note the movement through the system. Inputs come into the system, they are changed in the process stage, then outputs leave the system, and all the while the control mechanism makes sure that the system operates properly. Also note that the system operates within an environment. In the case of a business, the environment includes elements such as suppliers, competitors, customers, and regulators. The environment provides the system with its initial inputs and receives its final outputs. Although our model is only a simplified version of a system, it should give you an idea of any system's basic operation.

For an insurance company, inputs include premium payments, applications for insurance, customer service requests, new office equipment, job applications, and a host of other "things" that are brought into the company from its external environment. Processing in an insurance company includes all the activities needed to interact with these inputs. Thus, processing includes activities such as accounting for premium and investment income, underwriting insur-

Figure 6–1
Basic System Model with Environment

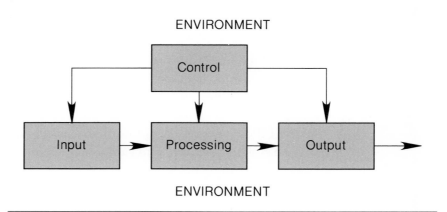

ance applications, determining the correct responses to customer service inquiries, installing office equipment, interviewing job applicants, and all the other activities required for the company to interact with its environment. Outputs include insurance policies that are sent to producers or consumers, answers to customers' inquiries, materials such as computer printouts produced by office equipment, job offers to job applicants, and any other functions performed, or objectives achieved, by the company.

A system does not always work as originally planned. Consequently, a company must monitor its system so that it can spot system problems or deficiencies as quickly as possible and take corrective action to help the system get back on target. The control mechanism is the element that ensures that the system functions effectively and efficiently. Two important aspects of the control mechanism are the standards that a company expects the system to meet and the measurements that it uses to ensure that the system consistently meets those standards. Standards relate to the effectiveness of the system — whether or not it is doing what you want it to do. Measurements relate to the efficiency of the system — how well it operates. Later in this chapter we discuss standards more extensively. In Chapter 7, we will concentrate entirely on measurements used to evaluate system performance.

Business as a System

Typically, when we think of systems and businesses, we think of computer systems and all the accompanying computer technology — the hardware and software — that a company needs in order to operate. We think of how the different parts of the computer network work together and how the people in the company interact with the network. Such a computer network is in all respects a system. However, it is only one kind of system, and it is only a part of the entire system that makes up a business. While computer networks are an essential part of almost every business system today, they cannot operate without the other parts of the business system. Before computers even existed, businesses were systems. These systems were made up of the employees in the company, the procedures those employees followed, and the financial and physical resources that were needed to keep the system working. That model of the business system still works, but computers have now become an essential part of the model. Today's company combines computers, employees, procedures, and financial and physical resources to form a business system that processes inputs into outputs. The more effectively and efficiently its system works, the more likely the company will be able to provide its customers with quality service.

Every insurance company is a system made up of many other systems. And just as a company can be organized in various ways, so can these systems. Some companies are organized along functional lines; some are organized according to geographical regions; others are organized by products or by customers. Each of these organizational structures can lead to a different system of systems. For example, consider a company organized by function — actuarial, marketing, underwriting, and so forth. Each function within such an organization is a system of its own and can be defined separately. But each function must cooperate with the others for a company to succeed.

Customer Service as a System

In addition to the systems that fit the established organizational structure of a company, there are other systems that help a company to operate. Although these additional systems are important, perhaps even essential, to a company's smooth operation, they may not appear on any organizational chart. These systems operate across functional and organizational lines and require the participation and cooperation of employees in various departments and divisions throughout the organization. One such system is a company's customer service system.

Most insurance companies have a customer service department. In fact, many insurers have several customer service departments to handle different lines of business. As noted earlier, however, customer service isn't handled just by customer service departments. Many other people and many other departments in a company are essential for providing quality customer service. Consequently, a company's customer service system includes many functional areas in addition to its customer service department. The customer service system consists of all the people, processes, and technology used by a company to provide service to its customers. From the receptionist who answers the company's telephone to the mainframe that processes policy transactions, each part of a company that directly or indirectly interacts with customers is part of the company's customer service system.

To get a better idea of how customer service works as a system, let's look at Customer Service in Action 6–1 and see what happens when customers interact with the Juniper Financial Group.

The Customer Service System at the Juniper Financial Group

Emily Grodin has decided to create a fund to help pay for her daughter's college education. She contacts her insurance agent, Bill Bolesley, a broker with TBT Associates. TBT Associates is an insurance brokerage firm that does a lot of business with the Juniper Financial Group, an insurance and financial services corporation.

Mr. Bolesley looks at Ms. Grodin's current finances and the amount of money she needs to save for her daughter's college fund. He describes a number of different strategies (such as mutual funds, variable life insurance, and annuities) to help Ms. Grodin achieve her goal. Ms. Grodin describes how much money she can afford to put into a college fund. Mr. Bolesley takes this and other pertinent information and sends it to Juniper Financial and two other financial services corporations, asking them to calculate the cost and the return on investment of various financial products that Ms. Grodin might use.

From the moment Mr. Bolesley sends this information to Juniper Financial, both he and Ms. Grodin begin interacting with Juniper Financial's customer service system. Mr. Bolesley will be acting as both a customer of Juniper Financial and as a part of Juniper Financial's customer service system. Ms. Grodin will see Mr. Bolesley as part of Juniper Financial's customer service system. As far as she is concerned, he will be the customer service system, at least for now.

The information that Mr. Bolesley sends to Juniper Financial will go to various parts of the customer service system. Some information will go to the actuarial department, which will calculate the cost of various products, such as variable life insurance or an annuity, that Ms. Grodin might use. Some information may also go to the company's investment department, so it can prepare an investment proposal. Juniper Financial's customer service system must work quickly and accurately if it wants Mr. Bolesley to remain a satisfied customer and Ms. Grodin to become one.

Juniper Financial sends several proposals back to Mr. Bolesley, who presents them to Ms. Grodin, along with proposals from the other two companies. After much discussion, Ms. Grodin and Mr. Bolesley decide that the product that best suits Ms. Grodin's needs is a four-year annuity certain from Juniper Financial. The annuity is deferred 10 years with monthly premium payments payable for the next 10 years, at which time Ms. Grodin's daughter will be 18 years old. Ms. Grodin then completes an annuity application, stating that she would like to have her monthly premiums withdrawn from her paycheck. Mr. Bolesley sends the application to Juniper Financial's new business unit of the underwriting department. Juniper Financial must once again respond quickly and accurately if it wants to satisfy Mr. Bolesley and Ms. Grodin.

The application is approved, and Juniper Financial prints an annuity contract and sends it to Mr. Bolesley, who delivers it to Ms. Grodin. Ms. Grodin accepts the contract and hands Mr. Bolesley the first monthly payment. Mr. Bolesley sends the check to Juniper Financial, where the accounting department will establish an account for Ms. Grodin and approve a commission check for Mr. Bolesley and an override commission for TBT Associates.

So far, the system has worked smoothly, and both of these Juniper Financial customers have been satisfied. But when the first premium payment is withdrawn from Ms. Grodin's paycheck, she realizes immediately that Juniper Financial has withdrawn $20 more than it was supposed to. Needless to say, Ms. Grodin is upset and calls Mr. Bolesley. Once again the customer service system is brought into action. Mr. Bolesley calls the billing department at Juniper Financial and explains the situation. The billing department verifies the error and makes arrangements to correct it. The billing department calls Ms. Grodin and explains the different ways that Juniper can correct the error. The company representative gives Ms. Grodin a toll-free number that she can call if she has any future questions. Six months later, Ms. Grodin uses this toll-free number to verify the value of her annuity. At the end of each fiscal year Juniper Financial sends Ms. Grodin a financial statement and also sends a copy of the statement to Mr. Bolesley. After 10 years, Juniper Financial begins making annuity payments to Ms. Grodin.

This case demonstrates that a company must maintain an intricate and powerful system if it is to provide even the minimum amount of service that customers expect in order to be satisfied. The example also illustrates that customer service is not the responsibility of a single department responding to customer inquiries. In fact, the example we have given didn't even involve Juniper Financial's customer service department, although it could have.

The Invisible System

Looking back at the Juniper Financial case, you could say that Juniper does a good job of maintaining an invisible system. An *invisible system* is one that is designed so a customer is not inconvenienced by, or even aware of, all the steps a company must take to fulfill the customer's request. No matter how complex the system is, as long as it allows employees to do their work without inconveniencing customers, then the system is invisible, and it is at least one step closer to being effective.

Some companies still seem to forget that the ultimate purpose of a business system is to make it easier, not just for employees to do their work, but for customers to do business with the company. A company's rules and procedures, its software and hardware, should be flexible enough to let its employees deal with a customer's needs in a manner that is most convenient for the customer. If a company's service system is designed so that its employees cannot easily respond to customers' requests, then the system is not invisible. It is far too visible. It intrudes on the company's attempts to provide customer service. Customers should not hear phrases like, "You can't do it that way," or "The system won't let me do that for you," or "But our procedure is . . . ," especially when they have requests that they think are both reasonable and within the levels of customer service that the company says it will provide.

Today, many insurance companies are operating with computer systems that do not allow them to respond quickly to the needs of their customers and they are looking for solutions. Michael E. Treacy of MIT's Sloan School of Management has suggested a radical solution to the problem. Speaking of systems technology in particular, Mr. Treacy suggests that some insurance companies must "blow up and destroy existing systems technology. . . . It's not that companies are too big; they're too inflexible. And Information Systems is part of the problem. Old systems have become baggage."[5] Dynamite is probably an excessive means of dealing with the problem, but Treacy makes an important point. The challenge now facing insurance companies is to develop invisible systems, systems that meet the needs of the employees who use them and the needs of the customers who are trying to do business with the company.

In the next few pages, we will talk about some of the formal steps that any company needs to take in order to develop systems that are efficient, effective, flexible, and invisible to the customer.

Systems Analysis

According to most quality-control experts, fully 85 percent of all errors in any business are caused not by employees but by the system that the business uses. If the system is flawed, the results produced by the system will be flawed. As W. Edwards Deming, one of the world's leading quality-control experts, puts it, "You only get what the system will deliver."[6]

Although the term *systems analysis* is often associated with computer networks, the term can be much more encompassing. For our purposes, *systems analysis* is defined as the process of examining how a company's employees, procedures, technology, and financial and physical resources work together to achieve a specific goal. When applied to customer service, systems analysis is used to ensure that the company's entire customer service process is working effectively and efficiently to provide the services its customers expect and need.

For the rest of this chapter, we will discuss the process of systems analysis, especially as it applies to the customer service system. In particular, we will discuss four aspects of a system — the analysis of services, performance standards, resources, and the actual work flow or procedures for completing tasks — that should be studied in a thorough systems analysis.

Who Should Conduct Systems Analysis?

Typically, when a company begins a systems analysis, it calls in people who are specifically trained to do such an analysis. Some large companies have people on their staffs whose full-time job is to analyze company systems. Other companies call in outside consultants to help them analyze their systems. These analysts are identified by a variety of titles, such as *systems analyst, industrial engineer,* or *organizational development expert,* but their jobs are generally the same. For simplicity, therefore, we will use the term *systems analyst.* A **systems analyst** is trained to analyze every aspect of a business from a systems point of view and to develop plans to make the system work in the most efficient way possible. Systems analysts evaluate the physical arrangement of work areas, system performance standards, and the system's work flow in order to identify problems in the system and suggest improvements. Although systems analysts evaluate a system from a statistical point of view, using mathematical formulas to determine a system's efficiency, they are also expected to consider the needs and concerns of the people who work in, and are affected by, the system. Systems analysts must be prepared to deal with employees' reactions to changes in their assigned work.

While it is difficult to complete a thorough analysis of a system without a systems analyst, the analysis is usually more effective when it is done with the assistance of the employees who are part of the system. Over the years, systems analysis has been conducted in a variety of business settings, and unfortunately, it has sometimes developed a bad reputation among employees. Employees tend to view systems analysts as outsiders who come into the company to snoop around and tell them how badly they're doing things and how they need to change their operations. Employees are afraid they'll be poked and prodded by old fashioned *efficiency experts*, people who stand around with clipboards and stopwatches, raising fears and self-doubts among employees. Often employees are afraid that systems analysis will lead to staff reductions and new procedures that aren't nearly as efficient or effective as they're supposed to be.

One of the best ways to prevent such problems and perceptions is to have employees participate in the analysis process. Therefore, it is useful to establish a mixed task force of employees and systems analysts who work together to make recommendations for improving the system. A mixed task force approach has a number of advantages. It

- helps reduce frontline employees' anxiety and increases their level of "buy-in" because they are involved in analyzing their jobs and recommending changes,
- provides managers with fresh insights because it allows them to analyze work from their staff's point of view,
- provides staff with opportunities to see their work from their manager's point of view, and
- provides an objective third party (the systems analyst) who can see problems in the system that those who actually work in the system might not see.

Analyzing Services

Analyzing the services that a company currently provides is the first step in a thorough systems analysis, because if those services aren't the ones that customers really want, then no matter how efficiently the system is operating, it will be flawed. Insurance companies can evaluate the effectiveness of their services by conducting customer-satisfaction surveys as discussed in the last chapter. Such surveys typically provide companies with the most accurate picture of their customers' needs and of the types and levels of services that their customers want and expect.

Another excellent point of reference for examining a company's services is its customer service mission statement. A clear and up-to-date mission statement, as we discussed in Chapter 3, should function as a useful guide during the company's analysis of its services. If the services it offers do not support its mission, then the services should be modified until they do support the mission.

Finally, the company can survey its own employees and ask them which services they think are most important to customers. In a recent study by Berry, Parasuraman, and Zeithaml, the authors found that when interviewing company employees about a company's services, the two most revealing questions asked were

1. What is the biggest problem you face in trying to deliver quality service, day in and day out?
2. If you were president and could make only one change to improve service quality here, what change would you make?[7]

Analyzing Performance Standards

After conducting an overall analysis of the services provided through its customer service system, a company can (1) begin evaluating the performance standards that have already been established in order for the system to be able to provide those services and (2) determine the need for any new or additional performance standards. As we discussed in Chapter 3, companies use the objectives stated in their customer service plans to develop their performance standards. A *performance standard* is an established level of performance against which actual performance is to be measured. A performance standard can be defined as the minimum level of service quality and quantity that any part of the customer service system must reach in order to meet established customer service objectives. For example, if one of the company's customer service objectives is to provide immediate, error-free turnaround on claim processing, then one of its performance standards will specify the amount of time it takes the health claims department to process a standard claim with no errors. Meeting this standard requires the company's employees to work at a certain level of efficiency. It requires the company's computer system to provide employees with the level of support they need. It also requires that the company's procedures allow employees to do their work effectively. Because the claim department's operation relies so heavily on sound performance standards, the standards must be evaluated to make sure they are valid, realistic, understandable, and measurable. Performance standards for other departments should be similarly evaluated.

Valid Standards

Standards are valid when they measure what they are intended to measure. For example, suppose an insurance company wants to measure the overall effectiveness and efficiency of its claim operations. As a performance standard, it specifies the number of claims to be processed each day. Does this one measurement of claim volume measure effectiveness and efficiency? Not really. It doesn't take into account whether claims are processed accurately, whether they are processed with a minimum of expense, or whether they are processed to customers' satisfaction. Unless the standard measures these factors, it is not a valid standard for effectiveness and efficiency. It is not valid because it is not measuring what it was intended to measure.

Realistic Standards

From a systems perspective, standards are realistic when they are set at a level that challenges the system, but at a level that the system is capable of achieving. In terms of human resources, standards are realistic when they can be achieved by employees who are reasonably competent on the job. For example, assume the unit in charge of answering an 800 number at The ABC Insurance Company has been given a performance standard of answering all incoming calls within 10 seconds of the first ring (about two additional rings). However, the number of incoming calls far exceeds the number of operators available to answer the calls. This situation makes the standard unrealistic for the system, because even if all the employees in the unit are reasonably competent in their jobs, they will still not be able to perform according to the standard. Standards that are set unreasonably high often discourage employees from even trying to perform well on the job.

As another example, suppose a company's standard for payment of benefits is that 70 percent of the payments made each month must be accurate. Employees know they can achieve a 90-percent accuracy rate, and many can achieve 100-percent accuracy. A 70-percent standard is too easy to achieve and, therefore, is not a realistic measure of performance. By setting standards too low, companies send the message to their employees that standards are not important. In effect, they encourage employees to perform below their abilities.

Understandable Standards

A company's overall customer service standards must be understood by all of its employees. Similarly, departmental standards that have been established for specific functional areas of the company must also be understood by employees who work in those areas. For performance standards to be truly understandable, they should meet a number of criteria. They should be stated in writing, clearly defined, and effectively communicated.

- *Stated in writing.* By putting the standards in writing, the company helps to make sure that the exact requirements of the standards are accurately recorded and can be referred to if questions about the standards are raised.
- *Clearly defined.* The standards should be written in such a way that there are no doubts about their meaning and intent. The standards should be specific and written in a clear, direct manner.
- *Effectively communicated.* The company must make sure that the standards are communicated to the employees. The written standards should be made available in easily accessible locations. The standards should be explained to all employees, and managers and supervisors should make sure that all employees agree with the standards and understand them.

Measurable Standards

Performance cannot be monitored unless the standards designed to monitor the performance are measurable. Standards that cannot be measured are not really standards at all, because no one analyzing the system will be able to determine whether the standards have been met. In Chapter 7, we will discuss in detail some of the measurements that are used to compare the results produced by a system to the standards established for the system.

Asking Employees to Help Set Standards

One of the worst mistakes that a company can make is to establish standards that employees don't believe in. Employees need standards that are reasonable and suited to the current situation. Furthermore, every employee should know how to achieve the standards and *why* they should be achieving them. Otherwise, employees may have little more than a general notion of what is expected of them, even less of how they are performing on the job, and no clear-cut goals or objectives toward which to direct their efforts. One of the best ways to make sure that employees believe in the standards and know why they exist is to ask the employees to help set the standards. Experienced employees know the practical necessities of their daily work routines. They know the obstacles they must deal with and how to achieve specific goals. And they typically set high standards for themselves. By establishing standards through a collaborative effort, a company and its employees can develop standards that employees are willing to work toward and that the company believes will help it achieve its goals. After a thorough examination of its standards, a company should modify or replace any standards that are not effective and then move to the next step in systems analysis: resource analysis.

Analyzing Resources

Typically, a company's resources include (1) human resources — from frontline employees through top management; (2) physical resources — including such things as office space, telephone systems, and computer software and hardware; and (3) financial resources. When looking at these three resource areas from a customer service perspective, a company should ask itself several questions:

- Do we have enough resources to fulfill our company's customer service mission statement? Are there enough employees to do the work? Have we budgeted enough money and enough equipment to make sure that the system operates properly?
- Are we using too many resources? Are there too many employees and are they spending too much money to do the work?
- Are our resources properly allocated? Even if our company's system as a whole has the right level of resources, does each subsystem have the right level? Do some subsystems have too many resources while other subsystems have too few?
- Are our resources being properly used? Is the staff well trained? Are they doing the work they were trained to do? Do employees have enough equipment and the right equipment to do their work?
- How does our level of resource commitment compare with that of our competitors? Do we use our resources as well as they do?

- What resource applications used in other industries could we adapt to our advantage?
- Are we using resources to maximize customer satisfaction in our key markets? Are some customer service areas causing too much of a drain on our resources? Should we continue to offer these services? How can we change these services to allow us more efficient or effective use of our resources?

Work-Flow Analysis

Besides asking very pointed questions about its services, standards, and resources, a company must also consider its procedures. It must consider how its current procedures are conducted and its reasons for using those procedures. One of the best ways to determine both the effectiveness of a company's procedures and the efficiency of its use of resources is doing a thorough analysis of the work flow throughout the system.

Work-flow analysis examines all the steps or tasks involved in a particular process. In this case, a *process* is a series of steps that, when completed, provide a finished product of some kind—such as a particular customer service. As we noted earlier in our discussion of systems analysis, a process in its most basic form consists of an input, a process step, and an output. Most processes are more complex, however, consisting of several input stages, several process steps, and several output stages.

For example, suppose Emily Grodin (our customer from earlier in this chapter) calls Juniper Financial Group's customer service department and asks for a printed report showing the current value of her annuity. This call, which will begin a work flow process in the customer service department, is called the *initial input* of the process. The next part of the process is a process step in which the customer service representative calls up a computer screen or possibly a succession of computer screens to identify the annuity's current value. Each new computer screen is an output, but these outputs don't complete the process. They are called *process step outputs*, and each one becomes the input for the next process step. Each new input is called a *process step input*, which continues the process to the next output. The *final output* is the last output that a process provides, and represents the purpose of the entire process. In this case, the final output is the printed report that Ms. Grodin requested.

Once all the processes that make up the work of a subsystem

have been examined, then the relationships among these processes are studied to make sure they are logical, effective, and efficient. No reasonable analysis of the customer service system can be concluded until the work flows of all processes in the system have been analyzed.

The work-flow analysis for any process follows five general steps:

1. Identify the work processes required to perform the function.
2. Rank the processes in order of importance.
3. Analyze each step involved in each process.
4. If necessary, rerank the work processes.
5. Modify work processes so that they serve the needs of the customer more logically, effectively, and efficiently.

Identify and Rank the Processes

Before actually analyzing each process step in a work flow, the company needs to identify and rank all work processes according to their importance to the company. When ranking the processes, the company considers factors such as those listed below:

- *Legal requirements.* In a regulated industry like insurance, certain processes must be conducted in order to comply with the law. Such processes become important because they are required by regulators.
- *Value of the information provided by the process.* Some processes, such as collecting information about customers' purchasing histories, provide valuable information. The value of this information is an indicator of the importance of each process.
- *Time spent in the process.* The amount of staff time spent each month on a certain process may be an indicator of the importance of a process.
- *Difficulty of the process.* The amount of skill and training needed to do a process may be an indicator of its importance.
- *Revenues from, and expenses caused by, the process.* The amount of money generated or saved by performing the process and the amount of money spent performing the process may be indicators of importance.
- *Impact of the process on the company's objectives.* The impact that a process has on the company's ability to achieve its objectives is a major indicator of its importance.
- *Customers' perceptions and expectations.* The effect that a

process has on customers, as indicated by customer service research, is one of the most useful criteria for ranking processes in a department.

The last criterion is especially important, because it requires the company to think about its customers. All too often when companies rank the importance of internal processes, they turn their attention inward and base their rankings on what seems most important to the people who are performing the processes. They forget to look outside to gain a perspective on how their internal processes affect customers. A company must remember to look outward, even when it is evaluating its own internal activities. Keeping its customers in mind can help a company maintain the proper perspective when the company is ranking its work processes.

Conducting Work-Flow Analysis

By identifying and ranking all of the processes performed by a specific subsystem, the company should have a good overall picture of the work that is done and the degree of importance placed on each process. The next step is to take a detailed look at each process and analyze what exactly goes on and what procedures are followed to complete that process.

To conduct such an analysis, the company should ask itself five basic questions as it goes through each task in a process. The answer to each question should prepare the company for the next question. The five questions and an explanation of each question's purpose follow:

1. *What is worked on?* (That is, what is the input?) The answer to this question should allow the task force to identify all the major inputs.
2. *Where does the input come from?* The answer to this question should tell whether the input is an initial input or a process step input. It also tells who the customers are in the process.
3. *What are the finished products of each process step?* The answer to this question identifies the outputs.
4. *Where does the output go next?* The answer to this question differentiates final outputs from process step outputs. If the answer is a process step output, the company would select the next task in the sequence and repeat the first four ques-

tions for that output. This step also helps identify who the receiving customer is in the process and whether the output meets the needs of that customer.

5. *What must be done to turn initial inputs and process step inputs into process step outputs and final outputs?* The answer to this question identifies the process steps.

To simplify the task of explaining the workflow of a process, systems analysts map out the work flow in charts. Figure 6–2 illustrates the process flow chart for a request for information on an annuity.

Rerank and Revise Processes

Once the analysis is completed, the company should have a better understanding of the work flow required to provide the specific service being analyzed. The company might find that the order in which it had originally ranked the processes does not accurately reflect the importance of some processes. In addition, the company may determine that some of the processes are not as customer-oriented as they should be. The processes and their rankings should be changed accordingly.

Conclusion

By conducting a thorough systems analysis, a company takes an important step in making sure that it is providing customers with the services they want and providing them in the most efficient manner possible. Systems analysis can help a company identify inefficiencies, inadequate standards, or missing resources in its systems and so make modifications that will improve customer service. Further, a thorough systems analysis also provides a company with a means of identifying the customer service processes that need to be measured and the best ways to measure them. In the next chapter, we will discuss some of the measures that are currently being used by insurance companies to help them monitor and control the performance of their customer service systems. However, before you go to the next chapter, look at Issues in Customer Service 6–1, which describes some of the practical problems that can occur when establishing a particular kind of system — a toll-free number for customer service.

Figure 6–2
Sample Process Flow Chart for a Request for Information on an Annuity

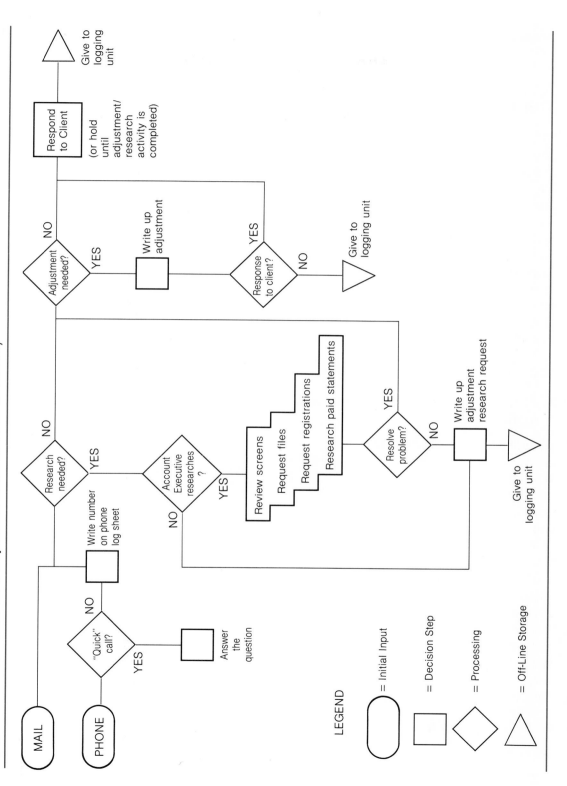

ISSUES IN CUSTOMER SERVICE 6-1

The Pitfalls of System Roll-Out

TARP has noted numerous pitfalls while observing and assisting companies in the implementation of 800 numbers. Ten of these pitfalls are discussed below. Some are not serious; others can lead to corporate embarrassment or even disaster. Companies considering or using 800 numbers must be wary of all pitfalls, however, even those that are not deemed major or serious. These "minor" pitfalls can and do drain an operation's cost-effectiveness, leading to high staff turnover and obstructing the flow of useful information. Major errors have even greater impact, leading, in some cases, to upheaval within the company.

1. Failure to do a cost/benefit analysis in advance.

Several systems have been launched without formal specification of their role. Without knowing the system's purpose, costs, or anticipated benefits, the company tends to evaluate the system on criteria which are neither important nor applicable. At the same time, benefits from the system that were not originally anticipated or articulated are overlooked and go unmeasured. In any case, failure to know what the system is supposed to accomplish before the fact leads to (1) dissipation of effort, (2) ineffective evaluation of the system, and (3) ineffective use of funds. The toll-free system lacks both a clear mandate and an evaluation plan by which it can be judged.

2. Going too fast in the system roll-out.

There are several classic examples of toll-free systems that went from being literally nothing to being nationwide, nationally advertised services. Where the company underestimated the response, the effects of this speedy roll-out were (1) massive system overload, (2) embarrassing publicity for the system's sponsor, and (3) overall negative customer feedback.

By starting small and then scaling up, the company prepares itself for possible future difficulties. Even using this slow scaling up, however, a company can still have problems unless it takes care to evaluate the impact of *all* the system's characteristics, including (1) number of products, (2) scope (local, regional, national), (3) product maturity and complexity, and (4) characteristics of the communication mechanism. Overlooking a system characteristic can be disastrous. The number of products carrying the number, the choice of a local or a nationwide system, the size, color, and location of the system's number on the product, the types of calls selected (positioning), and channels of communication used to communicate the system's number (such as national advertising) are system characteristics and scale-up factors. Each of these factors individually results in an increase in the magnitude of operations. Failure to take the impact of these factors into account can result in a system that is dangerously overloaded.

In addition, scaling up an 800 system can have consequences that, while not disastrous, can render the system less effective that it could be. TARP has found that speedy scale-ups of systems result in several key functions falling by the wayside. These functions include:

- Development of effective data collection systems
- Development of effective data analysis systems
- Evaluation of system outputs
- Development of personnel management and incentive systems

Once the phones start ringing, it is very difficult to implement these functions in an orderly manner.

3. Failure to evaluate during pilot testing.

Often in pilot testing, the predominant attitude is: "Let's just get the system up, running, and bug-free before we get fancy and get data on productivity, call content, or customer satisfaction." The problem here is that, unless a data-gathering mechanism is built into the pilot test from the start, there is little time to establish and implement such a mechanism once the system is up. Before you know it, the pilot test is over, and still no data has been gathered. Without data on productivity, call content, and satisfaction, no cost/benefit analysis can be conducted. Having no cost/benefit analysis, the company has great difficulty justifying full-scale implementation of the system.

4. Failure to give customer representatives guidance, access to information, and adequate authority.

TARP's research shows that telephone representatives can be most productive and achieve the highest levels of customer satisfaction and job satisfaction when they receive three types of support. First, they must be fully trained. Second, they must have ready access to needed information

and guidance. Finally, they must have full authority to solve any customer problem.

Training and access to information tend to be deferred due to time constraints and a feeling that providing all the needed information is simply too costly. In fact, by deferring these items, the company has cheated itself. By saving a little money up front, it has, in effect, reduced the effectiveness of representatives by (1) not giving them adequate training and (2) placing on them the burden of gathering information and/or being creative in developing responses. The necessity to invent responses not only produces misleading, negative, or inefficient answers, but also adds stress to the job, leading to increased staff turnover.

In addition to providing inadequate training and information, companies tend to give representatives inadequate authority. Fearing that representatives will "give away the store," the company often requires them to get authorization for problems involving anything above a selected dollar amount. The effect of this policy is that representatives tend to mirror the company's lack of confidence. The authorization procedure thus becomes the representatives' crutch. They use it to avoid dealing with difficult problems. And the customers on the other end grow more angry and dissatisfied because once again they are talking to someone who does not have the authority to solve their problems. A major Midwest bank survey recently found that to "talk to someone who can solve my problem" was the most important factor in customers' service expectations. Besides all this, when a representative is required to submit a case to someone else, the company has to create a tracking and control system to prevent cases from "falling through the cracks."

In direct contrast with this is the fact that representatives with full training, information, and authority tend to have a much higher rate of calls closed on first contact. And that dramatically increases both customer satisfaction and employee productivity.

5. Failure to provide adequate pay and incentives.

Many companies still view telephone customer service representatives as glorified telephone operators. In the case of some retailers, they are paid the minimum wage. And in many companies, the only incentive for staff to perform well is reported to be: "If you do well, you have the privilege of keeping your job." As one company's representative stated: "I know that if I give bad service often enough and *get caught*, I won't be here."

Low-paying, production-oriented environments lead to less effective customer service. The more competent personnel experience burnout, which causes high staff turnover. The staff who are willing to remain in such a pressurized, low-paying environment tend to be less sensitive and less effective. Companies with effective systems are generally those that treat frontline telephone representatives as professionals.

6. Not gathering data on unimportant calls.

A large number of companies view inquiries and status calls as "nonsubstantive" and, therefore, not meriting data collection. Nevertheless, the company still spends a significant amount of money in handling those telephone calls.

If a company can identify why thousands of calls on unimportant issues are being received, there is an opportunity to prevent those calls, freeing up valuable staff time so that other functions such as outgoing telemarketing can be performed. Also, many inquiries are pre-purchase calls, up to 80 percent of which can lead to product sales. Therefore, it is critical to note both (1) the nature and cause of all calls received by an 800 system and (2) the cost of handling them by category, so that priorities for prevention and customer education can be set.

7. Failure to conduct a preventive analysis of the data gathered by the system and package it so that senior management can use the information.

Many organizations report the number of complaints and inquiries received, but do not address their root cause. They use broad categories that preclude any analysis which is useful to managers. For example, one food processor reported the number of complaints on "flavor, taste, and texture." To make the data useful, the specific attributes of "taste" should have been broken out so that it would have been possible, for instance, to report 15 complaints about products tasting too salty. The lack of specific data and their market implications precluded any significant use of the information.

8. Using measurement systems that emphasize employee productivity at the expense of customer satisfaction.

The measurement system in many telephone service systems is based almost totally on productivity, such as number of calls handled or number of calls closed on first contact. TARP has observed environments (especially when large automatic call directors are used) where representatives will purposely disconnect a call that seems complex because it will decrease their productivity. Disconnecting such a call leaves them with a record of very short calls, for which they are rewarded. Also, upon approaching a certain time limit, many representatives will quickly bring the call to a close even if customers indicate they do not fully understand an answer. In other words, representatives will declare a call to be closed on first contact even if customers are left confused.

To avoid this pitfall, companies should monitor service given by individual representatives by mailing surveys to a limited number of customers who have talked to each representative. Representatives who receive high ratings should then receive recognition, if not more material rewards.

9. Failure to expand the 800 system into a proactive marketing tool.

One of the best times to sell additional products or services to a customer is right after a company has effectively resolved a problem, thereby demonstrating its willingness to stand behind its products. Very few companies have taken advantage of this telemarketing capability. Nor have they taken advantage of the fact that a company representative not only has a customer on the line but has probably already established a potentially profitable relationship with that customer.

10. Failure to calibrate data derived from phone systems with rigorous, projectable baseline studies.

A legitimate concern of the marketing and market research departments about information derived from toll-free telephone systems is that the data may not be statistically projectable for the company's customer population as a whole. The best methodology for dealing with this concern is periodically (perhaps once a year) to conduct a survey to a random sample of the entire customer base to identify (1) the incidence of problems and questions and (2) the level of satisfaction among the customer base as a whole. The data derived from this statistically projectable survey can then be compared with data derived from the ongoing telemarketing system, so that the telemarketing system can be calibrated and interpreted on an ongoing basis.

Source: Adapted from TARP working paper, "The Benefits of Toll-Free Telephone Numbers and the Pitfalls of System Roll-Out" (Washington, D.C.: Technical Assistance Research Programs, 1983), pp. 2–7. Adapted with permission of TARP, (202) 544–6312.

Key Terms

efficiency
effectiveness
system
input
processing
process step
output
control
invisible system
systems analysis
systems analyst
industrial engineer
organizational development expert
performance standard

valid standards
realistic standards
understandable standards
measurable standards
resource analysis
work-flow analysis
initial input
process step input
process step output
final output
system roll-out
system characteristics
scale-up factors
pilot testing

Notes

1. Peter F. Drucker, *Management: Tasks, Responsibilities, Practices* (New York: Harper & Row, 1973), pp. 45–46.
2. Drucker, *Management*, p. 45.
3. Peter F. Drucker, *Managing For Results* (New York: Harper & Row, 1964), p. 6.
4. Many ideas presented in this chapter are based on a seminar called "Measurement Processes," by Susan Shepard of The Travelers and on interviews with Susan Shepard.
5. LOMA, "Technology Can Enhance Radical Strategies," *Interchange* 1 (Spring 1988), p. 1.
6. "Deming's Demons," *The Wall Street Journal*, June 4, 1990, pp. R39, R41.
7. Leonard L. Berry, A. Parasuraman, and Valarie A. Zeithaml, "The Service Quality Puzzle," *Business Horizons*, September/October 1988, p. 43.

CHAPTER 7

Measuring the Performance of the Customer Service System

After studying this chapter, you should be able to

- Define standards, benchmarks, and benchmarking
- Describe the advantages and disadvantages of using internal standards, industry standards, and general business standards
- Identify essential criteria for developing and maintaining an effective measurement system
- Describe the uses of quantitative and behavioral performance measures and the differences between them
- Describe the various performance measurement techniques that are particularly effective in customer service

Introduction

As we discussed in Chapter 6, a customer service system must have a control mechanism if it is to operate effectively. The control mechanism compares the results of work done with the performance standards established for the system. In order for the control mechanism to operate properly, companies must establish various ways of measuring results so they can be compared to standards. The purpose of this chapter is to describe performance measurements — what they are, what kinds there are, and how they are used. Before we begin our discussion of measurements, however, we need to make a few additional comments about standards.

Benchmarking and Standards

In order to measure the performance of its customer service system, a company must compare the results of its performance measurements with some previously established benchmark. A *benchmark* is a standard by which something can be measured or judged. The process of comparing actual performance results with a benchmark is called *benchmarking*. Benchmarking allows a company to determine how well it is performing in relation to the standard. While the performance standards that a company uses for benchmarking are based on the system's objectives, they come from many different sources — from inside the company, from companies in the same industry, from a variety of companies both inside and outside the industry, and from customers themselves.

Internal Standards

Internal standards are developed inside the company, based on the outputs that the company's own customer service system produces. Internal standards are used by every business, and we will use such standards as the basis for much of our discussion of measurements. Companies use internal standards because (1) they are fairly easy to gather, (2) they reflect actual processes or practices followed in the companies that have developed them, and (3) they allow the companies to compare their current performance with their past performance. Internal standards, however, tend to provide a fairly narrow and introverted perspective on a company's customer service performance.

Industry Standards

Most insurers like to stay abreast of how other insurance companies are handling customer service. One way insurers stay informed is to study *industry standards* concerning basic customer service processes and then to compare them with their own results. Look at Customer Service in Action 7–1, on the facing page, for a summary of a study of industry standards published by LOMA.

Leaders in Customer Service

While industry standards allow a company to compare itself to other companies in the same business, such standards tend to narrow a company's focus, just as internal standards do. As we noted earlier in the book, customers tend to compare the customer service they receive from one company with that of every other company they do business with. They don't differentiate among insurance company customer service, grocery store customer service, and bank and department store customer service. As far as customers are concerned, it's all customer service.

By looking beyond its own industry and studying the strategies of businesses that are considered leaders in customer service, an insurance company can improve its chances of establishing superior service standards. It can analyze the annual reports of excellent service providers and study articles written about those provisers. As we noted earlier, some customer service leaders even offer seminars

CUSTOMER SERVICE IN ACTION 7–1

Service Turnaround Times: Individual Insurance

LOMA developed the Service Turnaround Time Study in 1988 to satsify its member companies' requests for industry norms to compare with their own service times. The first survey was completed by the 44 companies who were members of LOMA's Individual Insurance Services Committees I and II. But widespread interest in the results prompted LOMA to open the survey to the entire industry.

One hundred thirteen companies participated in the 1991 survey, which measured 20 service functions: 4 new business functions and 16 policyowner service functions. Respondents submitted either the number of days or the range of days necessary to complete a specific transaction.

The graph at the right shows the average of service turnaround times by function. Because companies measure their turnaround times differently, they had the option of calculating their survey responses two different ways:

• *Industry Average A:* Turnaround is measured from the time a request is submitted to the time it is completed, regardless of any intervening activities, such as work done by other departments or by outside sources, such as requesting a physician's statement. In other words, the clock starts ticking when the request is received in house and it doesn't stop until the reply is mailed to the client. So turnaround time includes all the time necessary to fulfill the request, including work done outside the service department.

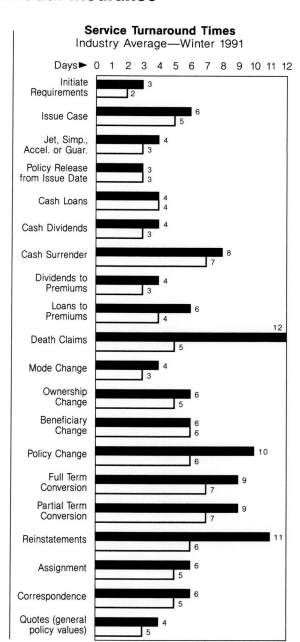

Service Turnaround Times
Industry Average—Winter 1991

Days► 0 1 2 3 4 5 6 7 8 9 10 11 12

Function	Value 1	Value 2
Initiate Requirements	3	2
Issue Case	6	5
Jet, Simp., Accel. or Guar.	4	3
Policy Release from Issue Date	3	3
Cash Loans	4	4
Cash Dividends	4	3
Cash Surrender	8	7
Dividends to Premiums	4	3
Loans to Premiums	6	4
Death Claims	12	5
Mode Change	4	3
Ownership Change	6	5
Beneficiary Change	6	6
Policy Change	10	6
Full Term Conversion	9	7
Partial Term Conversion	9	7
Reinstatements	11	6
Assignment	6	5
Correspondence	6	5
Quotes (general policy values)	4	5

- *Industry Average B:* Turnaround is measured as the time a particular area takes to complete a transaction. As with Formula A, the clock starts ticking when the request is received in house. But with Formula B, the clock stops every time the service department stops working on the request, for example, when it requests a physician's statement. So turnaround time includes only the time the service department itself spends on the request.

  Participants reported that their companies provide information on their internal time standards to:

- Agents

- Policyholders
- Client service personnel
- Executives and other home office personnel
- Regional offices
- Regional management
- Field offices
- Management staff
- All employees

Fifty-five companies send time standards to agents, but only four companies send time standards to policyowners. Forty-two companies send time standards to other groups. Forty-nine companies include a quality standard with the time standards they send.

Source: Adapted with permission of the publisher from Stephanie Consie, "Survey Measures Service Times," *Resource*, LOMA, April 1991.

to teach other companies how they conduct their customer service operations. Consequently, in order to put the quality of its own customer service in the proper perspective, an insurance company must compare its service with the best customer service being provided, regardless of the source.

The Baldrige Award

One of the best ways that businesses in the United States have to compare themselves with other companies, no matter what industry they are in, is to participate in the competition for the Malcolm Baldrige National Quality Award. This award, which was named after a former Secretary of Labor and was inspired by Japan's Deming Prize, was established by Congress to recognize outstanding achievement in quality.

When a company applies for the Baldrige Award, it must fill out an application that requires answers to 133 detailed questions about the company's leadership, information gathering and analysis, strategic planning, the use of human resources, quality control, and customer satisfaction. Although the award is designed to evaluate the entire company, 300 of the potential 1,000 points that a company can earn are based on the company's skill at customer service. Customer service is the single most critical factor in earning the Baldrige Award.

Curt W. Reimann, director of the Baldrige Award, identifies eight critical factors that the judges look for:

- A plan to keep improving all operations continuously.
- A system for measuring these improvements accurately.
- A strategic plan based on benchmarks that compare the company's performance to the best companies in the world.
- A close partnership with customers that feeds improvement back into the operation.
- A deep understanding of the company's customers so that their wants can be translated into products and services.
- A long-lasting relationship with customers, going beyond the delivery of the product to include sales and service.
- A focus on preventing mistakes rather than merely correcting them.
- A commitment to improving quality that runs from the top of the organization to the bottom. [1]

If the panel of judges rates the application highly enough, the company will be awarded a site visit, during which information on the application is verified and judged more closely. Very few companies do well enough to earn a site visit. However, no matter how well or how poorly a company does, the judges will explain where the company did well and where it fell short. Many competitors for the Baldrige Award consider the feedback they receive to be the most important aspect of the entire process. Some compete only for that reason. They receive sound business advice, and they don't have to pay consultants.

Winners of the award include Xerox Corporation, Westinghouse, and Cadillac. Although no insurance companies have yet won, Paul Revere Insurance was a runner-up in 1988, and USAA Insurance earned a site visit in 1989. Other insurers are either planning to compete or have actually begun competing for the Baldrige Award.

Choosing Performance Measures

Once a company has a clear understanding of its customer service system, the standards it should follow, the work flows in the various subsystems, and the rankings of those work flows from most important to least important, the next task is to develop ways to measure its work. This task forms part of the control mechanism of the system model. The control mechanism is needed to ensure that the system is operating according to plan and to serve as a basis for recommending necessary adjustments to the system.[2]

When developing its measurement systems, a company should observe several basic concepts:

- The information about system performance that the company gathers through its control mechanism must be accurate. Otherwise, its measurements are useless.
- Measurements should be made on a regular basis, and the results should be used as soon as possible to evaluate performance. As measurement results grow older, they become less applicable to the current situation.
- Measurements should be objective and understandable. Employees should understand them and feel that the measurements are fair and applied without bias.
- The measurement system should be used to measure only the important processes.
- The measurement system should concentrate on those activities where corrective actions can be taken. Although companies should be aware of activities that can't or won't be modified, they should not focus their efforts on measuring them.
- The measurement system must be realistic. Performance standards must be attainable, and the company must provide enough resources for employees to meet the standards.
- The measurement system must fit into, not disrupt, the normal work flow.
- The measurement system should do more than measure. It should also prescribe ways to correct problems.
- The measurement system should be accepted by the people who are being measured by it. Just as employees should help to develop standards, they should also help to develop the measurement system.[3]

Certain practices can disrupt a measurement system. When planning its measurement systems, a company should be careful *not* to

- measure only those factors that are easy to measure (measurements should be based on the importance of each activity, not the ease with which the activity is measured);

- place too much emphasis on short-run factors while ignoring the long-term good; or
- establish an inflexible system that cannot be modified to reflect the changing importance of various processes and the changing needs of the company's customers. [4]

In addition, companies should try to keep their measurement systems from being over-controlling. Measurement systems should take into account the independence that employees need to serve the customer. Ideally, a company develops measures that evaluate and encourage initiative and independence. In addition, the number of measures used must not create such a glut of reports that managers and staff spend more time measuring work than doing work. Employees should also receive adequate education and training so they have the background and skills required to perform the work that is being measured. Finally, while employees and managers should not be overwhelmed with measurements, a company should use enough measurements so that all work can be appraised from several points of view, thus helping managers evaluate work in a complete and balanced manner. [5]

Quantitative Measures and Behavioral Measures

Two types of measures are generally used to evaluate the quality of a company's customer service: quantitative measures and behavioral measures. A balanced system of measurements should include both types of measures.

Quantitative measures are used to evaluate how quickly, how often, and how accurately processes are completed. A quantitative measure might be used to monitor the number of telephone calls a unit answers in an hour, the length of time it takes a unit to respond to correspondence, or the amount of time a customer service representative spends assisting each customer. As the name implies, quantitative measures are numbers-oriented. They are highly objective in that they indicate either that something was done or that it was not done. Quantitative measures do not require a great deal of subjective judgment by managers or staff members—either 95 percent of telephone calls were answered within 20 seconds or they weren't;

either 90 percent of benefit checks were mailed within seven days after a claim was filed or they weren't.

Because of the nature of quantitative measures, people sometimes get the impression that they have little to do with the quality of work done. Such impressions are wrong. Quantitative measures have a lot to say about quality. The speed and frequency with which processes are completed are an important part of the *quality* of service that a company is providing. After all, as far as a customer is concerned, quality customer service occurs not just because a customer service representative is polite but also because the representative works quickly and accurately and doesn't waste the customer's time. A recent study by American Family Insurance indicates that customers rank responsiveness and efficiency at least as high as, or higher than, the courteousness of its employees. [6]

Most quantitative measures are simple and straightforward. They are easy to gather and present in management reports, and they provide objective information that a company can use to evaluate customer service performance. In addition, they often measure activities that directly affect income and expenses, the bottom line on which companies are judged. On the other hand, quantitative measures can be so easy to use that they can be misused. If not analyzed properly, they can mislead managers and encourage them to attach an oversimplified interpretation to a given situation. For example, one quantitative measure sometimes used in customer service activities is the number of telephone calls answered each day. If a department handled 150 calls a day last year and handles only 130 calls a day this year, the manager may interpret the measure to mean that the department is less efficient this year than it was last year. But remember the difference between efficiency and effectiveness, between doing things right and doing the right things. It could be that this year, customer service representatives are providing each caller with more complete and satisfactory customer service, with the result that fewer customers need to call a second time to get complete service. Or perhaps the department has initiated some new procedures that help customers receive certain services without calling the company. Companies must be careful not to misinterpret their quantitative measures.

Behavioral measures are used to appraise the actions or reactions of employees under specified circumstances, such as those involving interactions with customers. Often called *qualitative measures*, behavioral measures are not typically associated with numbers or statistics. In a customer service situation, for example, behavioral measures would be used to analyze the amount of knowledge employees display when interacting with customers, the level of courtesy employees display, their ability to communicate effectively, to make customers feel that they have received the service they deserve, and their ability to negotiate and resolve problems.

Behavioral measures are more complex than quantitative measures, and therefore are more difficult to interpret. When using behavioral measures, an evaluator doesn't have a set of numbers that tell whether employees are extremely courteous or merely civil. All the evaluator has is evidence of how the employees have acted in various situations. The evaluator must rely on accurate, unbiased reports and then display a high degree of insight into human behavior to interpret the reports accurately. Therefore, in order to use behavioral measures correctly, a company must have (1) specific, well-constructed standards and measures and (2) managers and supervisors who have been thoroughly trained in how to use such measures.

Measurement Techniques

Now that we've discussed some measurement basics, let's investigate some specific measures that insurance companies use and the manner in which they use those measurements.

Customer Satisfaction Surveys

In Chapter 5, we discussed customer satisfaction surveys as a way of understanding the perceptions and expectations of a company's customers. Now we will look at those surveys from the point of view of evaluating various customer service subsystems.

Customer satisfaction surveys generally are not designed to gather information about the work done by individuals. Rather, they are designed to help a company measure whether a specific type of customer service is being delivered in a manner that lives up to customer expectations. Such surveys should be done on a regular basis. Some insurance companies send out short surveys to randomly selected customers every three months or so and a longer survey once a year. These surveys should measure the service dimensions described in Chapter 4: reliability, assurance, empathy, responsiveness, and, where appropriate, tangible factors. The responses to these surveys should then be used to evaluate how well each part of the customer service system is fulfilling its customer service mission and to provide the company with the information it needs to make any necessary adjustments.

The great advantage of using customer surveys for performance measurement is that the system itself and the people who work in it are being evaluated by the people the system has been developed to serve. This keeps the customer in the foreground of customer service system analysis. The primary disadvantage of surveys is that designing, developing, and administering them can be a difficult and time-consuming task. If not carefully developed and correctly administered, surveys can provide a company with a lot of erroneous, useless, and, in cases in which it is misinterpreted, dangerous information.

Observation

Observation is a data-collection method in which a person's behavior is observed and evaluated. Observation can involve everything from simply walking around a department or company to get a feel for how customer service interactions are being handled to standing over employees and checking everything they do. (Please note that we are not recommending the latter since it would probably not provide the kind of measurement information needed and would very likely irritate and de-motivate any employee subjected to it.)

Monitoring

In most insurance company service operations, where customer contact is typically made by telephone or through written correspondence, observation is performed by managers or supervisors who listen in on customer service calls or who review employees' customer correspondence files. These forms of observation are called *monitoring*. Monitoring is considered one of the most effective ways of

- evaluating the level of each employee's customer service skills,
- recognizing any problems an employee or group of employees may be having in using these skills,
- modifying new employee training programs,
- providing information that can be used to apprise employees of how they are performing and to identify needs for skills training, and

- determining—from an internal perspective—whether a company's customer service system is achieving its objectives and meeting overall standards that have been established for it.

Monitoring and other forms of observation sometimes have a bad connotation that managers must try to dispel. Some employees equate monitoring with snooping, and managers must understand these impressions and try to allay employees' concerns. First of all, managers must be honest about their monitoring process. They should ask employees to help them determine how the monitoring should be carried out and for what purposes. Typically, managers do not want to tell employees exactly when they will be monitored—especially when the monitoring involves listening in on customer service calls—as such disclosure may reduce the chance that the managers will be listening to a spontaneous and representative conversation. On the other hand, managers should give employees an idea of how often they will monitor correspondence and conversations and make sure that enough of each form of communication is monitored randomly to give a representative sample.

Next, managers and employees should discuss what factors management will be evaluating in correspondence or in a conversation. When monitoring telephone or written correspondence, managers will normally evaluate each employee on factors such as

- the accuracy with which the representative provides the service,
- the representative's knowledge of the subject being discussed,
- whether the representative uses correct grammar and syntax,
- the appropriateness of the tone used in the communication,
- whether the representative recognizes opportunities to convert a satisfied customer into a prospect for an additional sale,
- personal idiosyncrasies that customers might find disturbing, distracting, or confusing (such as breathing too heavily into the receiver, unconsciously making noises, or using jargon),
- adherence to established procedures,
- initiative displayed by the representative (such as the willingness or ability to be flexible when faced with an unusual circumstance), and
- interpersonal skills (for example, how personable the representative is, the manner in which the representative addresses the customer, and whether the employee thanks customers and encourages them to call back if they have additional questions).

Employees should be properly educated and trained so that they have the knowledge and skills needed to perform well on these factors. If the manager uses a checklist to evaluate employees, this checklist should be provided to employees in advance so they know exactly which behaviors are being evaluated.

Finally, the purpose of the monitoring should be presented in a positive manner. Employees should be reassured that monitoring is designed to help locate problem areas and to help them improve their performance, not to punish them. The purpose of monitoring is not to catch employees on every little error they make but to detect errors that groups of employees are generally making and serious problems that particular individuals may be experiencing. Serious problems encountered during monitoring should be brought to the immediate attention of the employees making those mistakes. Commonly made errors, however, are often best discussed in group sessions where they can be presented as problem areas on which most employees need improvement. (Many companies have found that when employees review calls, they are often more critical of themselves than their managers are.)

Although monitoring is often associated only with interactions between customer service personnel and outside clients, this technique can also be used to evaluate how well employees deal with internal customers and agents.

Mystery Shoppers

Another means of gathering behavioral information is through the use of mystery shoppers. A *mystery shopper* is a trained evaluator who approaches or calls a customer service employee and pretends to be a customer. The mystery shopper conducts a transaction with the employee and then evaluates the way in which the employee handles the transaction. The same advantages of monitoring also apply to the mystery shopper technique. Plus, there are two additional advantages:

1. The mystery shopper technique is far more effective than monitoring in situations in which there are direct, face-to-face interactions between employees and customers.
2. A mystery shopper can manipulate the circumstances of the interaction to see how the employee responds to various customer situations, whereas a monitor can only listen while the customer directs the interaction.

Unfortunately, the mystery shopper technique can be more expensive and may require more planning than the monitoring approach. To reduce employee anxiety about the mystery shopper approach, employees must be educated about a company's mystery shopper program, and they should have some say in its development. The company should do whatever it can to present the program in a positive light and assure employees that the results will be used to help their performance, not to punish them for mistakes. For example, Great-West Life used the mystery shopper technique combined with a contest to reward employees for positive interactions. Their "Focus on Service Contest" rewarded people who handled the calls properly, in accordance with published guidelines, by entering those employees in drawings to win prizes.

Some companies use a variation on the mystery shopper technique by having managers make anonymous phone calls to the company to gather information such as the length of time it takes to get through to the appropriate department, how many rings it takes to reach a particular person or department, the number of times telephone lines are busy, how long or how often a customer might be put on hold, and so forth. Managers can also gather similar types of information by making follow-up calls to inquire how customers perceived the service they received during recent, specific interactions with the company.

Complaints as a Performance Measure

Complaint letters should be monitored at all times. Although isolated complaint letters typically cannot be used to measure a customer service system's performance, a study of the source, number, frequency, and nature of complaint letters may indicate trends in customer concerns or customer service problems. As we indicated in Chapter 5, many companies keep a log of all complaints. Further, by categorizing its incoming complaints (as to their source, number, frequency, and nature), a company is in a much better position to eliminate the problems that are causing the complaints.

It is important to remember that a lack of complaints does not necessarily mean that a company's customer service system is performing well. Recall from the TARP studies discussed earlier that most of a business's dissatisfied customers do not bother to complain to the business. They simply tell other people how dissatisfied they are and take their business elsewhere. On a brighter note, TARP studies have also indicated that the way in which a complaint is handled affects customers' willingness not only to repurchase a product, but also to purchase additional products from the company that satisfactorily handled their complaints. When their complaints are satisfactorily resolved, between 54 and 70 percent of customers who register a complaint will do business again with the company.[7] Keeping track of and resolving customer complaints, therefore, should be high on a company's priority list.

Other Customer Service Performance Measures

While surveys and observation provide a great deal of measurable information on employee behavior, insurance companies also gather a wide variety of performance information based on quantitative measures. Some of this information and its uses in measuring customer service performance are described below:

- *Turnaround times.* Turnaround time is the amount of time it takes to complete a particular customer-initiated transaction, such as the time it takes to process a claim, underwrite an application, cut a commission check, or complete a contract change. Reports on turnaround times provide information on how responsive a system is to its customers. One problem with measuring turnaround time relates to deciding when a transaction begins and ends. Traditionally, turnaround time has been identified as starting with a request and ending with the moment the request is answered. To get a more accurate measurement of customer satisfaction, however, a growing number of companies are measuring turnaround time from the moment the customer makes a request until the time the request is *satisfied*.
- *Number of processes completed.* Another measure of customer service responsiveness, information on the number of processes completed, measures transactions such as the number of applications, claims, or policy changes made each week, month, or quarter. This measurement provides insight into how quickly and efficiently a system works.
- *Error rate.* Error rate measures the accuracy of the work done either by individuals or by a work group.
- *Call abandonment.* Call abandonment occurs when a customer makes a telephone call to a company, is put on hold

to wait for assistance, but hangs up before receiving assistance. The number or percentage of callers who abandon their calls is an indication of the system's responsiveness. A high abandonment rate may indicate that calls are not being handled efficiently enough (and staff needs better training), that too many phone calls (and possibly the wrong types of phone calls) are being routed to a particular department, or that the department needs more staff or better equipment. In addition, the length of time that a customer is willing to wait before abandoning a call gives the company some criteria on which to base its call-waiting standards and procedures.

- *Wait time.* Wait time is the average amount of time that customers must stay on the telephone before they receive assistance. Typically, the shorter the wait time, the lower the call-abandonment rate. Companies need to follow their wait-time measures very closely, so they can shorten their wait times to the maximum period acceptable to the customer. If a company hires additional operators to reduce wait time below the maximum level acceptable to customers, it may experience excess service capacity in the form of idle operators who are themselves waiting to receive telephone calls from customers. As a result, the company will incur the unnecessary expenses associated with idle resources. On the other hand, if the company does not have enough operators, it will have too little service capacity, will experience increased wait time, and as a result, may lose customers.

- *Misdirected calls.* A misdirected call occurs when an operator transfers a customer to the wrong part of the company. Measuring the number of misdirected calls gives the company an insight not only into the accuracy of the work done by its employees but also into employees' understanding of company operations and how each part of the company relates to the other parts.

For customer service processes that rely heavily on telephone communication with customers, a variety of quantitative measures can be used to evaluate the system in one way or another. These measures include phone usage rates (number of incoming calls, number of outgoing calls), number of calls getting a busy signal, average length of a call, and number of hours per day that each staff person spends with customers on the telephone. All of these measures can provide insights into such things as the level of service provided and the effectiveness of the technology being used. Many companies have computerized telephone systems that are programmed to automatically record these types of information.

Other measures, such as reductions in the number of lapsed policies, replaced policies, and policies applied for but not taken, or increases in the number of add-ons, updates, cross sales, and referrals to producers, can be used to indicate the ability of a customer service system to affect the company's bottom line.

Sampling and Measurement

As mentioned earlier in this chapter, the overuse of measurement can actually disrupt work flow and make it more difficult for employees to do their work and for the system to operate smoothly. One way to keep measurements from getting out of hand is to use sampling techniques so the company doesn't have to measure every single action but rather a representative portion of those actions.

As we discussed in Chapter 5, sampling allows researchers to examine a portion of a given population in order to make conclusions about the entire population. In Chapter 5, the subject was customer service, so the population we were talking about consisted of customers. The purpose was to select a representative sample of the company's customers and learn about their perceptions and expectations so the company could react to the needs of all its customers. In this chapter, we are concerned with measuring the performance of the company's customer service system, so the sampling has more to do with the inputs, outputs, and processes that are part of that system. For example, suppose a company uses the number of errors made in processing policy loans as one of its measures of quality. In this case, the population to be measured will be all policy loans. However, the company does not have time to check the accuracy of every policy loan transaction. Therefore, the company will sample a certain portion of them. If the samples are taken in a statistically sound manner, they should provide a representative picture of the entire population of policy loan transactions. In this way, sampling allows the company to measure its customer service performance without taking too much time away from its mission — serving the customer. Randomly selecting and monitoring customer service telephone calls and correspondence are also examples of sampling.

Putting Performance Measures to Use

The control component of the customer service system cannot be limited to gathering information and monitoring the work that is done. Instead, measurements must be used to initiate change in the system. Simple, understandable reports should be developed to present the results of measurements. These results must then be communicated to, and reviewed with, employees individually or in groups and thus used to help improve performance. The frequency with which such review sessions should be held varies, depending on factors such as the amount of change occurring in the organization and the experience or performance level of the people on the job. For example, companies or departments undergoing a great deal of change will require more frequent review sessions (perhaps monthly or even weekly), as will new employees or those experiencing performance problems.

Frequent, regularly scheduled, or even impromptu individual performance-review sessions are important because they help keep everyone on track toward achieving the standards that have been set for them. Such sessions are especially important in cases involving employees who are exhibiting poor performance. If caught early, most performance problems can be corrected before they become serious. These sessions also help avoid "unpleasant surprises" at an employee's annual performance appraisal time.

If these sessions are to be instructional for both managers and employees, then the sessions should not be performance lectures. Both the manager and employee should be expected to express

- their understanding of the standards,
- their assessment of the employee's successes or failures in meeting the standards, and
- their ideas on any steps the company or employee should take to improve performance.

The results of the monitoring and measurement process can provide companies with much valuable information. In addition to helping companies evaluate employee performance, monitoring and measuring also help point out deficiencies in the processes involved in executing policies and procedures as well as in the policies and procedures themselves. As problems are discovered, a company's ineffective processes or procedures should be revised, its technology updated, and its staffing levels changed to help the company's customer service system better meet the needs of its customers.

A Final Note about Measurement

Measurement is needed to maintain control of the processes in a company and to make sure that the processes continue to meet the needs of customers. However, if the performance measurement system measures the wrong things, it will actually lead to decreased performance rather than improved performance. As Karl Albrecht says in *At America's Service*, "In the minds of employees, it's not what you *expect*, but what you *inspect* that counts."[8] Employees will concentrate on doing the things that are measured, regardless of whether those things are most important in serving customers. Companies must avoid putting too much emphasis on efficiency and not enough on effectiveness. As Drucker observed in a seminar for federal executives held during the Eisenhower administration, "The greatest temptation is to work on doing better and better what should not be done at all."[9]

Further, when too many things are measured, employees become inhibited by the sense that they are being watched all the time. They feel handcuffed by a system that puts so many restrictions on them that they can't serve the customer. Insurers must strike a balance between measuring and controlling their customer service systems and allowing their employees enough independence to serve customers in the best way possible.

Key Terms

benchmark	monitoring
benchmarking	mystery shopper
internal standards	turnaround time
industry standards	number of processes completed
Baldrige Award	error rate
quantitative measures	call abandonment
behavioral measures	wait time
customer satisfaction surveys	misdirected call
observation	

Notes

1. Jeremy Main, "How to Win the Baldrige Award," *Fortune*, April 23, 1990, p. 108.
2. Many ideas presented in this chapter are based on a seminar called "Measure-

2222222

ment Processes," by Susan Shepard of The Travelers and on interviews with Susan Shepard.

3. James A.F. Stoner and R. Edward Freeman, *Management*, 4th ed. (Englewood Cliffs, NJ: Prentice Hall, 1989), pp. 572–73.

4. Stoner and Freeman, pp. 573–74.

5. Leonard L. Berry, David R. Bennett, and Carter W. Brown, *Service Quality: A Profit Strategy for Financial Institutions* (Homewood, IL: Dow Jones-Irwin, 1989), pp. 175–76.

6. Annette Zacher and Nancy M. Johnson, "Consumer Education: Strategies that Work," *Resource*, LOMA, March 1990, p. 26.

7. TARP, *Consumer Complaint Handling in America: An Update Study — Executive Summary* (Technical Assistance Research Programs Institute for the U.S. Office of Consumer Affairs, 1986), pp. 3–4.

8. Karl Albrecht, *At America's Service* (Homewood, IL: Dow Jones-Irwin, 1988), p. 214.

9. As quoted in Stoner and Freeman, p. 10.

CHAPTER 8

Developing a Dedicated Customer Service Staff

After studying this chapter, you should be able to

- Explain the importance of human resources in customer service
- Describe the basic steps in human resources planning and recruitment
- Describe the various types of training and education appropriate for employees who work in customer service
- Describe various types of performance appraisal
- Describe the various types of rewards and incentives that insurers use to motivate customer service representatives

Introduction

In Chapter 2, we identified the four elements that are essential for the development of a customer-oriented company. These four elements are customers (the central element), strategy, systems, and people (or human resources), and we have organized this book around those elements. In Chapter 3 we described the development of service strategies in insurance companies. In Chapters 4 and 5 we discussed insurance customers—what they expect and how to get to know them better. In Chapters 6 and 7 we discussed the importance of establishing and monitoring an effective customer service system. Now, in Chapter 8 we describe the human resources needed to provide excellent customer service.

The Importance of Human Resources

Every company needs a variety of resources in order to operate—financial resources to pay expenses, technological resources to serve customers and support employees, and human resources to make use of all the other resources. Without the human resources, without the people who work for a company, none of the other resources would amount to anything. People make a company work. This is true for the entire company, and it's especially true when we talk about customer service.

The people who work for a company determine whether or not

the company's customer service strategy will be successful. They implement the strategy, and how well they implement it determines how successful the company is in achieving its strategic goals. The people who work for a company also determine how successfully a company's customer service system operates. They not only operate the system, they should also be involved in developing the system. Their actions can determine how well the system operates and whether or not the system is the best one for serving the customer. Finally, the people who work for the company compose the critical link between the company and its customers. To a large extent, they determine whether or not customers will be satisfied with the products and the services that the company offers. As far as customers are concerned, the people they deal with *are* the company.

To develop and maintain the human resources necessary to provide excellent customer service, a company must

- examine its customers' needs,
- examine the work it does,
- determine the number and type of people it needs to do its work and satisfy its customers' needs,
- determine the best way to recruit those people to work in the company,
- develop educational and training programs to help guarantee that its employees can serve customers effectively,
- develop effective means of evaluating its employees' performance, and
- plan various rewards and incentive programs to encourage employees to continue providing excellent customer service.

We already discussed the first two steps in earlier chapters. In this chapter, we will discuss the remaining steps in human resources planning. We talk about determining human resources needs, recruiting employees for customer service work, training and educating employees to offer the best customer service, evaluating employees' performance, and motivating employees with rewards and incentives so they continue to provide the best customer service possible.

Analyzing Human Resources Needs

Once an insurance company has determined the amount of service that customers expect, it must then determine the number of employees it will probably need to fulfill those expectations. It must also analyze the technical and interpersonal skills and the personal characteristics its customer service employees will need to do their jobs properly and satisfy customers.

Job Descriptions and Job Specifications

Based on its analysis, a company develops job descriptions and job specifications to define the various roles that it needs employees to fill. A *job description* explains what a job is. It identifies the duties, responsibilities, and accountabilities of a job. A job description identifies (1) the name or title of the job, (2) the actual work done on the job, (3) the immediate supervisor or manager for the job being described, and possibly, (4) how the job relates to other jobs in the company.

Typically, a job specification is part of, or at least attached to, the job description. A *job specification* describes the qualifications and characteristics that a person must have to perform a job. A job specification indicates the required level of education, amount of experience, type of training, and personal characteristics that a person must have in order to be considered a candidate for a certain job.

By developing these job descriptions and job specifications, a company has a better idea of the kinds of human resources it needs to do its work. In addition, people who apply for jobs in the company will have a fairly accurate understanding of the kind of work they would be expected to do. Look at Figure 8–1 for an example of a job description and a job specification currently used for a customer service position in the insurance industry.

Who Develops Job Descriptions and Job Specifications?

Developing job descriptions and job specifications should be a cooperative effort between human resources managers, customer service managers, and customer service employees. Human resources managers have expertise in analyzing personnel needs and developing job descriptions and specifications. They understand the steps involved with each of these processes. However, the customer service managers and employees know what is needed to get the job done. They may not understand the best way to conduct a human resources needs analysis or the best way to develop a job description,

Figure 8–1
Sample Job Description and Job Specification

POSITION TITLE: Customer Assistant III
DEPARTMENT: Customer Service Organization
REPORTS TO: Office Manager
DATE: April 13, 1989

GENERAL ACCOUNTABILITY:

Accountable for providing expert sales support to marketing staff and professional customer service to all customers; ensuring policyowners, marketing, head office, and other divisions receive accurate and timely assistance to conserve business and promote good public relations with our clients, thereby contributing to new sales and conservation of existing business. Also acts as a technical resource for other Customer Assistants and back-up support to the Office Manager.

NATURE AND SCOPE:

The general sales division's sales activities are targeted to professionals, businesses, and upper-income individuals. It is important that our company be distinguished as the leader in customer service in the complex up-scale market.

The role of the Customer Assistant is to provide front line sales and service support. C.A.'s are assigned to support, on average, 3.5 representatives. C.A.'s are instrumental in morale building for these representatives as well as providing training on product/service procedures.

Customer Assistants frequently have the first, critical contact with the client and provide "moment of truth" service. Representatives are often out of the office and unavailable.

The Customer Assistants complete the service circle from inquiry to resolution and must deal face-to-face with our policyowners, often under stressful conditions, as well as meeting demanding deadlines.

In the senior position, the Customer Assistant has developed breadth and depth in knowledge of our company's products, business systems, and office operations.

1. **Support to Office Manager:**

   Accountable for assisting with the training and managing of the administrative staff; participates in special projects as assigned; accountable for the effective operation of the office in the absence of the office manager.

   Measures: Effective operation of office in office manager's absence; procedure manuals and training aids current and effectively used; quality projects completed on time; contribution to daily operations.

2. **Customer Service:**

   Provides superior customer service to clients though correspondence, telephone, and face-to-face interviews for the purpose of conserving business in force, which contributes to the achievement of growth in our business. Acts on behalf of representative in his/her absence and supports in sales efforts.

Figure 8–1 (Continued)

Measures: Number and materiality of complaints/compliments; turnaround time; depth and breadth of product/procedure knowledge; ability to deal with complex situations.

3. Conservation:

Contributes to the conservation of existing policies by timely follow-ups and effective interaction with policyowners to retain existing policy base, promote repeat business, and reduce replacement.

Measures: Ability to conduct a conservation interview; timely follow-ups on loans, expiries, lapsables; net controllable terminations.

4. Productivity and Innovation:

Contributes to operation improvement by suggesting, implementing, and becoming involved in initiatives to improve effectiveness of office operation and customer service, which results in higher profits, better returns to policyowners, and better overall position in the industry.

Measures: Number and acceptability of ideas; involvement in campaigns; materiality of ideas accepted and implemented.

KNOWLEDGE/SKILLS:

- Superior letter-writing skills in corresponding with upscale target market
- Develops and applies complete knowledge of all aspects of the business
- Comprehensive knowledge of plans issued (including their features, peculiarities, and limitations, as well as the features and limitations of each benefit), and full knowledge of new-wave products
- Awareness of premium scales used, substandard ratings, modes of payment, etc.
- Excellent human relations skills, competent secretarial/administrative skills
- Knowledge of applicable taxation and government legislation
- Ability to utilize all regional office systems
- Thorough knowledge of office and company procedures, as well as regional managers' attitudes and preferences
- Organizational and problem-solving skills

but they understand what is actually needed to do the work in their areas. They have firsthand knowledge of the problems they face, and they understand the kind of person who is most successful in the type of work done in their area. Therefore, the development of job descriptions and job specifications should be a cooperative effort that takes advantage of the experience and knowledge of a variety of people in the company.

Recruitment

After developing job descriptions and job specifications, the company faces the task of recruitment. *Recruitment* is the process of identifying and attracting job applicants who match job specifications and are capable of performing the duties outlined in job descriptions. It is also the process of screening out job candidates who are not appropriate for the positions that the company needs to fill. Recruitment is usually left to human resources professionals, since they are familiar with the best ways to locate prospective employees and how to inform them of job opportunities at the company.

Sources of Potential Job Candidates

There are two general sources of job candidates: internal and external. The *internal* source is the pool of potential job candidates who are currently employed by the recruiting company. The *external* sources are the various pools of potential job candidates who come from outside the recruiting company.

All businesses hire employees from both internal and external sources, and both sources have advantages and disadvantages. One of the greatest advantages of hiring from within the organization is its ease and low cost. If a company maintains a *human resources inventory*, that is, a list of all its employees, including their experience, education, and particular skills, it can identify without too much difficulty whether or not it has the right people to fill positions that become available. By hiring people from within, the organization is hiring people whose qualities it knows and who know the organization. People who work for the company understand the company's procedures and culture. They know who to talk to in order to get something done. They understand what is required of them and what the company expects. They need less training than employees hired from external sources. And, finally, companies that have a policy of hiring and promoting from within often find that their employees are more motivated, because they know their performance has a direct effect on their opportunities to advance in the company.

On the other hand, when companies hire from within, they take the chance of missing out on new ideas. The employee who is hired or promoted from within generally has learned to work within the company's corporate culture and its standard operating procedures. Because of this internal conditioning, the internal hire may be less likely to question why things are done a certain way and less likely to suggest novel ways to approach a situation. On the other hand, employees who are hired from outside the company carry no such baggage. They perceive the company's operations from a fresh perspective. They may make mistakes through inexperience, and they may take longer to train, but they may also see opportunities for improvement that people inside the company don't see. Coming from different environments, people hired from external sources bring experiences with them that can help the company see new ways of doing things. In addition, external sources also provide a company with a larger pool of human resources than the company can provide by itself. Frequently, the right person for a certain job cannot be found inside a company, or if people can be found in the company, they might be needed in other jobs. Whatever the reason, a company cannot always, and should not always, hire from within. External sources offer a large and useful pool of potential job candidates.

Methods of Recruiting

Businesses have a variety of options for recruiting employees. These options or methods of recruiting include

- posting job notices within the company,
- advertising in newspapers and trade journals,
- recruiting in colleges and universities (and occasionally in high schools), and
- having current employees refer job candidates to the company.

Job Posting

Job posting is an internal recruitment method. It is a way of letting current employees know about new job offerings or vacancies in old jobs. In a properly administered job-posting program, any job that becomes available in a company is announced to all employees. Typically, a job description and job specification are posted on bulletin boards in centrally located places in the company. All employees are encouraged to read the job postings and apply for any job they feel qualified for. By giving everyone a chance to apply for a job, the company reduces the possibility of favoritism or bias in choosing job candidates. Plus, by using companywide job posting, the company can draw from the largest possible pool of current employees. Usually, a job posting is left up for a few days. If no suitable job candidate is found among current employees, the company will then turn to external recruiting.

Advertising in Newspapers and Other Media

Probably the best-known method of job recruiting is the use of advertisements—typically classified advertisements in newspapers or magazines but also, perhaps, advertisements on radio or television. This form of recruiting allows companies to reach a large number of potential job candidates. The success of a job advertising campaign relies primarily on two factors: (1) how well the advertisement is written and (2) the number of qualified candidates that are exposed to the ad.

A good advertisement gives as complete a description of the job as space allows and lists the basic requirements that applicants must have to be considered for a job. The advertisement should make the job and the company attractive to readers or listeners, and the writing should be clear and honest.

When choosing the type of medium (for example, newspaper or magazine) in which to advertise, a company must consider the most cost-effective way to reach the largest number of qualified candidates. If a company is advertising a job that it believes a wide range of people can apply for, then the company is likely to advertise in a low-cost medium that will reach the widest possible audience, such as a large-circulation local newspaper. However, if it wants to target its audience more carefully, it may choose other media. For example, if a company needs computer programmers, it will probably advertise in computer magazines. If a company has a large number of jobs that it thinks will appeal to young adults, it may advertise on radio programs directed at that particular audience. Similarly, if a company has part-time jobs that may appeal to retired people, the company may advertise in magazines with an older audience.

Figure 8–2
Examples of Classified Advertisements

CUSTOMER SERVICE REPRESENTATIVE

ABC Life, a Fortune 500 company and a leader in the life insurance industry, has an immediate need for an experienced Customer Service Representative.

The individual we seek will develop and maintain customer relationships through effective communication skills.

The successful applicant must have a minimum of 5–7 years customer service experience, preferably in the financial industry. Production schedule experience is a plus. The ability to work in a fast-paced dynamic and professional environment is a must.

We offer an excellent salary and a top-rated benefits package. If you qualify and are seeking a career with an industry leader, please send your resume, including salary history, to:

ABC LIFE
Dept. RP
P.O. Box 00000
Atlanta, GA 30348

Due to the volume of response,
we are unable to respond
to all inquiries.

Equal Opportunity Employer, M/F

Customer Service Representative

As one of America's most respected leaders in financial services, XYZ Financial Corporation now seeks a highly organized individual to oversee timely and accurate processing of loan documents and customer payments.

The successful candidate will greet customers and provide service information on general inquiries, process documents, receive payments, and perform administrative/clerical duties.

A high school diploma (or equivalent) and a minimum of 6–12 months of related office experience is required. Strong communication skills and a sharp math aptitude are important. The ability to work flexible hours is also required.

In return for your expertise, we can offer an attractive salary and top benefits including medical/life/dental, savings, tuition reimbursement, and more. For immediate consideration, call John Smith at 212-000-0000. An Equal Opportunity Employer.

XYZ FINANCIAL CORPORATION

If a company is looking for candidates who are already working in the insurance industry, it may advertise in a trade magazine like the *National Underwriter*.

College and University Recruiting

Generally, recruiting at colleges and universities is an expensive means of finding potential job candidates. Companies must pay the salaries of recruiters who visit campuses and meet personally with students. The cost of such recruiting ranges from $1,500 to $6,000 per person hired. Because of this expense, not all companies can afford this type of recruiting. However, by recruiting in colleges and universities, businesses can focus their recruiting efforts on a very specific market — college students working toward degrees in academic areas that businesses feel will make the students particularly suited for work in their companies. Aside from using college and university recruiting to fill specific jobs, many businesses use this kind of recruiting as a form of public relations. It allows the company to maintain a high profile among the kinds of people it would like to hire in the future.

Companies and colleges can also work together to develop *intern programs* in which students work full-time for a company during a defined period (such as six months) and receive credits toward graduation. Intern programs give students a chance to learn about a company and give companies a chance to identify job candidates who have a high potential for success.

Job Referrals

Job referral occurs when an employee of a company recommends that the company hire someone that the employee knows. Typically, job referral is an efficient and inexpensive way to recruit new employees. Because a current employee is recommending the job candidate, the company should feel fairly certain that the candidate is potentially suited for the job. Furthermore, because the candidate is identified for the company, the amount of time and effort spent in the recruitment process is greatly reduced. Because this method often provides good candidates, companies frequently pay recruitment bonuses to employees who refer successful candidates. On the other hand, people hired through a job-referral system are frequently similar to the kinds of people who already work for the company. Therefore, a company that relies too heavily on job referrals can run into a problem much like the one suffered by a company that relies too heavily on hiring from within — not enough new ideas enter the company. In addition, a company that relies heavily on job referrals may be accused of bias or favoritism in its hiring practices.

Qualifications of Customer Service Personnel

As we noted earlier, a job specification describes the qualifications needed in a candidate for a particular job. These qualifications include the educational level, the technical training and experience, and the personality traits of candidates it is considering. At one time, people who were recruited to work in customer service areas were not expected to meet very extensive qualifications. Typically, no more than a high-school education was required, and candidates were not expected to have much experience working in customer service. Today, more and more insurance companies are raising the qualifications for customer service representatives. They are looking for people with college degrees. They're also looking for people with strong interpersonal skills, such as the ability to communicate effectively in conversation and in writing, the ability to remain calm under pressure, and the ability to manage unhappy customers. Companies look for people who enjoy helping other people. Finally, because of the widespread use of automated administrative systems in customer service operations, companies are also looking for people who are comfortable working with computers.

Personality Traits for Success in Customer Service

With the proper education, training, and support, most people can become proficient customer service providers. On the other hand, there are also certain personal characteristics and attitudes that make some people more likely than others to do well in customer service. Some of these traits may be part of an individual's personality. Others may be developed through training and personal experience. Listed below are some of the traits that many experts believe are desirable in a person who works in customer service. In many ways, these are traits that employers would like to see in most of their employees. But they are especially important for customer service personnel.

- *Positive attitude.* People with positive attitudes believe that they can make things succeed for their customers and themselves. A positive attitude is often the first step toward reaching a successful resolution to any problem.
- *Cheerful manner.* When customer service personnel are cheerful, customers enjoy doing business with the company and co-workers enjoy working together. A cheerful manner can overcome a lot of obstacles in customer service.
- *Desire to serve.* Some people feel the need to help or serve other people. This kind of person has often been attracted to

work in areas such as health care and community services. Many potential employees see customer service as a means of helping other people, giving them the opportunity to educate people about the company and its services. Companies that want to be proficient in customer service should try to attract people with this desire to serve.

- *High energy level.* Customer service work can be highly demanding. It can be fast-paced and emotionally demanding. A person with a high level of energy, a person who is "up" most of the time, is likely to do well in customer service.
- *Flexibility and creativity.* Responding to customers' needs means that a customer service worker must be ready to take unexpected courses of action and adapt company procedures to the needs of the customer. A flexible, creative person can handle unexpected situations and turn them into positive experiences.
- *Articulateness.* Employees in customer service deal with customers either on the phone, in person, or by mail. Customer service specialists must be able to express themselves clearly and pleasantly.
- *High self-esteem.* Customers are not always happy with the service that a company provides them, and employees in customer service must work with these unhappy customers. Listening to complaints on a regular basis can be quite demoralizing. Taking these complaints personally can lower a worker's sense of self-worth. Therefore, it is helpful for people working in customer service to have an inherently high sense of self-esteem. It helps them deal with the bad times.
- *Calm demeanor.* A person who remains calm under trying circumstances is a special sort of person. A patient, calm demeanor can help a person deal with some of the difficult and unexpected problems that sometimes arise in customer service.
- *Ability to work well with others.* A company can provide a high level of customer service only if it has employees who work well together. Customer service employees need to develop a high sense of cooperation — with other employees as well as with customers.
- *Proactive insight.* Companies need customer service employees who have the ability to spot areas of customer dissatisfaction before they become full-blown problems.

This is only a partial list of the personality traits that employees may need while working in customer service.

Applicant Testing

As a means of screening job applicants and identifying the most qualified people, businesses today use a variety of tests. These tests can be divided into six categories — aptitude tests, psychomotor tests, job knowledge tests, skills tests, interest tests, and psychological tests. These categories are described briefly below:

- *Aptitude tests* measure a person's potential ability to perform a job. Aptitude tests do not measure a person's current knowledge of, or skill in, a specific job. Rather, they measure more general abilities, such as a person's ability to use language, numbers, or logical thought. Great care must be used in developing such tests to make sure they are not culturally biased. The Job Effectiveness Prediction System (JEPS) offered by LOMA is one example of a validated test. JEPS is designed to help insurance companies take the guesswork out of hiring entry-level employees. To complement JEPS, LOMA is currently developing an aptitude test to help the insurance industry identify job candidates who are likely to succeed in customer service. The primary component of the system is a videotaped "situations test" that presents job candidates with a series of difficult customer service scenarios. After viewing the scenarios, the candidates will be asked to describe how they would handle the scenarios.

- *Psychomotor tests* measure a person's physical strength, dexterity, and coordination. These tests seldom apply to work in insurance companies or customer service.

- *Job knowledge tests* measure a person's understanding of a particular job. A test on using a computer terminal and a particular software program might be a type of knowledge test.

- *Skills tests* measure a person's ability to perform the functions required for a particular job. Typing tests are skills tests. Such tests are closely related to job knowledge tests but are even more specific. Both job knowledge tests and skills tests are considered very useful as screening tools, because they correlate so closely with actual jobs. SEEK is a skills test offered by LOMA to help companies screen typists, data entry operators, and word processors.

- *Interest tests* are designed to determine what a job candidate's particular interests are and then compare these interests to those of people who have been successful in the type of job that the candidate is applying for. Insurance companies sometimes use interest tests as career-planning tools.

- *Psychological tests* (also called *personality tests*) measure an individual's personal charactistics. The purpose is to determine if the job candidate has the type of personality that is likely to be successful in a particular kind of job. Many critics believe that the interpretation of psychological tests is too subjective and that their validity and reliability are too low. However, a growing number of companies see psychological testing as a tool that can help them choose the kinds of personalities who are likely to succeed in customer service. Therefore, more companies and consultants are working to make psychological tests effective predictors of success in customer service.

Training and Education for Customer Service Employees

In today's business world, training and educating employees is a never-ending concern. Businesses must be prepared to train and educate employees, not only when they first begin working in the industry, but throughout their careers. The business environment is constantly changing and demanding more and more from companies and their employees. Therefore, businesses must ensure that their employees develop and maintain the skills and knowledge that are needed to respond to the changing business environment.

Training and education in business cover a wide range of areas, from first-day orientation to on-the-job training all the way up to university-level courses. In the next few pages, we will describe some of the basic types of training and education that businesses provide for their customer service employees.

Job Orientation

When any new employee starts work, job orientation is called for. *Job orientation* introduces employees to the company they are joining and to the work they are about to do. Job orientation does not make an employee an expert on the job, but it should give the employee enough information to function adequately. In addition, it can help make sure the employee begins work with a positive attitude and an understanding of the company's culture.

Three areas of orientation are particularly important for someone entering a customer service role in the company. The first area is orientation to the company. This orientation is typically handled by a company's human resources department. It introduces the new employee to the overall structure of the company and explains how the employee fits into that structure. Typically, such an orientation will include an explanation of the company's organizational structure, its policies and procedures, and its fringe benefits, such as group insurance and vacation time. But more than that, the company orientation should introduce the new employee to the company's culture and its mission. This orientation should let the employee know what the company expects of all its employees, how the company and its customers benefit from the work of the employees, and how the employees are benefited by the company. Ideally, a company with a strong customer service mission will make that mission known during this first companywide orientation.

After the company orientation, a new employee is given an orientation to the unit in which the employee will be working. This orientation introduces the new employee to the basic operations of the unit and to the other employees in the unit. In addition, the orientation reinforces the ideas presented earlier about the company's mission, culture, and commitment to customer service, stressing the activities that are specific to that unit.

Finally, there may be an orientation to the concept of customer service itself. This may introduce the idea of a customer service culture, the economic importance of customer service to the company and the employee, and some of the basic rules of providing service to the customer.

Look at Customer Service in Action 8–1 (on the next page) to find out what Metropolitan Life Insurance Company is doing to orient its new employees to a customer service culture.

How MetLife Gets Its Employees Started

From the employee's first day on the job, a companywide orientation program at MetLife emphasizes quality and accountability.

MetLife's companywide employee orientation program *Quality from the Start* was developed with the input of more than 2,000 MetLife personnel. *Quality from the Start* introduces the newcomer to the company's businesses, customers, expectations, and corporate values. The program consists of two video presentations and a variety of printed materials that give the new employee an overview of MetLife's family of companies and its scope of business.

Quality from the Start officially begins with a welcome letter to the new employee after the individual accepts a job offer. The program is officially completed on the employee's one-year anniversary.

Quality from the Start pairs the new employee with a mentor and builds in opportunities for the employee to talk with managers and associates.

The program places responsibility on the new employee to take an active role in learning about the company and his or her job responsibilities.

It also embraces the philosophy that giving an employee 'the best possible start" translates into an employee who will deliver service excellence and contribute to MetLife's success.

The company believes that just as the first day on the job is an important step in a person's career, that first day is also an important step in a company's investment in the individual as well as the company's future.

Quality from the Start is designed to help employees:

- develop a sense of pride in working at MetLife,
- become aware of the scope of the company's businesses and its impact as a major financial institution,
- reduce the anxieties associated with starting a new job,
- become productive, contributing members of the MetLife team quickly and efficiently,
- understand that quality customer service is a primary source of competitive advantage,
- understand the standards of quality by which performance is measured, and
- share responsibility for individual growth and development.

Before *Quality from the Start*, MetLife had no official orientation program. Instead, the different business lines and departments used materials each developed over the years to orient new employees.

Susan Berger is the Assistant Vice President responsible for Human Resources Development and Training at MetLife. Berger explains that the human resources department began developing the program in the fall of 1986. The year-long development phase was required because all areas of the company were asked to participate in the development. *Quality from the Start* debuted in the fall of 1987.

"*Quality from the Start*," Berger remarks, "is not something the human resources department constructed in an

Ivory Tower. It is built on the expressed needs and issues of our lines of business." A majority of the planning involved research and interviews.

- MetLife studied how other excellent companies, both in and out of the insurance industry, oriented the new employee at every level. "A unique and successful aspect of our program is that it's not directed at only clerical-level employees or professional-level employees," comments Berger. "We built it to serve the entire employee population."
- An internal survey gathered information on what MetLife's businesses and departments were already doing to orient employees.
- Employees who joined MetLife within the previous six months completed a questionnaire. The questionnaire asked them to describe the good and bad aspects of their orientation experience as well as their feelings about joining a company of 33,000 employees.
- Executives and managers were asked their opinions about a companywide orientation program.
- MetLife vice presidents and upper middle managers formed focus groups to discuss the research compiled from the outside companies.

These focus groups developed 11 excellent employee practices, which serve as the cornerstone of *Quality from the Start*. These practices center on three areas of on-the-job action and offer a blueprint for the excellent employee.

Area 1: Quality and Customer Focus

The excellent employee:

- knows who his or her customer is,
- is service and results oriented,
- does it right the first time and on time,
- demonstrates high personal standards, and
- pursues self-development.

Area 2: Accountability for Results

The excellent employee:

- is personally accountable for high-quality results, takes responsibility for getting the job done,
- demonstrates a sense of urgency in getting the job done,
- asks questions, finds out why, is curious, and
- is decisive.

Area 3: Teamwork

The excellent employee:

- communicates with associates, management, and customers, and
- shares ideas and sells new ideas.

The research phase of the project unveiled recurrent themes about the orientation program. Managers did not want restrictive procedures. They preferred materials and tools they could mold to their needs.

Second, the orientation materials should be appropriate for all employee levels. In addition, the materials should be valuable to existing employees to avoid a "new employee versus old employee" culture.

The size and complexity of MetLife often means that even long-service employees are unaware of operations outside their areas. Videos would prove to be an ideal way to present information about MetLife's history, current business, customers, and future plans to both the new and old employee.

Orienting through Videos

Quality from the Start is composed of two video presentations. The total running time is 26 minutes.

"Looking Back to See Ahead" takes the employee to the Civil War and traces the company's beginning as the National Union Life and Limb Insurance Company. The video moves into modern times and covers recent developments at MetLife, such as the acquisitions program and international expansion.

Several executive officers address the challenges MetLife faces in "Our Businesses." This segment presents an overview of MetLife's major lines of business and insight into how these businesses are interrelated.

The Manager's Role

The emphasis on a manager's participation in *Quality from the Start* is made clear by the management guide that details all facets of the program. The guide gives managers an overview of each program segment as well as a suggested timeframe to follow.

In addition, the management guide describes an important component of the orientation process—the mentor. Each new employee is assigned a mentor for the duration of orientation. The manager can serve as the mentor or can appoint a co-worker to act as the mentor. The mentor assists the employee in learning about MetLife and its environment.

The manager's guide contains an orientation checklist for the mentor to follow. This checklist groups the mentor's activities

under categories that cover touring the work facilities, introducing staff members, describing the telephone system, reviewing local policies and procedures, and providing relocation information if an individual is new to the area. A new employee also receives the checklist. It serves as a road map the employee uses to chart orientation activities and the specific resources (such as organization charts and videotapes) that are available to accomplish the activities.

Though *Quality from the Start* is structured to operate over a one-year period, Berger describes the program as "a process that enables people to become as productive as they can. The process," she continues, "can take up to a year depending on the employee and the type of job and business."

Planning a Program

What advice can she offer to companies interested in implementing a comprehensive employee orientation program? Berger cites four guidelines.

First, talk to the managers who will orient new employees to discover needs and wants. "Don't assume that management has nothing else to do but orient new employees," she cautions. "Managers have jobs to do, and they are protective of their time and energy."

Second, interview employees hired within the last six months. These employees are valuable information sources and can point out areas they didn't learn about when they started.

Third, design an easy-to-use program. Test materials as they are developed to remove the trouble spots.

Finally, make the program flexible so managers want to use it. Managers will want to use it if they don't view their participation as one more job they must do.

"At MetLife," Berger summarizes, "we want employees to be active in their orientation and career development. To deliver quality service to all customers, they must feel accountable for what they do. This feeling must start right at the beginning, and this is what *Quality from the Start* is all about."

Source: Adapted with permission of the publisher from Chris Breston, "MetLife Gives Employees the Best Possible Start," *Resource,* LOMA, November-December 1988, pp. 22–27.

On-the-Job Training

Orientation is only the beginning of a career-long process of training and education. The early training usually concentrates on the skills and knowledge that new employees need to do the work they were hired to do. This training frequently begins with **on-the-job training (OJT)**, during which a co-worker or a supervisor of the new employee explains the step-by-step operations of a job and watches while the new employee does the job. The person who is supervising the OJT shows the new employee how to do the work, watches the employee do the task, notes where he or she has made mistakes, and shows how to remedy those mistakes. Ideally, the trainer gives the employee written job aids for later reference.

On-the-job training includes training in a variety of areas, such as filling out reports, answering telephone calls, or operating computer equipment and software. The advantage of OJT is that it is conducted while the new employee is working, so the situations that the employee learns about are the actual ones that he or she will have to deal with on a day-to-day basis. In addition, the person who teaches the new employee is someone who actually does the work for a living, someone who has firsthand knowledge of the job.

Unfortunately, OJT can be an inefficient form of training. It takes the person who is doing the training away from the work that he or she would ordinarily be doing. Furthermore, while the person providing OJT may be an experienced employee, he or she may not be trained in OJT techniques and, therefore, may not be an effective trainer. In addition, because the training is done in the actual work situation, errors made during training are, in fact, errors on the job. Because the situation is real, the trainee may feel more pressure than in a training situation away from work.

Classroom Training

In order to avoid, or at least alleviate, some of the disadvantages caused by OJT, most companies provide a certain amount of training away from the work unit. This training may be conducted by the new employee's supervisor or a co-worker, but it is more likely to be conducted by a person whose primary job is to train the company's employees. This training is often presented in a classroom format in which an instructor lectures to the group, leads the group in discussion, or directs the group as they do various exercises, such as role playing. Videotapes are frequently used to supplement the information taught in the classroom format.

The advantage of classroom training is that it removes trainees from the pressure of the work unit and allows them to concentrate completely on the skills and knowledge they are supposed to acquire. In addition, it is usually supervised and conducted by professional trainers, people whose primary responsibility and expertise are to teach the company employees how to work more effectively. The big disadvantage of this kind of training is the flip side of one of its advantages: the training occurs away from the work unit, away from the actual conditions under which the employee will be expected to use the skills he or she has just learned. Because the training occurs away from the work unit and is provided by trainers who may not be aware of all the conditions at the work unit, the training may not be completely applicable on the job.

Simulation Training

To overcome the disadvantages of classroom training, some businesses try to create training conditions that are as much like actual working conditions as possible. This type of training, called *simulation*, is designed to give employees the opportunity to see what it's like on the job without putting them under the pressure of actually being on the job. With simulation, employees can feel free to apply their training and not be afraid to make mistakes. They can practice the procedures and techniques they have learned in classroom situations and learn from whatever errors they make during the simulation. Simulations vary greatly in their attempts to match working conditions. Some are highly sophisticated and replicate working conditions almost exactly. An example of such sophisticated simulations is the flight-simulation cockpit used by pilots and astronauts, which matches actual flight conditions almost exactly. A typical business example is a situation where a company with a large volume of telephone calls puts trainees in an office with telephone equipment and assigns trainers to play the role of customers. The trainees practice making and answering business calls and dealing with problems that commonly occur on the job.

The great advantage of these exact replicas is that they make the trainees feel that they are actually on the job. They feel real stress and they deal with what appear to be real problems. Employees coming out of such sophisticated training can feel almost like seasoned veterans before they even get on the job. The disadvantage of simulations that replicate working conditions to a high degree is that they can be very expensive. To avoid this expense, companies create less exact replicas or use computer software to simulate business situat job.

Computer-Based Training

Computers can be used for a variety of training situations, not just simulations. Many companies are using *computer-based training (CBT)* to increase their employees' skills and knowledge. Typically, a trainee sits at a terminal or a personal computer and uses a software program to learn about a specific topic. These CBT programs vary widely in complexity and effectiveness. Some programs are little more than electronic page-turners, requiring the trainee to read the text on a screen and then push the return key to go to the next screen and the next page of text. Other programs are far more interactive and, as indicated above, attempt to simulate actual working conditions. These software programs require trainees to deal with complex business situations and come up with workable solutions. Once the solution is offered, the software will tell the trainee how close he or she came to the best answer and then suggest that the trainee either go on to another topic or continue to work with the current topic.

To create a more interesting and realistic training situation, videotape and computer software can be combined in a type of CBT called *interactive video training (IVT)*. In this format, a videotape is made and then transferred to a video laser disk (similar to the kind of disk that is used for music in a compact disk player). A software program is also developed and transferred to the same laser disk. The result (when done properly) is a training videotape, viewed through a computer, that does not allow the trainee to be a passive observer.

IVT requires the trainee to respond to the information presented, to choose various responses and courses of action. It then shows the trainee where he or she made errors and suggests ways to correct those errors. With IVT, the trainee is allowed to go to any part of the video at any time just by telling the computer. The advantage of IVT over standard CBT is that the video portion can make the training more interesting and more realistic. Unfortunately, it also makes the training more expensive.

Education

Typically, *training* is designed to give employees the skills they need to do specific kinds of tasks most effectively. For example, training may teach customer service representatives how to use computer software, fill out forms, conduct interviews, listen effectively, communicate effectively, influence people, or manage time. Training may also teach people about the products that a company offers. In the case of an insurance company, the training may include an explanation of the company's different policies, including a description of each policy's benefits and provisions and how they are administered. Through training, employees of a company become efficient at using the company's operating procedures and knowledgeable about the company's products.

In addition to training, though, many companies encourage their employees to attain a broader level of education, because they realize that they need employees who have a wide range of knowledge about a variety of subjects. While employees who are trained to do specific jobs may contribute significantly to the company, employees who also have a broad knowledge of many different areas provide the company with a reservoir of talent and wisdom that can benefit the company for years to come. Because of their broad backgrounds and knowledge, such employees may be able to respond more quickly and imaginatively to unexpected situations.

This broader education may be attained by employees when they attend seminars or participate in independent study programs, such as the FLMI Insurance Education Program or the CLU (Chartered Life Underwriter) program, or when they attend university courses. Many businesses pay for all or part of their employees' fees when they participate in educational programs.

In addition, many insurers are growing more concerned about an apparent decline in the basic math and verbal skills of their new employees. These employers are creating, or paying for, programs that help them provide their employees with at least a minimum level of knowledge.

Job Rotation and Mentoring

Other forms of employee development include job rotation and mentoring. In a sense, both are a type of extended OJT. In *job rotation*, employees are moved periodically from one job to another, staying in each job long enough to learn how the job is done and how it relates to other jobs in the company. The advantage of job rotation is that it gives an employee the opportunity to gain a broad understanding of the company's operations and of the people involved in those operations. The disadvantage (according to some people) is that it forces the employee to stay in each role just long enough to learn the basics but not long enough to become really proficient in the role. In addition, job rotation requires the company to commit the resources necessary to train the employees who are rotating through various jobs.

In *mentoring*, an inexperienced employee is assigned to work with a more experienced employee, or *mentor*. The idea behind mentoring is that it provides an inexperienced employee with a specific person who can answer questions, offer advice, and provide general guidance as the employee gets accustomed to new responsibilities and a new environment. However, for a monitoring program to be effective, the company must make mentoring an official part of the mentor's responsibilities. If mentoring responsibilities are not worked into the mentor's job description, the mentor either will not take the mentoring responsibilities seriously or will not be given enough time to give the new employee the needed direction.

Continuous Training and Education

As we mentioned earlier, training and education must continue throughout a person's career. Every new job will require new skills and different levels of knowledge. Even when a person keeps the same job, aspects of the job will change so that new skills and knowledge will be needed and old skills will have to be reinforced and kept from getting stale. No company can afford to let that happen. Training and education are an integral part of a company's investment in its employees.

Look at Customer Service in Action 8–2 for a description of some of the steps to take when training employees for work in customer service. Although the company profiled in this selection is not an insurance company, it is a leader in providing customer service. The steps it takes to train its employees in customer service apply to any company that wants to achieve excellence in customer service.

CUSTOMER SERVICE IN ACTION 8–2

Customer Service Training at Arkla Incorporated

Fact: Unless frontline employees develop a sense of competency and confidence in what they do, they will pass the buck to the manager.

What to do? Train them in the skills they need to gain the confidence that is necessary to deal competently with even the most difficult situations.

"If you equip frontline employees with the skills, confidence, and knowledge to handle problems on their own," says Bob Brewer, Manager of Organizational Development for Arkla Incorporated (Shreveport, LA), "you [the manager] will have more time to do what you should be doing—planning and managing."

Developing the Program

Brewer has been training employees in customer service techniques since the early 1970s. When he came to Arkla in 1978, one of his first assignments was to create a comprehensive training program for the customer service representatives in the company's gas utility division. Eventually, the program, called "Positive Customer Relations," spread to *all* employees in the division's five states who had contact with

customers, whether in person or on the phone. These included customer service representatives, meter readers, service technicians, and construction personnel.

Brewer also expanded the program to cover issues related to building even better relations with the majority of customers—those who are *not* angry, who don't cause problems, who pay their bills on time, and who always cooperate. "Those who seem to fall between the cracks and frequently feel that they are not appreciated and valued," he explains.

To Brewer's way of thinking, effective customer service training involves more than just the classroom experience. There are three steps involved in the training process:

1. Preparing employees for the training experience.
2. Conducting the training.
3. Measuring results after the training and providing follow-up coaching.

Preparing for the Training

"It is important to create a sense of involvement in the training among the employees before they even begin the program," stresses Brewer. Employees will have questions that need answering before they can mentally and emotionally prepare themselves to receive the training:

- Why am I being chosen for the program?
- How successful will I be?
- How "professional" will this training be? How serious is this company about the program?
- What do I need to do to prepare for the training?
- What will be expected of me after the training?

To answer these questions, Brewer arranges for a great deal of preparation for participants before the training begins.

First, he gains top management support and has the CEO send a letter to all training participants explaining the importance the company places on customers, its commitment to service and quality, and the importance of employees projecting positive images to customers. The letter explains that the trainees have been individually selected and that the training is something special.

Brewer also explains to the participants why the training will be a positive experience for them. For many of the participants, this is the first training or educational experience they have had since being in school. "It is very important, therefore, that we make this a positive experience," states Brewer. If they view it as negative or threatening, or as a drudgery before they even start, the purpose will be defeated. To overcome these problems, Brewer emphasizes to the trainees that they have been selected because they are important to the company, not because there is anything wrong with them.

Brewer also lets the participants know what they need to do to prepare for the training. He provides the trainees with pre-course materials to read, fill out, and complete, including surveys on

- how much they already know about serving customers properly,
- how they are currently treating customers, and
- how much they know about the company's business (its goals and operations).

Some of the material is pre-course reading designed to bring everyone up to the same level before the training begins.

In many organizations, training is not a highly regarded activity. "Frequently," says Brewer, "training is viewed as an 'if you have the time' endeavor. If a prospective trainee takes a casual attitude toward the experience, the probability for significant results will be minimal. We want to make sure that the employees take the training seriously." Therefore, employees who do not complete the pre-course materials are not allowed to attend. In addition, Brewer emphasizes to employees that the program will be organized, efficient, and effective. "We want to establish credibility *before* the training."

Before the training begins, employees sit down with their supervisors (who have already participated in the training) and discuss

- any apprehensions or concerns the employees have about going into the program,
- what the employees need to concentrate on in the program, and
- what performance outcomes the employees should be able to exhibit after training.

The employees then sign a "learning agreement" with their supervisors, covering expectations and outcomes. "This kind of commitment between employee and supervisor helps to underscore the vital link that training played in the employee's performance expectations," says Brewer.

The Training Program

Introducing the Program. The first step once the trainees actually enter the program is to create positive expectations—the training should be a good experience for them *and* it will help them and the company in the long run. Employees view a videotaped two-minute speech from the CEO. No matter where the program is conducted in the field, employees view the videotape and understand the importance the company is placing on training. "This seems to set the tone and get across the message that the program will be a good experience for them."

Enhancing Self-Esteem. The way people feel about themselves affects the way they perform their jobs. "I feel that all training should enhance self-esteem and self-image," says Brewer. "When you feel better about yourself, you enhance your ability to contribute to your company."

Employees who deal with customers all day, every day—particularly those in entry-level positions—frequently catch flak and abuse from customers. They feel like doormats. They often don't get respect from customers, particularly the irate ones. "If you are constantly being berated on the phone and made to feel useless, you can eventually begin to feel that you are not very significant."

Thus, Brewer emphasizes to employees that the training program will help them feel better about themselves, subsequently helping them perform their jobs better and more enjoyably.

Building Bridges with Customers. Employees then learn 10 steps to help build bridges and break down walls with customers:

1. Create a positive first impression with customers when you first meet them or talk with them on the phone.
2. Allow the customers to talk. Don't interrupt. If they're upset, let them "dump" and get their anger out.
3. While customers are talking, listen not only for facts, but for underlying feelings and causes. In other words, besides getting information like names, addresses, account numbers, what happened, who was involved, and so forth, find out if the customers are angry, hurt, afraid, frustrated, ignorant, uninformed, or confused.
4. When the customers finish talking, respond with empathy and "active listening"—feeding back to the customers what you heard them saying.
5. Learn to manage the "stressure" that builds up during the conversations. "Stressure" is a word Brewer coined to represent a combination of stress and pressure.
6. Work toward defusing the criticism. When someone is arguing with you, one way to "take the wind out of one's sails" is *not* to argue back. "It's no fun to argue alone," points out Brewer. If you or your company make a mistake, admit it right away and stop the confrontation. Sometimes, you may just have to ride out the storm until the customer is exhausted.
7. Learn to manage the negative feelings with which you are being bombarded by

the customers. This involves learning how to be physically, mentally, and emotionally fit.

8. Involve the customers in the solutions to the problems. Explain that the only way you can help them is for them to help you. Offer to negotiate and solve the problems. Consider saying slowly, in a calm but firm voice, something like "I would really like to help you, but it is hard to do when you're talking to me in that tone of voice," or "It's hard to help you when you're interrupting. I want to help you, but you need to help me."

9. Sell the customers on the solutions. Instead of talking about what you *can't* do for the customers, concentrate on what you *can* do for them. Part of this involves never using the words "no" or "can't." Instead, for example, you can say, "I wish I could give you the answer you would like to hear, but based on my understanding of the situation, here is our best option."

10. Create a final positive impression. In most cases, people are more impressed by the employees with whom they deal than with the specific answers these employees give. "In other words, customers may not like your decision, but you don't want them to be able to argue with the way you treated them," he points out. It is critical that when you end conversations or meetings with customers—especially if the conversations and results have been unpleasant—you emphasize caring and consideration.

To train employees in these 10 steps, Brewer relies heavily on role-playing in small groups. Participants alternate among roles of customer, employee, and trainer and provide one another with supportive feedback about how they react in various situations.

Commitment and Follow-up

Before leaving the training, employees view another videotaped message from the CEO. His message in essence: "Now that you have learned new ways of handling customers and of dealing with yourself and fellow employees, you need to make a commitment to implement some of these new things on the job."

Employees then fill out "commitment sheets" (individual action plans) covering the following items:

- Here is what I learned.
- Here is what I am going to start doing differently.
- Here are the benefits to me, the company, and our customers.
- Here is how other people will know that I am making these changes.

Then they sign these sheets and share them with their supervisors.

For the next six months, supervisors are instructed to

- observe changes in employee behavior,
- document those changes regularly,
- note how what they are doing differently is affecting their jobs, and
- determine how their new behaviors are enhancing the productivity and morale of the employees, the supervisor, and the overall department.

After the first six months, Brewer sends letters to the employees asking them:

- How are you doing?
- How do you rate yourself?
- Where are you getting your best support?
- What difficulties are you still trying to manage?

On the back of the forms, the supervisors fill out their observations on the employees.

"Over a two-year period, we were able to document a significant return on investment in terms of productivity increases and the amount of time supervisors and managers saved by having the employees handle complaints on their own."

Source: Copyrighted material reprinted with permission of CUSTOMER SERVICE MANAGEMENT BULLETIN and Bureau of Business Practice, 24 Rope Ferry Road, Waterford, CT 06836.

Performance Appraisal

All businesses appraise the performance of their employees in one way or another. Through performance appraisal, companies try to (1) evaluate the work that their employees are doing, (2) let their employees know what they think of their work, and (3) suggest ways to make their work better.

Salary increases, bonuses, promotions, demotions, and firings are all based on performance appraisals. Therefore, to both employees and employers, performance appraisal is one of the most important activities in a company. In the next few pages, we will briefly describe some commonly used performance-appraisal methods and suggest some rules of thumb that can help assure the effectiveness of any performance-appraisal system.

Methods of Appraising Performance

Among the most commonly used performance-appraisal methods are management by objectives (MBO), essay appraisal, critical incident appraisal, and graphic rating scales. We will describe each of these methods briefly.

Management by Objectives

The *management by objectives (MBO)* method of performance appraisal creates a situation in which a supervisor and an employee agree upon certain goals that the employee should achieve during the upcoming appraisal period. The employee's success or failure at achieving these goals is then evaluated, and the performance appraisal is based on how well the goals were achieved.

To begin the MBO process, the employee and the employee's supervisor sit down together at the beginning of the appraisal period (the period may be a month, a quarter, or a year), and together they agree upon clear and attainable work objectives for the employee to strive for. In addition, they develop a plan for achieving those objectives. During the appraisal period the employee and the supervisor measure the employee's progress toward the objectives and, if necessary, agree on ways to improve the employee's performance. At the end of the performance-appraisal period, the employee and supervisor

- determine how successful the employee was in achieving his or her goals,
- discuss any problems that occurred during the appraisal period, and
- agree upon goals for the next appraisal period.

The employee should be rewarded based on how well he or she achieved the objectives agreed upon at the beginning of the period.

When developing an MBO performance-appraisal system, the company must be sure that the objectives set forth for the evaluation period are (1) measurable, (2) challenging, (3) achievable, (4) clearly stated, (5) presented in a written form, and (6) agreed upon by both the employee and the supervisor.

Figure 8–3 presents a list of objectives that might be used in a customer service situation. Some of these objectives will apply more to managers; others will apply more to professional and technical staff members.

Essay Appraisal Method

The *essay appraisal method* is a much less structured form of performance appraisal than the MBO method. The only requirement for essay appraisals is that at the end of the appraisal period the supervisor of an employee must write a description of the employee's performance during the period. While some supervisors do a very good job using this highly unstructured format, the method opens the door to a number of problems:

- Because objectives or other criteria for judging performance

Customer Service in Insurance: Principles and Practices

Figure 8–3
Sample Performance Objectives in Customer Service

- Respond to all inquiries and complaints within 24 hours.
- Resolve all complaints within five working days.
- If a problem will take more than one day to resolve, inform the customer and keep the customer updated on your progress in solving the problem.
- Within four months become competent (as defined in your job description) in the use of the annuities administration software.
- Assure that your team achieves a 95 percent customer satisfaction rating, as measured by the quarterly customer survey.

do not have to be established, essay appraisals can be highly subjective.

- Because of the format used, the supervisor's ability or willingness to express herself or himself in writing has an enormous impact on the appraisal.
- Because of the subjective nature of the method, it is fairly easy for the supervisor's personal biases to influence the appraisal.
- Because the method does not require strict record keeping during the appraisal period and does not provide any aids to help the supervisor remember the employee's performance during the period, many important examples of good and bad work may be forgotten and left out of the essay.

Despite all of its drawbacks, however, the essay appraisal method is still widely used, probably because it is simple to use.

Critical Incident Appraisal Method

The *critical incident appraisal method* calls for the supervisor to record good and bad examples of an employee's work during the appraisal period. Any incident that appears significant to the supervisor, such as "trained two new employees while still completing all of her normal duties" or "was chronically late for work during the month of April," is written down and used by the supervisor to establish the criteria for appraising the employee. The advantage of the critical incident appraisal method is that it calls for the supervisor to keep accurate records of an employee's specific activities, so the appraisal is based on concrete evidence and not on the supervisor's generalized recollections. On the other hand, the supervisor's record keeping may not be accurate, and his or her interpretation of what is and is not critical might differ from the employee's interpretation.

Graphic Rating Scale Appraisal Method

Under the **graphic rating scale appraisal method**, the supervisor grades an employee's work during the appraisal period based on a number of factors identified at the beginning of the period. The factors used in the scale are intended to identify the personal characteristics and work characteristics that are needed on the job. Look at Figure 8–4 for an example of part of a graphic rating scale. As indicated in the figure, the supervisor is required to rate the employee, from excellent to poor, on each factor on the scale.

The advantage of the graphic rating scale is that it provides the supervisor with an objective, structured format on which to base appraisals, and the employee knows in advance what basis the evaluation will be based on. The major flaw of the rating scale is the possibility that the rating factors themselves might not reflect the most important factors involved in doing the employee's work. When establishing the rating scale, supervisors and employees should meet and develop factors for the rating scale that reflect their actual activities on the job.

Rules of Thumb for Performance Appraisal

Listed below are some general guidelines to keep in mind when planning and conducting performance appraisals:

- Train managers to conduct appraisal sessions effectively.
- Train employees to accept and learn from the feedback offered in performance appraisals.
- Use the performance appraisal to coach the employee and identify development needs.
- Use performance appraisals to point out an employee's strengths as well as weaknesses.
- Offer specific suggestions for improvement and growth.

Figure 8–4
Portion of a Graphic Rating Scale

Quality of Work Accuracy and completeness of worked performed	☐ Poor quality, frequent errors, seldom meets standards	☐ Quality is usually acceptable but frequently doesn't meet standards	☐ Consistently meets standards	☐ Good quality; often exceeds standards	☐ Excellent quality; consistently exceeds standards
Quantity of work Volume of worked performed in an average work day	☐ Does not meet minimum requirements	☐ Does enough to get by	☐ Consistently meets standards	☐ Industrious; does more than required	☐ Superior work production record
Job Knowledge Information necessary for satisfactory performance	☐ Poorly informed about most work duties	☐ Understands routine aspects but has frequent gaps	☐ Can answer most questions about job duties	☐ Understands all phases of the job	☐ Complete mastery of all phases of the job
Dependability Ability to follow directions and work without supervision	☐ Requires close supervision	☐ Requires normal level of supervision with occasional follow-up	☐ Requires normal level of supervision	☐ Requires very little supervision	☐ Requires absolute minimum of supervision
Overall Rating	☐ Poor	☐ Fair	☐ Satisfactory	☐ Good	☐ Excellent

- Appraise performance based on work done, not on the personality of the person doing the work.
- Make performance appraisal a two-way conversation. Ask the employee to evaluate his or her performance as well as the performance of the supervisor.
- Invite the people who will be appraised to help determine the performance-appraisal method that will be used. This step helps assure that both the appraiser and the appraised have similar expectations during the appraisal period.
- Although annual performance appraisals are most common, more frequent appraisals, even on an informal basis, are effective in keeping employees aware of how they are doing.

Motivating Employees

Not every company has employees who are committed to excellence, but every company wants such employees. However, in order to have such employees, a company must create an environment in which excellence is encouraged. And this encouragement must come not just in the form of words but also in actions. Motivating employees to achieve excellence is one of the most important activities that any manager and any company can participate in. And motivating employees, like creating a customer service culture, relies not only on the attitudes of individual managers but also on the attitudes demonstrated and encouraged by top executives in the company. For a company to reach its highest possible level of performance, the culture of the company itself should encourage employees to achieve excellence. In the next few pages, we will discuss some of the ways a company can create an environment that motivates its employees to achieve excellence.

Punishment as Motivator

The general management climate today tends to encourage the idea of motivating employees through positive reinforcement, that is, rewarding them for all of the good things they do. But companies also use negative responses or punishments to motivate employees. The ultimate punishment, of course, is dismissal. An employee who does not perform at a minimum acceptable level can be fired, and the employee knows that. Employees can also be demoted, or may receive minimal pay raises, if any. All of these punishments are available to employers. But usually just the threat of such punishments is enough to obtain the minimum required performance.

Use of punishment, however, has several drawbacks. Many researchers have found that too much emphasis on punishment or the threat of punishment causes employees to become so afraid of making mistakes that they limit their own potential. They learn what their companies expect them to do, and they do just that and nothing more. Most companies today prefer to create an environment that emphasizes the positive things that their employees do and encourages them to continue improving. In our discussion of motivation, we will also stress the positive.

Relating Rewards to Performance

Probably the most important thing to keep in mind when developing an effective reward system is that the rewards must be related directly to performance. If this relationship does not exist, then rewards are unlikely to achieve their primary goal — improving performance. In addition, the relationship between rewards and performance should be clear and well-publicized. Companies that excel at motivating their employees are also very good at communicating the relationship between rewards and performance. Their employees know what they must do in order to be rewarded, and the companies get what they reward.

Unit Performance

Typically, when we think of rewards for performance, we think of rewards that go to individuals, and we think of the efforts that individuals must put forth in order to be rewarded. But companies also direct their motivational efforts toward groups or units in the company. Motivating and rewarding unit performance are keys to a company's success. Stressing and rewarding unit performance help create team spirit and unit cohesion. It encourages the individuals in a unit to identify the unit's objectives and work together to achieve those objectives. Unit members know that their success depends not just on their own individual performance but on everyone's performance. Realizing this, unit members are more likely to help one another so the unit as a whole can achieve its goals. In this way, motivating unit performance can also motivate individual performance. For a unit to achieve excellence in its work, each person in that unit must also be striving for excellence.

Rewards and Motivation

Typically, when we speak of motivation we are speaking of various forms of rewards. A system of rewards is established and offered to employees to encourage them to perform at a certain level of production. Once that level of production is achieved, more rewards are offered to raise production or quality to even higher levels. The rewards that companies use to motivate employees to achieve excellence can be divided into monetary rewards, such as bonuses, and nonmonetary rewards, such as public recognition for work well done or simply a positive work environment. As companies develop reward systems, they need to keep in mind that the importance attached to any reward varies with each individual. What is a reward to one individual may even seem a punishment to another. For example, some employees view travel to conventions as a reward, while others hate to leave their families. Thus, companies should ask their employees what they perceive as important when designing reward systems. Figure 8–5 lists rewards commonly used to motivate employees. In the next few pages we will discuss some of the most important of these rewards.

Figure 8–5
Rewards to Motivate Employee Performance

Monetary Rewards	Nonmonetary Rewards
salaries	working environment
commissions	attitude of management
bonuses	promotion opportunities
profit sharing	travel
educational expenses	vacation
	new responsibilities
	flexible working hours
	special parking places
	benefits packages
	awards and other public recognition

Salaries

Most employees don't think of salaries as rewards. They think of salaries as their due. And so, in many respects, they are. Companies must pay everyone who works for them. And typically, there is a base pay for similar types of jobs. As long as an employee performs at a level that the company considers acceptable, the employee will continue to receive this base pay. When performance drops below this acceptable level, then the company normally takes some action to remedy the situation. The employee may be counseled or given further training to learn how to improve performance. Or the employee may be given a different job or demoted or even fired. However, if performance rises above the required level, then an employee's pay can be raised to reward the employee for superior performance. This kind of pay raise, called a *merit pay raise*, is related directly to an individual's performance on the job.

Not only is the use of merit pay raises an effective way to reward performance, but by varying the amount and frequency of raises according to job performance, a company creates an effective motivational tool and ties that tool directly to performance. Of course, for such a motivational tool to be equitable and accepted by employees, it must be based on timely and accurate performance appraisals.

Another type of pay raise, called a *cost-of-living pay raise*, is given by many companies to allow salaries to rise at a rate similar to the rate of inflation. Cost-of-living pay raises may be given together with merit pay raises but normally have little or nothing to do with an employee's performance.

In addition to using raises to motivate behavior, the base pay itself can also act as a motivator. Adequate salaries and wages make people feel that they are receiving appropriate rewards for their work. Unfortunately, for a number of years, the base pay of many customer service employees was not on a par with the pay in other types of jobs in the insurance industry. This discrepancy made it difficult not only to attract employees to customer service jobs but also to use salaries as an effective means of reward. Today, salaries in customer service positions have increased and are much more effective as part of a reward system.

Commissions

While the primary monetary reward system for most home office employees is a salary, the primary monetary reward system for most producers (agents, brokers, and so forth) is a commission. While salaries are set amounts that are agreed upon for a certain period (usually a year), a ***commission*** is a variable amount that fluctuates according to the amount of insurance a producer sells.

The great advantage of the commission system is that rewards are directly related to performance, at least to sales performance. It is a dramatic and effective way of rewarding performance. The more a producer sells, the more money he or she earns in commissions. There is no upper limit on income. Unfortunately, there is no lower limit either. A commissioned producer can make a great deal more money or a great deal less money than a salaried home office employee. To modify the system, some businesses use a salary-plus-commission system, which provides a base pay that can then be increased by commissions. The base pay is usually small, but it does supply at least some sense of security for the person on commission. In the insurance industry, producers who are new to the industry typically start with a salary-plus-commission contract. But eventually the salary is dropped, and producers earn their income entirely through commissions.

Although the commission system has the advantage of being closely related to performance, it is not necessarily suitable for every type of person or every type of job. Some people simply don't have the personality to work effectively under the amount of uncertainty the commission system can create. They want more assurance that they will be paid some agreed-upon amount on a regular basis. In addition, not all jobs are structured so that workers have the opportunity to go out and actively do the work necessary to get commissions. Furthermore, it is fairly easy to base commissions on sales. But if a job does not involve sales, then commissions would have to be based on some other factor, and this may be difficult or simply impractical to do.

Bonuses

Like commissions, bonuses have a direct and apparent relationship to performance. Unlike commissions, however, a bonus is just what the name implies — an additional amount added to the normal pay. Some bonuses, such as Christmas bonuses and executive bonuses, are given regularly, although they are not a guaranteed part of employee compensation.

Other bonuses can be given at any time in amounts that range from a few dollars to thousands of dollars. Typically, such bonuses are given when a manager believes that an individual or a unit has performed at a such a high level of excellence that a special reward is called for. As with all other reward systems, the bonus system can lead to problems. For example, employees may feel that bonuses are not given often enough, that they are not large enough, or that some people have more opportunities to earn bonuses than other people. Therefore, any company that uses a bonus system must be sure that the criteria for bonuses are fair and well publicized among its employees and that everyone has an equal chance to earn a bonus.

Educational Expenses

Some companies pay for the costs of their employees' educations. Many companies will pay these costs, however, only if the employee who is taking educational courses is doing his or her work at an above-average level and if the courses are job-related. Companies may reimburse educational costs for high-school equivalency education, college and university education, professional designation and certification programs, and skill-related training programs.

Nonmonetary Methods of Motivating Employees

As we have mentioned before, there are many different ways of motivating employees. Money, of course, whether in the form of salaries or commissions or bonuses, is generally the first motivator considered. There are, however, a number of other ways to motivate employees. A few of these additional motivators are discussed below.

Working Environment

Workers spend close to a third of their lives in a business setting. And typically, they want to work in a place where they feel comfortable. This doesn't mean they need expensive furnishings or an atmosphere that is so casual that they are not expected to work. But they do want a place that doesn't make them feel alienated or too pressurized.

Attitude of Management

When managers have a positive attitude, when they make their employees feel that they are valued individuals, when they treat their employees like responsible adults, workers tend to respond by working like responsible adults. The general belief among management experts today is that employees work better when they are treated better by their managers. This goes back to the idea expressed in Chapter 2 that managers are not just authority figures. They are coaches and helpers. Their job is to help their employees perform at the highest possible levels.

Promotion Opportunities (Career Paths)

Without a doubt, promotion opportunities are closely connected to monetary rewards. When people are promoted, they usually receive pay raises. On the other hand, even before employees receive promotions, it is important for employees to feel that when they start a job there will be promotional opportunities. A number of companies have spent a great deal of effort developing career ladders for their employees in customer service. Knowing that a career ladder is available encourages employees to work hard to move up the ladder and encourages good employees to stay in customer service rather than transferring into other parts of the company. Figure 8–6 shows the customer service career path developed by USAA Life Insurance Company.

Many companies encourage their employees to follow multiple career paths, crossing over from one career path to another based on their interests and the interests of the company. For example, an employee might begin his or her career on a customer service path, then over the years switch to a training path or a systems path, enter management training, and possibly switch back to customer service. Each crossover brings experience that increases the employee's value to the company.

Special Contests and Awards

Although we talked earlier about the fact that motivational campaigns cannot change a company's culture or create a customer service attitude all by themselves, they can be useful tools for motivating individuals and units for the short term. Having quality-service contests and awarding special prizes to individuals and units for their excellent work can have a positive effect on employee performance.

Figure 8–6
The USAA Customer Service Career Path

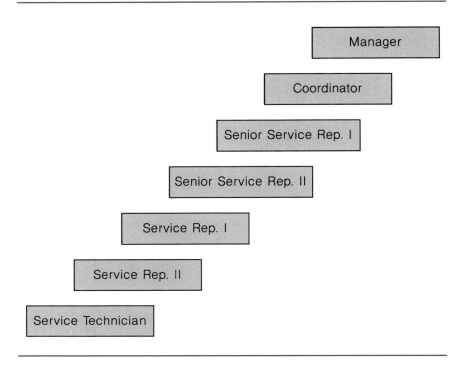

Some awards that can be given during such motivational campaigns are commemorative plaques, coffee cups, extra vacation time, special reserved parking places, bonuses, a meal paid for by the company, tickets to a sporting or cultural event, a trip to a resort, special recognition given by a top executive, and mention in the company newsletter.

Benefits Packages

Like promotions, the company's benefits package could just as easily be listed under monetary rewards, since the value of a benefits package can be worth as much as 25 percent of an employee's pay. When we say benefits package, we mean all the non-pay benefits that an employee receives from the company. For most employees, the benefits package includes health insurance and life insurance, the company pension program, and annual vacation time. But the package can also mean (1) inclusion in a savings plan outside the regular pension plan, (2) a company car, (3) investment advice, (4) participation in a stock plan, in which employees receive shares of company stock which, on retirement, they can sell for cash, (5) day care provided or paid for by the company, and a variety of other benefits.

Conclusion

Throughout this book we have emphasized the management aspects of a successful customer service operation. Understanding the principles that underlie customer service enables us to build the kind of organization that provides excellent service. To a large extent, however, customer service "happens" on the front line. For that reason, employees at all levels who are involved in customer service need to understand human behavior and develop interpersonal skills for dealing with all kinds of people. Thus, LOMA has developed a companion text—*Customer Service in Insurance: Improving Your Skills*—that discusses various aspects of human behavior and gives you a chance to explore the interpersonal skills that every employee needs to be a successful provider of customer service. To hone your customer service skills, continue your studies by reading *Customer Service in Insurance: Improving Your Skills*.

Key Terms

job description
job specification
recruitment
job candidate
human resources inventory
job posting
classified advertisements
want ads
college and university recruiting
intern programs
job referral
job candidate qualifications
job skills
personality traits
applicant testing
aptitude tests

psychomotor tests
job knowledge tests
skills tests
interest tests
psychological tests
job orientation
on-the-job training (OJT)
classroom training
simulation training
computer-based training (CBT)
interactive video training (IVT)
job rotation
mentoring
performance appraisal
management by objectives (MBO)
essay appraisal method

critical incident appraisal method
graphic rating scale appraisal
    method
employee motivation
monetary rewards
nonmonetary rewards
salaries
merit pay raise
cost-of-living pay raise
commissions
bonuses

profit sharing
educational benefits
promotion
work environment
vacation
flex time
benefits packages
merit pay raise
renewal commission
salary-plus-commission system

Glossary

advisory panels. Standing groups that provide insurance companies with qualitative research information; they may consist of producers, policyowners, contract holders, field office employees, or home office employees.

annual plan. A plan that defines specific activities and programs that will be conducted during the year to meet corporate objectives.

assurance. The competence and credibility of service personnel, including their ability to convey trust and confidence and the courtesy they show to customers; one of the five service dimensions.

behavioral measures. Nonquantitative performance measures that are used to appraise the actions or reactions of employees under specified circumstances, such as those involving interactions with customers.

benchmarking. The process of comparing performance results with a standard, or benchmark, by which that performance can be measured or judged.

benevolent autocratic culture. A corporate culture in which the relationship between management and frontline employees is fairly cordial, but decision making still remains completely in the domain of management, indicating a lack of trust in employees.

call abandonment. What happens when a customer makes a telephone call to a company, is put on hold to wait for assistance, but hangs up before receiving assistance.

consultative culture. A corporate culture in which top management generally shows a high level of confidence in its employees, seeking out their opinions when it makes decisions.

consumer. Anyone who is a current or potential buyer or user of insurance products.

control. A mechanism that monitors a system to ensure that it is functioning properly and then provides feedback to the system, so that the system can adjust its operation as needed.

corporate culture. The attitudes, values, perceptions, beliefs, and experiences shared by the employees of an organization and instilled in new employees when they enter the organization.

corporate objectives. Statements that describe the long-term results a company intends to accomplish in carrying out its mission.

corporate strategies. The long-term methods by which a company intends to achieve its corporate objectives.

customer-oriented data base. A data base that can be used to call up all pertinent information about a particular customer.

customer service. The broad range of activities that a company and its employees undertake in order to keep customers satisfied so they will continue doing business with the company and speak positively about the company to other potential customers.

customer service mission statement. A statement that tells why a company is providing customer service and how customer service relates to the company's goals.

effectiveness. The ability to establish and achieve appropriate objectives.

efficiency. The ability to achieve objectives with a minimum of waste.

empathy. The process of understanding the customer's emotional state and imagining how you would feel in a similar situation; one of five service dimensions.

empowerment. A process in which a company gives its employees the authority and responsibility to make certain types of decisions without having to wait for approval.

environmental analysis. A component of a situation analysis in which a company gathers information about various ongoing events and relationships in its environment in an effort to understand how those events and relationships are likely to affect the company.

expectation. What people believe likely or certain to happen.

exit interviews. Interviews with employees who are leaving the company.

expected service. The quality of the service customers expect to get.

exploitative autocratic culture. A corporate culture in which managers, expecially top-level managers, make all decisions and maintain a high degree of secrecy about the company's intentions.

exploratory research. *See* **qualitative research.**

external customer. Any person who is not on an insurance company's employee payroll and who is in a position either to buy or use the insurance company's products or to advise others to buy or use its products.

external data sources. Sources of research located outside the company, including a variety of research firms, advertising agencies, and professional and trade associations.

final output. The last output provided by a system, the purpose of the entire process.

focus-group interviews. Unstructured, informal sessions during which six to ten participants are asked to discuss their opinions about a certain topic.

gap analysis. The process of identifying and studying the differences between expected service and received service.

human resources inventory. A list of all of a company's employees, including their experience, education, and particular skills.

industrial engineer. *See* **systems analyst.**

input. Something that needs to be worked on by a system in order to achieve the system's objective.

internal assessment. A component of a situation analysis in which a company examines its current activities and its ability to respond to potential threats and opportunities in the environment.

internal customers. Employees of an insurance company who receive service from other employees of the company.

internal data sources. Sources of research located within the company itself.

invisible system. A system that is designed so that a customer is not inconvenienced by, or even aware of, all the steps a company must take to fulfill the customer's request.

job description. A statement that identifies the duties, responsibilities, and accountabilities of a job.

job rotation. The process of periodically moving employees from one job to another.

job specification. A statement that identifies the qualifications and characteristics that a person must have to perform a job, including the required level of education, amount of experience, type of training, and personal characteristics.

mission statement. A statement that describes a company's fundamental purpose, defines the scope of its business activities, and specifies what business the company is in.

moment of truth. Any occasion when there is contact between a company and a customer; any opportunity for the company to create a good or bad impression in the mind of the customer.

monitoring. Observation performed by managers or supervisors who listen in on service calls or who review employees' customer correspondence files.

mystery shopper. A trained evaluator who approaches or calls a customer service employee and pretends to be a customer.

observation. A data-collection method in which a person's behavior is observed and evaluated.

operational plans. Detailed business plans that outline the actual steps needed to implement a strategy.

organizational culture. *See* **corporate culture.**

organizational development. *See* **systems analyst.**

output. The final result produced by a system.

participative team culture. A corporate culture in which employees at all levels are involved in making decisions.

perceived service. The quality of service that customers believe they have received.

perception. The process by which people select, organize, and interpret information in order to give it meaning.

performance standard. An established level of performance against which actual performance is to be measured.

policy-oriented data base. A data base that can be used to call up information only on one particular policy at a time.

population. The total of all members of a group that is being studied. *See also* **sampling.**

primary data. New research that is gathered to help a company understand a specific problem.

process step. *See* **processing.**

process step inputs. The output of one process step, which becomes input for the next process step.

process step outputs. An output that does not complete an entire process, but leads to the next process step.

processing. The work that a system performs on the input it receives.

producers. Agents and brokers who sell a company's insurance products.

qualitative performance measures. *See* **behavioral performance measures**.

qualitative research. Research designed to examine what people think and how they feel about a subject, so the researcher can learn about the general nature of a problem, including its causes and solutions and the factors that need to be considered in addressing the problem.

quantitative measures. Performance measures that are used to evaluate how quickly, how often, and how accurately processes are completed.

quantitative research. Research that can be quantified or summarized statistically.

reliability. Performing promised service dependably and accurately; one of the five service dimensions.

responsiveness. A willingness to help customers and the ability to provide them with prompt service; one of the five service dimensions.

sampling. Examining a portion or subset of a group being studied (the sample) in order to develop conclusions about the total group (the population).

secondary data. Data that has been collected for a nonspecific purpose either by the insurance company itself or by some other organization.

service dimensions. Five criteria that customers typically use to judge the quality of the service they receive: reliability, assurance, empathy, responsiveness, and tangible factors.

service gap. The difference between expected service and perceived service.

service objectives. The specific goals that a company must meet to fulfill its customer service mission.

service strategies. A company's general plans for achieving service objectives.

strategic planning. The process of determining an organization's long-term corporate objectives and deciding the overall course of action the company will follow to achieve those objectives.

survey. A data-collection method that uses structured data-collection forms, such as questionnaires, to gather data directly from the population being studied.

syndicated data. Secondary data that is collected and sold by commercial marketing research firms.

system. A group of elements that work together to perform a specific function or to achieve one or more desired objectives.

systems analysis. The process of examining how a company's employees, procedures, technology, and financial and physical resources work together to achieve a specific goal.

systems analyst. Someone who is trained to analyze every aspect of a business from a systems point of view and to develop plans to make the system work in the most efficient way possible.

tactical plans. *See* **operational plans.**

tangible factors. The physical aspects of a company and its employees; one of the five service dimensions.

turnaround time. The amount of time it takes to complete a particular customer-initiated transaction.

value-added services. Services that provide customers with additional benefits (whether tangible or intangible) that do not routinely come with a product or service they have bought.

wait time. The average amount of time that customers must stay on the phone before they get assistance.

work-flow analysis. An analysis that examines all the steps or tasks involved in a particular process.

work groups. Small groups of employees who work together on a regular basis.

Index

W

Wait time, 177
Work-flow analysis, 151–54
Work groups, 37, 53

Z

Zeithaml, Valarie A., 88, 100,
    109, 128, 147
Zemke, Ron, 56